Out
of
Ireland

Babe Toner

Order this book online at www.trafford.com
or email orders@trafford.com

Most Trafford titles are also available at major online book retailers.

Printed in the United States of America.

ISBN: 978-1-4269-6320-9 (sc)
ISBN: 978-1-4269-6321-6 (e)

Trafford rev. 03/21/2011

 www.trafford.com

North America & international
toll-free: 1 888 232 4444 (USA & Canada)
phone: 250 383 6864 ♦ fax: 812 355 4082

In memory of my mother
Bina Abigail O'Riordan Toner
3-12-1905 —11-27-1997

And

My sister Theresa Toner Jones
2-27-1934—2-20-2001

ACKNOWLEDGMENTS

I would like to give special thanks to my wife Pat for encouraging me to write this book and my two sons Jerome Jr. and Joseph for taking an interest in the story.

Special thanks as well to Ann McKelvie my editor
Dick Bowman my toughest critic.
Debbie McCann for her literary input.
Abby and Tim Looney for their Irish connection.

Betsey Berwick for helping me solve my Microsoft problems

My friends at Staples, Prices Corner Brian P. Joel, Frank, and Thomas
Most all of the Ireland sources came from my mother sitting with me over a hot cup of tea in our kitchen on 29th. St. She would get very excited telling me about her brothers and sisters and all the things that they did from day to day. I remember her showing me a picture of her mother smoking a white stone pipe, and how she loved to have a smoke at the end of the day

She loved telling me about her school in Renanirree and her teacher Master Lynch, and how they all eventually lost interest one by one until they had all dropped out by there age fourteen.

My mother had told me that Jerem had paid Julia's way to America, and Julia paid Bina's way to America

Uncle Jerry didn't make friends with too many people. I think because he was my God Father he confided in me a lot, especially about the shooting I can still remember to this day drilling him on how he got rid of that rifle. I never forgot him telling me how scared he was and afraid of being caught. Uncle Jerry was quite the character and loved it when we could be together and have our one on one talks over a cup of tea.

My Gaelic came from the book Irish Proverbs by Fionnuala Carson Williams.

The Michael Collins web site to find the name of the town where he was shot (Beal na mBlath)

Tim and Abby Looney my first cousin would get together with Pat and I and tell me stories for hours at a time. They gave me a lot of information about the towns and villages around Cork. Some insights on the family and my grand father and mother. Timsey Jerh Liam and his wife Margaret (Binas parents) that I would have never known. Abby and Tim grew up in Ireland and knew our family history well, the good and the bad.

That's what the story is all about the good and the bad in the life of the O'Riordans and the Toners.

Tim O'Riordan for showing my family the house our grand mother died in, and is haunted to this day, everything is still lying around where the repairmen left it when they ran out of the house.

1

The soft clouds opened early in the morning and let the sun shine down on Timothy O'Riordans dark green pastures and modest two-story white stucco home, which provided the shelter the family needed to survive the cold strong winds that they could rely on to come each winter. Timothy would often stand by the milk house and see that he had a good piece of land for grazing or farming, but he needed help with it because it was too much for one man to farm. His wife Margaret couldn't help him that much; she was busy having babies or future farm hands. But for now, Timothy needed someone to care for and help milk the twelve cows. To the cows it was the same thing every morning. Around 5:30 someone had to milk them, so Timothy would hire someone to help him until the children were old enough and could replace the hired hand. At least that was his plan.

Timothy liked going down to the pub after dinner, having a few short ones with the boys, and listening to the latest gossip from around the village. Often this was the only way they heard the news from the surrounding villages. When you worked your farm you didn't get to hear the local news, and there weren't any newspaper deliveries to their farms. Most all of the neighboring men would be at the pub some evenings, and a familiar face there was his neighbor Dan Kelleher who was related to his wife Margaret, a Kelleher from County Kerry. Timothy was known to everyone through the community as Timsey Jerh Liam. There were so many O'Riordans in the area of GortNamill, Renanirree, and Macroom that by altering the first name in conversation it became easier to identify which O'Riordan was the topic of conversation. And Timothy was a very popular name in the area of County Cork, as well as in the whole of Ireland.

Timsey was well liked and respected in the community of Renanirree, even though he had a reputation of being a hell raiser. To him it was just having fun. He was respected enough that some of his drinking mates would ask him to co-sign some notes for the bank's approval so they might get money for long overdue repairs and equipment on their farms. Timsey didn't take the time to think out what he was being asked to do; he would sign anything his mates would put in front of him. He trusted everyone and took them at their word, but this trust and his neglect in not having an attorney look over the papers would later hurt him.

Timsey was more concerned about his 100-plus acres and how he could keep it up to his standards. His farm had been handed down through the ages and he wanted to do the same for his children someday. He made a good income selling the milk and hauling it down to the milk platform for the 8:30 a.m. pick up at the end of their lane where it ran into the main road. Timsey never failed to have his milk ready for pick up, even though the truck for the milk pickup was always late.

Margaret helped with the chickens, did the wash by hand, and made all the meals. Her favorite time of the day was after dinner, when she loved to take a moment off on a winter evening and sit in her rocking chair by the fire, enjoying a good smoke from her white stone pipe. There was no reason for anyone to interrupt her, just rocking slowly, which she looked forward to all day. My grandmother never smoked her pipe in public, mind you, and in the summer she would sit on the porch in her rocking chair and have a good smoke and watch the sun go down. She was not a talkative person; she was happy just sitting there and taking everything in. It was very hard to get her to join in the conversation; she just preferred to sit and enjoy her smoke. She would have a smile on her face that could only come from a woman who was thoroughly satisfied with her life with Timsey, living on the farm, and having his babies.

Early in the morning on the twelfth day of March, 1905, it was crystal clear outside and cold. In the field, Timsey could hear his son Jerem calling for his father to come quickly, that mommy was going to have a baby. Jerem was both delighted and frightened as he urged his father to come right away and see the baby being born. Jerem was so excited he was crying with happiness. His eyes were full of water from crying, so when he ran behind his father, trying to keep up with him, he often fell down. There was a pathway to the house but it was made from flat stones that were purposely laid to keep people from walking on the wet ground and bringing wet shoes in the house. Jerem didn't do that badly for a two-and-a-half-year old.

The father knew he had to wash well because his boots were caked with cow manure; there was no way the women were going to let him in the room with dirty clothes or boots on. So he took the boots off first, then he pulled off his overalls. He washed his hands with soap because he was going to hold the baby, so he had to be clean. He carried Jerem up the steps to see his newborn child on this near perfect day. Thank God his mother-in-law, Mrs. Kelleher, was there to help with the birth; she was known throughout the area as a midwife, assisting in the birth of children in the Gortnamill, Renanirree, and Macroom area. Some friends also come along to help out. When Timsey finally saw his daughter, my mother, he immediately named her Bina. She was to become the third of nine children. He was hoping for more boys, but as fate would have it only three of his nine children were boys: Jeremiah, William, and Timothy. The five other girls were Julia, Bridget, Johanna, Nora, and Mary O'Riordan.

Life on the farm was hard for the O'Riordan family, but life was hard for everyone then, so they didn't pity themselves. Everyone had their chores to do. Timsey was strict, and there could be no excuse for not getting them done. If things weren't done properly, someone was going to get a beating. The boys would do the tough jobs, such as digging for potatoes, going down to the bog and cutting the turf, and milking the cows. While Timsey ruled the roost, the mother ran the nest. The girls were given the light chores, like feeding the chickens, sweeping, and keeping the milk room clean. They would also lend a hand with the milking if needed, fetching the eggs, and when they were older they helped with the meals. The children took turns collecting the turf and wood for the stove.

As they grew, in addition to feeding and milking the cows, Jerem, Tim, and William would also keep busy maintaining the farm's 100-plus acres. Often the boys would work from sunup to sunset. While the entire family would go to Mass on Sunday at different times, the cows didn't wait for them to come home from Mass to be milked, so occasionally the brothers had to stay behind to finish the milking and would miss church. Whether permitting they would walk to Mass, and in bad weather they would have to take one of the horse-drawn wagons. There were times that they just couldn't go because of the weather.

After a hard day's work on the farm, Timsey would wash up and go down to the local pub and have a drink with his friends. Occasionally Timsey had more than his limit and he would raise a little hell, often returning home still in the mood for some confrontation. The one thing he wasn't going to do was to get into a fight with his wife Margaret. He knew that any confrontation was not going to be acceptable to her or the children. Nevertheless the target of his anger at times was usually Jerem, and he would often get into heated verbal exchanges with the teenaged son. On one occasion things got so bad that Jerem struck his father after being hit for what Jerem thought was no good reason.

Their relationship started to erode. Jerem was not happy working on the farm after that incident; he was restless and wanted to do more. Jerem would often show his disgust for his father's drinking and hell-raising and how he was running the house and farm; if the weather permitted he would sleep in the barn and love it. This made the air too thick for compromise. Timsey was also deeply hurt and never got over that incident. Jerem would have had to be pushed very hard to strike his father and was concerned that this could happen again. Jerem's sleeping in the barn made him look like a strange young man, but he wasn't; this was Jerem's way of keeping the peace. His mother would often ask Jerem to come into the house and say that with the work he was doing on the farm, he had as much right to be in the house as anyone else did. If she could say that to Jerem what must she have said to his father?

While the work was hard, the play was too. The boys loved teasing the girls and the girls loved being teased. When the wind would rattle the shutters on a cold windy night, the girls imagined ghosts or worse to be at the windows trying to come in out of the cold. The boys felt it was their duty to take every opportunity to maximize the girls' fears. There was always a grizzly tale to tell around the fire, and the tales would always include the noisy shutters. When it was bedtime the petrified girls were scared to go up the stairs to bed. One time, as they reached the top of the stairs the window shade sprang up, scaring them all, causing them to fall backwards against each other, tumbling down into a heap at the bottom of the steps. They never resolved the dispute about which one it was who wet herself from laughing so hard that night.

The only heat in the house was the fireplace and the kitchen stove. During the cold and damp season the children would go to bed with hot stones in their woolen socks and place them under the blankets. The stones didn't stay hot long, so it was best to get to sleep as quickly as possible.

Getting up during the night to go to the bathroom was rough, not to mention getting up in the morning and standing on the cold floor and trying to wash up with cold water. That was the hardest thing the girls had to do; Bina often remembered the many mornings that she poked through the thin ice that formed on the water in her wash basin overnight just to wash up. It was hard to really get up to full speed until they were fully dressed. Then they would work in twos to collect the wood for the stove and dig the turf while the sun was overhead in the sky.

The children walked to school about a half mile one way, to a little one-room schoolhouse in Gortnamill, just outside Renanirree. The children had a lot of respect for their teacher Master Lynch. Their school had a big fireplace to heat the one room. So each student had an assignment, to make sure there was plenty of turf available to do the job. Each child would take turns bringing the wood and turf to school each day. When the weather was really bad, with high winds, Timsey would put the children in the hay wagon and cart his brood to school, but the weather would have had to be very bad for their father to give them this treat. The children wore their scarves, which they knitted themselves, wrapped high around their faces and necks. (Knitting scarves, hats, sweaters, and mittens was a must for survival. Thank God they became good knitters. Margaret taught the girls how, and the wool was easily available in Macroom.) Everyone's clothes were variations on black; it was a common color. Their garments had very little color like what we know today.

The children liked going to school in the hay wagon. Jerem would sit up front with his father for his ride to school. Jerem was the oldest and no one would dare take his seat away from him. Although all the children maintained that their memories of school were all good ones, none of them went on to what we would call high school. There was never any emphasis to go to high school; Timsey couldn't run a farm without his children. Jerem was only twelve when he quit school, and the girls went until they were thirteen. Bina went until she was fourteen. As they grew older, life on the farm was boring for the girls. They couldn't do the big jobs, just a bunch of small jobs that were important but didn't challenge their intelligence.

There wasn't much time to play; the girls would take turns helping out in the kitchen. The girls learned to cook helping their mother prepare the meals. They would also sit on the milk platform at the end of their lane, just to see who would walk by or ride by on their bikes. In some cases this was the only way the children would get their news from farm to farm, or from around the village. There also was plenty of gossip to enjoy.

There was a dance in town every weekend, and Jerem was the first of the clan to check it out. They could hear the music coming from the dance hall in town while they sat on the milk platform; Jerem would go down to watch through the windows. It could get really hot inside the hall, so they had to open all the windows and try to cool off. Jerem was too shy to dance. Nevertheless he would have a good time watching and laughing. He loved to see the people he knew dancing; it just looked like fun to him. His mother knew he went and she would ask him what it was like; he would just start laughing without saying any more. He would laugh so much that it was contagious and they all would start laughing.

Eventually some of the girls would walk down on a Saturday night to see the fun first-hand. They weren't alone; there were plenty of other girls looking in the windows. They could see Jerem standing inside with some of his mates, just having a good time and laughing all the time. Everyone dancing would be stamping their feet in unison. The noise from their stomping was deafening but thrilling. Julia was the first to sneak in to the Saturday night dance hall and join her brother. It wasn't long before Julia was really kicking those legs up in the air, while Jerem watched and laughed. Bina could not be convinced to go. She was shy and she doubted the sincerity of the boys who frequented the dance hall. They usually smelled of alcohol and had that crazy look in their eyes when they were drinking. She said the alcohol gave them false courage. Bina would sometimes stay home with her mother and bake. Bina's favorite dessert, which she never forgot, was apple cake.

Jerem wasn't cheerful the morning after a dance—not that he had been drinking, but five o'clock came early. Those dance halls were full of smoke and all the dust kicked up from dancing would be enough to give anyone a bad feeling in the morning. It was hard for Jerem to feel good about getting the cows ready for milking, and he was starting to show signs that farming was not for him. He was losing all his enthusiasm, but he couldn't get any other work unless he had a trade. Then he would probably have to move to a big city to get work.

The word got out that Julia and Bina were looking for work, such as caring for children, what we would call a nanny. They were both hired, and they would work weekdays and have off the weekends. They would live in with the families and take care of the young children, cook meals, and do laundry. This was really tough in those days—no machines, so everything had to be done by hand. It wasn't farm work and they didn't miss the farm, but it was fun to go back home on the weekends. Julia and

Bina were thinking about their life at this point. They knew this was not the kind of life they wanted to live, so they always had their ears open for better opportunities to improve their lifestyles.

Jerem would always talk to Julia and Bina about going to America. Their response would be, "Whatever you do don't say anything to our parents. They would be angry with that kind of talk! Who would help them on the farm?" That was a really good question because 100-plus acres, with cows and pigs, were too much for one man. The farm had been handed down through the generations and Timsey was not going to lose it, but his children were getting restless, causing more conflict and tension in the home. Timsey also didn't realize that his drinking was not going to keep the family together. Although Bina and Julia were happy working out of the house and earning an income, Timsey would often take their pay and Bina and Julia never had a chance to save that much for themselves. Some of the money could have been used for the family to live on, and this worsened the relationship. They knew their father was getting drunk on their hard-earned money.

Meanwhile, Jerem knew fighting was going on throughout all of Ireland for Irish independence. He didn't understand all the issues other than freeing Ireland from British control, nevertheless all the skirmishes were all around them. The young men like Jerem were just right for plucking into the cause. Jerem was not happy at home, and he thought that if he joined the cause, the republicans, he would feel important and appreciated, and would gain stature among his peers. He was nineteen and needed a pat on the back instead of a punch from his father. The one good way to find out about this war was to go to the Republican meetings at the different farms around Macroom. At times the meetings got very heated. The message being passed around was that one of their trusted leaders had gone to London and betrayed the cause by signing a treaty with the British that the more conservative faction of the Sinn Fein considered treason. A lot of people didn't agree with the treaty; Jerem said they were called the Anti-Treaty Republicans. The men at the meeting said they needed some good dedicated men.

Jerem went to the meetings often enough that he was asked if he wanted to join and help the cause. He did, and he never missed a meeting. The leaders believed he could be trusted. He was young and healthy, just right for the republicans. It didn't hurt that he was an angry young man, too. The leader held up a rifle and bragged about where they got their rifles from. He said he would take them from the dead British soldiers as well as the .303 caliber bullets. Jerem was asked to stay after the meeting and was offered a rifle and ammunition and was told to take better care of it than the soldier they took it from did. They gave Jerem a .303-caliber British rifle and five rounds of ammunition, saying there was a shortage of ammunition so doesn't waste any of it. He was sworn in and told that some day they would be calling on him for his help. He was to become familiar with his rifle inside and out, and when called on he could not refuse. Like most farm boys he was already experienced with rifles, so every night Jerem cleaned his rifle out in the barn. At times the tension wasn't any better between him and his father and he would still rather sleep out in the barn, weather permitting, than argue needlessly. Jerem kept his well-oiled rifle wrapped in burlap and hidden behind some old bales of hay where he slept. He felt it was very safe there, and he inspected it every day.

Jerem later told me that at one meeting they were talking about the provisional Chairman from their county who sold out the Republic to the British. There were rumors that he was coming to the south for a meeting in West Cork. He was going to hold a political meeting to patch up some differences with the treaty that was in force. One of the leaders screamed that this man had to be stopped, and he had the men to do it. After that meeting Jerem was asked to stay behind for further discussion. At least a half dozen of other conspirators were going to meet more men later on that evening. Jerem recognized the men and knew one in the group as Kelleher. Jerem was asked to meet the next morning and to bring his rifle and ammunition at 4: 00 a.m. Jerem didn't get a bite to eat that early so he grabbed a chunk of bread and left quietly. He didn't want anyone to know he was leaving, so he had to make sure the front door was closed carefully. It was dark and a little humid but it didn't matter to Jerem. He had made plans to meet the leaders along the road for a ride down to where they would meet other conspirators and set up a good ambush site. They had a bicycle hidden in the bushes behind an abandoned old stone barn. Many of the men had different locations to pick up their bicycles for a successful retreat from the shooting scene, and Jerem knew where his bike was and felt he could return safely home.

A large number of men were stationed all along the road, and Jerem thought, "There were a lot of men here to shoot one person." He had counted more than thirty men hidden behind the bushes and on the higher elevated hills overlooking the road way. They needed people to send messages back and forth about the progress of the motorcade and to take part in the ambush. The leader said that the motorcade was hours late and would tell the men not to lose patience; he was sure the convoy was still going to show up.

It was after six o'clock in the evening now and Jerem was getting antsy and hungry. He asked the leader if he had anything to eat because his stomach was making such loud noises that he was afraid that the rumbling would give away their position. The man laughed and gave Jerem a half of ham sandwich. That really hit the spot and would have tasted even better with a nice cup of tea. Jerem lay there tired and trying to shake off that sleepy feeling that kept coming over him. The tension was high; he could see the men fidgeting with their rifles in anticipation of the convoy.

Impatient and doubting that the convoy would arrive, many of the men snuck off to the local pub not that far away. They must have thought that the convoy bringing this man wasn't going to show up. Jerem didn't believe that; he understood that the leader knew something because you could see the confidence in his reasoning in asking the men to hold their positions. Jerem half-heartedly left the original ambush scene with the group that was heading for the nearby pub. Only less then a dozen of them would remain on the hill overlooking the planned spot of attack. Once the departing force crossed the road, Jerem decided to take up a position where he could watch the ambush sight and at the same time stay in visual contact with his remaining compatriots; he looked over to see his friend Kelleher was one of them. It was almost eight o'clock when the word came that the convoy was in sight. It was too late to warn the men in the pub because he could hear the order to load their rifles and get ready. Jerem had loaded and unloaded his rifle so many times he could do it blindfolded.

Jerem could see the convoy get closer, so when it stopped it was perfectly off to the left of him and if he stayed hidden he could have a clear view. All of a sudden holy hell broke loose; everyone had opened fire on the convoy. Jerem withheld his fire following the orders not to waste his ammo, still maintaining his strong position in the gully below the road. He had no visible target and could see the ones that went to the pub bailing out onto the roadway running for cover and firing their rifles with not much effect. Jerem suddenly spotted someone in the back of the convoy who looked like he was shouting orders and directing his people to where the shooters were. Jerem took careful aim and shot at this lone visible target standing at the rear of the car. When he shot he saw the man fall to the ground and with four shots left he just fired indiscriminately, like everyone else, until he ran out of ammunition.

Suddenly Jerem felt sick and scared that he had shot someone. He knew that his shot had gone unnoticed because he was the only one not running around. He knew that his position would soon be overrun either by the boys from the pub or the vehicle that had a machine gun on it. Either way he was scared and wanted to leave. He looked over and saw that Kelleher wasn't looking any better; Jerem knew that he had to distance himself from this place. It was a quiet place called Beal na mBlath. Jerem thought, "Thank God there weren't any people standing around waiting to see who they thought was a traitor"; with all the wild firing, some of those people might have been killed or injured. He knew that if his father would have ever gotten wind of his son going on a mission to shoot someone he would have forbidden Jerem to go. As scared as he was, he couldn't believe how he ever wound up in the middle of a shootout. With all the wild firing coming from the men in the pub he thought, "It's a wonder I wasn't shot."

Jerem knew he had to find his hidden bicycle at the old stone barn some two miles away. He crawled on his elbows in a prone position until he was sure he was out of sight, hearing what he thought was a machine gun firing from behind him, and waited a while before he stood up and started to run through the countryside toward the old stone barn. It was still bright enough for him to see his way along the hedge rows and the stone walls the farmers used to section off their farms. All through out the meadows and hills toward the barns were fields walled off from each other. Running with his rifle wasn't as hard as he thought it was going to be; he was able to jump the walls, run through the streams and jump the ditches. Nothing could stop him from getting to his destination. His adrenalin must have been pumping to be able to keep up this rigorous pace. He didn't smoke or drink so he was very fit for what lay ahead of him.

Even though the air was warm it felt good on his lungs when he ran with his mouth open. He was not a track star. In fact he had trouble with his balance, so when he ran he would stagger just a little, but it was hardly noticeable. He had never had so much energy before. I guess that comes from being scared. He knew that if he stayed near the streams and stone walls he would finally come across the Old Stone Barn. This was one of many small obstacles that Jerem had to overcome before he could get home safely. Then he would have a lot of explaining to do to his father about where he was all day. He was definitely going to be missed.

He could see what little sun that was left shining on the Old Stone Barn through the cluster of trees up ahead of him. All of a sudden he had a surge of energy seeing the barn lit up by the setting sun. When he finally got to the barn he came across a large rock so he swung his rifle as hard as he could, breaking it in half on the first swing. Now he had to find a place to hide it. He looked over the barn's stone walls and found an opening between some of the stones, so he pushed the front end of the barrel into the space in the stone wall and banged it deep into the wall with the butt end of the rifle until it was completely hidden out of sight. He walked around to the back of the barn and found another space between the stones and pushed the butt end in as far as he could, but the butt end was still showing so he picked up a stone and banged the butt until it was out of sight and, he hoped, never to be found again. He walked around the barn to see if it was obvious that someone was there. Satisfied that the sight looked undisturbed he took his bicycle and started home to Gortnamill.

This bicycle was going to help distance Jerem from the shooting scene. As soon as he could get to the road a few miles away, he could ride the bike through the thick grass that would slow him down but not prevent him from getting to his destination. It took a while, but he knew that the road was on the other side of the hedgerow up ahead. What a relief. Jerem was ready now to do what he could do best and that was to ride his bicycle for a long distance.

The distance from the shooting to his home in Gortnamill was about 15 miles. Having just peddled a few miles closer to home, Jerem knew that if he kept a steady pace he could make it home with ease. There was hardly any traffic on the road this evening so it was going to be easy. He could be home in an hour or so in the mild August summer evening. But it was going to be a while before Jerem would stop seeing the man he shot fall to the ground. Later he would discover that only one member of the convoy was injured and died, and this upset him greatly. He peddled for the longest time and never let up until he saw some familiar landmarks and signs. The first road sign said Macroom, and he knew the next one would say Renanirree, so he kept on until he could see his white stucco home off in the distance. He had been instructed to leave the bicycle along side of the milk platform and someone would come by for it later that evening.

Jerem was able to get to the barn unseen and change out of his wet clothes into the dry ones he had stashed away just for this very reason. He sat on a bale of hay and tried to relax and calm himself down so when he went into the house it wouldn't be obvious that he had just recovered from a long ride on the bicycle and would not show signs of having been winded, such as a red face and a sweaty appearance. Having worked outside all his life, he did have a ruddy completion, with rosy cheeks.

Jerem prepared a good story to tell his father if he was pushed to explain his absence. He looked at his watch and it showed the time to be ten minutes before ten o'clock. Even though the sun was down he could still see very clearly outside. This was as good a time as any to go into the house and be confronted by his father. He knew that his mother would have been concerned the most, but Timothy would have dominated the interview. He also knew that his brothers and sisters would have stayed out of any confrontation with their father. Jerem knew that he would have to explain his whereabouts to someone, but most of all he wanted a nice hot cup of tea and something warm to eat. He was starving.

His father was waiting for him sitting at the kitchen table, and as soon as Jerem walked in the house the father wanted to know where he had been all day. Jerem had his story well rehearsed and told his father that he was making some inquiries for work in Cork as a factory worker so he could earn a wage and save some money for his future needs. Timsey was shocked to hear this news; he knew that things weren't good between them but didn't know that Jerem wanted to leave home and live in Cork. In shock, Timothy got up from the table and went into the sitting room and sat in his favorite chair near the fire place and just stared at the ceiling, very upset.

Jerem made himself a hot cup of tea, and warmed up some leftover supper, which he was eagerly waiting to sink his teeth into. His father came back in the kitchen while Jerem was eating and wanted to continue the conversation about his seeking work in Cork. Timsey was making a fuss about Jerem missing one day of work—maybe the only day he ever missed—and Jerem felt he had to tell his father that missing one day of work should not make him an outcast. The mother stepped between them and told Timsey to settle down and leave Jerem alone. "Can't you see that this is not an easy thing for him to do? You couldn't find a better man than Jerem to work on this farm with you so why do you want to run him off by bullying him all the time?" She took her finger to him and told him in Gaelic, "An rud ata sag cat ta se ina pisin." (What's in the cat is in the kitten.) The father looked long at her knowing that she was right, and he was heading in the wrong direction with Jerem.

Jerem was tired and had a long, not to mention a stressful day. He thanked his mother for speaking on his behalf, and she told him he was a good son and they relied on him a lot. With that he went to bed. He was exhausted from all the day's activities and wanted to be fresh in the morning, but he lay there thinking about what he had done and the next thing he knew it was time to get up. He and his two brothers were taking the milk down to the platform for pickup when the milk pickup truck came along. The driver and his helper jumped out and asked Jerem if he had heard the news that Michael Collins had been shot last evening by a single shot to the head. It happened in a small town, Beal na mBlath, and it was the republicans that are being blamed for it. There was news of it where they went. After the milk pickup the brothers hurried back to the house where they would usually meet for a big breakfast. They couldn't wait to tell their parents what happened, but the commotion being made by the others was making Jerem nauseous. He couldn't finish his breakfast, and just sat there quietly sipping his cup of tea, looking out the window with a queer look on his face. He was starting to worry if someone would come and arrest him or what the republicans were going to do to him to keep him silent. All these thoughts would come to mind often, especially when he went to bed. Laying there by himself he had plenty of time to think about what he did. He was more scared of someone coming to the farm and arresting him than anything else.

He remembered all the clamor and confusion at the ambush scene, but he was almost positive that no one knew he fired that fatal shot, so he promised himself not to claim credit for the shooting. The next evening his father went down to the pub and saw all the familiar faces, including his neighbor Dan Kelleher, a relative on his wife's side. His main reason for going this evening was to hear the latest news about the shooting. The only thing being talked about at the pub this evening was the shooting death of Michael Collins.

Someone said that an ex-British army marksman instinctively felt he might have hit the commander-in-chief of the National Forces, but most people didn't believe anything he had to say. The pub owner liked to speak Gaelic and said to the group at the bar, "Is beag an aithinne a dheanfadh do." (A spark may raise an awful blaze.) He knew this was not going to go unsettled, and all hopes of reconciliation between the republicans and the Free State forces were shattered.

Almost three years passed before Jerem went to Cork and applied for a visa to go to America. He had been writing to an aunt in Brockton, Massachusetts, who had painted a beautiful picture of America, and he needed a change from the worries that had been eating away at him. What if he were discovered? He still worried that the republicans might want to silence him forever, what would happen to him if he were found out, and if the republicans would stand up for him. He clearly wanted to go away to America.

One day Jerem went home and told his mother that he applied for a visa to go to America. She was worried that he may leave home still on bad terms with his father, but she wished him good luck. He told her he had a while to wait for his notice of acceptance and he would go to Cork again to pick up his visa. He waited for almost nine months, but finally his letter came saying that he was accepted to immigrate to America, and he would have to go to Cork to pick up his visa and passport, the best news he could get.

While in Cork in August 1926, Jerem booked passage for his trip to America. He had every penny he ever earned and could well afford his trip. When he went home his parents were sitting at the table drinking their evening cup of tea. Jerem sat at the table and told his parents that he would be leaving for America in a few weeks. His father stood up and left the table. Jerem told his mother that his father didn't try to be civil about him going away, and it hurt him and he would never forget it. Margaret knew that he didn't want to be a farmer, and completely understood him. His father didn't want to lose his son, whose help he needed on the farm. Jerem was not the bad guy here. He and his father had a clash of life styles, and Jerem had to go away and start a different life.

His father was visibly shaken because he could see that Jerem wasn't going to be the last one to go. Jerem said, "There's nothing around here to keep me at home. I know I can do better in America." What nobody knew was that he was going to be safer there as well.

Margaret was calmer. She knew the chickens were going to leave the nest; she cried a little and recovered quickly. Jerem knew his father was going to go down to the pub for a drink and some hell raising. His father hardly spoke to him after that. Although Jerem wasn't leaving for a fortnight, he would still do his chores. His brothers couldn't understand why he wanted to leave home and go to America when they felt he had everything right here at home. The last night Jerem was to spend in Ireland, his parents went to bed early. His mother said good-bye and good luck and please come home to visit. His father never said anything to him. His sister Julia helped him pack a suitcase and put two belt straps around it to keep it from opening. Jerem had to get up at 4:00 a.m. to start what was going to be the adventure of his life. He had made arrangements for his mate to drive him to the dock in Queenstown which is known as Cobh today. The only person he saw as he was leaving was his parish priest and a few parishioners who were going to Mass. Jerem didn't recognize any of them.

On ship, it was barely 8:00 when the ship's horn sounded loud and long to indicate the ship would be leaving in five minutes. The ride on the tender which was named Blarney to the ship anchored out in the channel which all Jerem needed to get his sea legs Although he had heard good stories about America, she was still apprehensive. His Aunt Mary on his mother's side was his sponsor and would meet him at the immigration pier and take him home with her. He was going to have eight days at sea to think. He was sure he had made the right decision, even though the smell of oil from the ship seemed to seep into his clothes and the food he ate didn't take away from his feelings about coming to America.

Jerem shared his room at sea with five other men. At night some of them had the sniffles. They were homesick before the second night. He noticed that everyone seemed to be in groups of two or three. Jerem was a loner and he didn't mind that at all. Early on the ninth morning the captain announced they could be in Massachusetts in two hours. Jerem couldn't see anything in the fog, but somehow it was beautiful. He knew his long voyage was over and was excited to meet his aunt and build a new life.

Everyone had to disembark the ship and go through immigration and customs. It wasn't that hard for Jerem because he had all his papers in order. They gave him an on-site short physical, and he was good to go. He decided to leave the O' off O'Riordan, because someone else had left it off at the immigration office. He felt that this would make it harder to be tracked down if someone was looking for him concerning the shooting. I guess when you think someone would be looking for you, you might think that way. Soon Jerem was on his way with Aunt Mary to her home, and he saw something he had never seen before—a black person. He couldn't stop looking at him. After dinner Jerem couldn't keep his eyes open so his aunt talked him in to going to bed.

Jerem was not comfortable in Massachusetts and work was hard to find, so after three months had passed and still no job he listened to Aunt Mary's suggestion that he should meet up with J.D. Kelly from Wilmington, Delaware (a good friend to the Irish who might help him find employment). Arrangements were made for Jerem to meet Mr. Kelly at the Wilmington train station on a Friday. The train ride was long and uncomfortable. He liked to stand up and walk a little just to keep his circulation going, and before he knew it the train was pulling into Wilmington early in the evening. He only had a vague description of J.D. Kelly and hoped that Mr. Kelly would recognize him. When at last

Jerem stepped off the train, suitcase in hand containing all his worldly possessions, wearing travel wrinkled clothes, there was Mr. Kelly standing in front of him and said "Mr. Riordan I presume." Jerem nodded his head saying, "That I am sir." Mr. Kelly replied, "A fine Irish brogue if I ever heard one." He introduced himself and said they just had time to catch the bus. "Come along, lad."

The bus took them near the J.D. Kelly home in the area of Wilmington called the Forty Acres, clearly an affluent neighborhood. (Forty Acres was a community on the outskirts of Wilmington where many Irish lived; there was strength in numbers.) Jerem could see that Mr. Kelly had done well for himself in America .Mr. Kelly asked Jerem if he was hungry and when Jerem nodded yes Mr. Kelly pulled out a ham and cheese sandwich and a soft drink. Jerem exclaimed that it was the best sandwich he ever had. Understandable after the long journey on the train and nothing to eat.

The first thing Mr. Kelly had Jerem do was to write down the Kelly address and phone number so if he got lost he could give an address or call the house for help. Mr. Kelly showed Jerem his room and told him to get a good night sleep that the weather was going to be good tomorrow. Jerem sat on the bed laid back and didn't awaken until seven o'clock in the morning. Mrs. Kelly made him a wonderful breakfast and a good cup of tea; Jerem told them that he wanted to take a walk around the neighborhood.

Jerem had put on a light jacket and found himself in front of St. Ann's church where he walked by a young priest reading his missal. He looked up and saw Jerem and asked where he was from. Jerem told the young priest that he was from Ireland and that he was staying with J.D. Kelly, and the priest said, "Ah Mr. Kelly, he's a good friend to the Irish." Jerem told the priest he was looking for a job. The priest told him that Archmere Academy, a private Catholic school for boys, was looking for a live-in janitor and gave him directions and bus numbers to get to the school east of Claymont.

When he got there, Jerem made his way to the office and asked about the live-in janitor's job. He was hired on the spot. He lived in one of the towers on campus and was paid $24 for 44 hours of work. Jerem didn't mind; he was working and was earning some money. He had a nice room that doubled as a bedroom at night. He had a sofa, and a nice radio. That's more than he had at home. Jerem said that he would need a few days to straighten out some of his personal affairs and start bright and early Monday morning. He hit it off with the students and the faculty, and the weeks flew by. When they paid him every Friday, he would put at least half his money away in a savings account.

It wasn't long before Jerem was in the swing of things. He wrote Julia about what he was doing and the money he was making. He told her he had a place to live that came with his salary. He praised the priest at Archmere and was happy about how well he got along with everyone. Julia wrote back, asking about joining him. She told him how she and Bina were working very hard for a pittance, really in a rut, and that they wanted out. Julia told him at the end of the letter that she wanted to come over. After she got her visa, she sent Jerem another letter telling him when she was leaving and her time of arrival, asking would he meet her. Julia was hoping that Jerem got her letter and was a little nervous if he would be there to meet her at Ellis Island.

2

Julia's parents were not happy that another child was leaving home. The last night was long and lonely for Julia. Bina was away with the family she was working for. Julia never slept, for she, too, had to be up at four to meet her ride into Queenstown and catch her ship to America. When she got to the ship it was drizzling. The priest gave everyone communion. He told them that America was a big place, and to be careful. She didn't have that much money on her because her pay had been used to keep the house, and Timsey was drinking a lot now. When they announced over the speaker system that they will be arriving in New York in the morning. She knew this was going to be a chance for her to start a new life.

Jerem, who was her sponsor, was waiting on the Ellis Island ferry platform. He spotted her carrying a big case. They weren't much on hugging, so Jerem took her bag and they headed for Penn Station. Julia told Jerem what had happened the last night at home. Her parents wouldn't say goodbye to her. They blamed him for breaking up the family. She told him the silence was deafening. She also told him that when her ride to cork drove down the lane to pick her up, she walked out and never looked back. On the train, Julia quickly fell asleep and slept all the way to Delaware. Jerem knew that with an Irish accent she was going to be a big hit in Delaware.

Jerem had heard that a woman in Westover Hills, an upscale neighborhood in Wilmington, was looking for a live-in house keeper. Julia went for an interview; the woman loved her and told Julia that eventually she could cook as well for more money. The pay was $16 a week, plus free housing and food. Julia was tickled pink to get such a good salary. She couldn't believe of all the opportunities here in America.

She was very happy with her new employers, Mr. and Mrs. Gibson. Julia was a big saver and was able to put most of her pay in the bank. Mrs. Gibson explained to Julia what food the family liked and what they would expect for dinner. She would place a three-by-five card on the kitchen counter every morning telling Julia what the dinner menu would be. With this addition to Julia's duties she received a $6 a week pay hike. This was very good money, but very hard work. At the end of the day Julia was a tired woman, she didn't mind because she had no other distractions from her work. To Julia, work came first, and there isn't anything wrong with that. The Gibson's were very happy with Julia, and they knew other families who could afford someone like her but couldn't find anyone. Julia told Mrs. Gibson she had a sister at home who would come over; Mrs. Gibson replied that she could get her sister a job sight unseen. Julia wrote Bina a letter and told her about the good news, even offering to pay her way. Bina was excited to hear more about the great picture Julia painted of her life in America. Julia told her what she could expect, and how much money she could make. This news couldn't have been timed any better, because Bina was exhausted and not making any money, having to have to turn some of her money over to her father, who drank it all up down the pub every night. So Bina went to Cork to fill out the paperwork to come over to America, and soon she got her visa and passport.

Bina had to give some notice to her employer, who hated to lose such a hard worker. She was afraid to tell her parents, but they weren't that upset because Bina had helped them so much that they were indebted to her. They never made her feel guilty for leaving. They wished her good luck, and asked her to write a letter now and then. Her brothers and sisters were very happy for her and said maybe some day they would come, too. The last night at home they all sat around the table having soda bread and tea. It was a very happy occasion; her parents were as nice as they could be, even though they were loosing another child to America. The way Bina had told her parents she was going to America made the occasion a happy one. She told her parents she had lived her life so as not to ever offend them and that they could be proud of her. She had done everything a girl could do for her parents, but it was time to move on and make a new life in America. It was the spring of 1928 and all the flowers and bushes had buds on them. Bina walked around and really looked the place over so she could form a picture in her mind forever.

That night her parents told her they were going to miss her. There were hugs and tears and it was over in seconds. They went to bed early, and it became very quiet. Bina's old employer took her to Queenstown to catch her ship. When they got there Mrs. Sullivan was crying and hugged Bina and told her to be safe. Then Mrs. Sullivan said in Gaelic, "Maireann Croi Eadrom I Bhfad." ("A light heart lives long.")

After her bumpy ride on the tender Bina walked up the gangplank to be greeted by her parish priest, who had gathered up about a dozen sad-looking women. He gave them communion and asked them to make a promise. He asked that they pledge, by placing their right hand on their prayer books, that they would never drink alcohol or smoke any tobacco for the rest of their lives. Those girls took that pledge not realizing what he was asking them to do. Bina kept her pledge and never drank any alcohol or smoked any tobacco for the rest of her life. I am proud of her resolve but feel it was unfair of that priest, to have those young ladies pledge to such a thing when they hadn't even started a life. It was unfair of him to ask those young ladies to do something he couldn't do himself. Those priests were invited to too many going away wakes and the parties before the Irish left for America not to drink along with the rest of the invited guests. They were known to get soused and find a chair to sleep in.

The ship's horn went off. Bina ran to the rail to see if anyone had come down to see her off. It was too far to see with the naked eye there was no one there for her. She knew her family didn't have a way to Queenstown; nevertheless it didn't stop the pain she felt in her stomach. She felt a little tug from the ship and knew it was leaving. It wasn't until they were at sea that she could feel the motion of the ship. Scared and cold, Bina went looking for her room. It turned out to be an all-female ward with twelve beds, each with a blue woolen blanket. The room was just at the water line, which she found very scary. She had one towel and had to share the bath room and tub with eleven other women. So many people used the hot water that it was rarely hot. They were afraid to complain. There was only one roll of toilet paper. Bina found more in a closet and hid some in her suitcase.

She would live out of a suitcase for the next eight days. There was a lot of commotion, but eventually it quieted down. She opened her suitcase and got out her needles and yarn. She thought it would be a good time to knit a sweater to take her mind off everything, especially her journey across the sea. She looked up to see a frail little girl struggling to walk down the narrow aisle to the only bed available. It was next to Bina's bed. The girl introduced herself as Nora Desman. They hit it off well and Bina made a friend on board. It wasn't long before they would do everything together, meeting every morning for breakfast and in the evening for dinner. Nora told Bina that her brother was meeting her, and they were going to Wilmington, Delaware. Bina said, "I think that's where I am going; my brother is meeting me too." After that bit of news they became inseparable.

The last night of the voyage one of the girls sat on the bed and started telling everyone a story about the only missing submarine of World War I and how it was creating havoc on all the ships in the Atlantic. She told them it was a ghost ship, sinking passenger liners and cargo ships cruising off the coast of America. Suddenly the ship was making loud noises; the story teller would pick up on the noises. She could change her voice in so many ways that the girls were shaking in their beds. Suddenly the ship jerked hard followed by a loud noise. When she heard a second noise, Bina felt this was the end. The lights went out, everyone was screaming, and Bina was right in there with them. It was pitch black. As they huddled together, holding hands, suddenly the lights came on. Where was the storyteller? They found her in bed with the blankets pulled over her head, shaking like she was freezing. A crew member came in and explained that the noises were caused by cargo coming loose and a blown fuse. Everything was OK now and they expected to be in New York by 10:00 o'clock the next morning.

That morning Bina and Nora walked together down the ship's ramp. When they got to the bottom, a man in a blue uniform was telling people to get in line according to the initials of their last name. Nora and Bina were split up quickly. Bina got in the "R" line just like Jerem and Julia had done. It was her turn to be interviewed. Bina answered all the questions and filled out forms. After about an hour she was told to see the doctor in the white coat. Nervously Bina gave him her papers. The doctor asked her if she ever had any serious illnesses, such as tuberculosis. She said no. He unbuttoned her sweater and blouse and put his stethoscope down her blouse to listen to her heart and lungs. He filled out a few papers and gave her an exit card. She was free to go. As she left the building, Bina could see the New York skyline, and Jerem sitting on the wall along the river. He walked toward her and took her suitcase. He told her that Julia wanted to come also but couldn't get off work. He was telling Bina about his trip to

New York and she was telling him about her trip to America. She told him she met a girl on board named Desman, who had a brother in Wilmington. Jerem wasn't sure if he heard of him or not.

They got to the train station early, and Jerem pointed out where she could get her ticket. Fortunately, Bina had changed all of her money into American dollars at Ellis Island. She paid for the ticket with a bill that had a 10 on it, and she got some ones for change. They sat on big wooden bench, with plenty of time to kill. She was hungry and walked over to a food stand and bought a ham and cheese sandwich. She was lucky to get a cup of tea as well. Bina filled Jerem in about the family at home, and how they had accepted her leaving home. Bina didn't think any of the others would be coming to America. Eventually Jerem asked if anyone had come to the farm looking for him. She told him she worked away all week, and only came home on weekends, so she wouldn't know. But Bina was curious who would be looking for him. Jerem, not knowing how to answer her said, "Anyone from town, you know, maybe any important people." Bina could see he had a worried look on his face, and told him that no one came around looking for him. He seemed and completely changed after that conversation. Then Jerem had some good news; Julia had made arrangements for Bina to interview with a family in Westover Hills in the same community where she works. Maybe she could live in with them, and all her meals would be included. Like Julia, Bina couldn't help but notice the differences in America: the way people dressed the food packaging. It was a simple thing, but the things that were supposed to be cold were cold. She could see that Jerem was different too. He seemed to have lost the chip on his shoulder. Even his name was different. Jerem told Bina, "By the way, everyone calls me Jerry here, so if you don't mind please call me Jerry from now on. I'm used to it now."

When they boarded the train Bina sat by the window. Jerry sat quietly while Bina slept all the way to Wilmington. As they walked out of the train station he told Bina they had to catch a bus back to Archmere Academy, where she could stay with him until she got her job. He had already cleared it with the priest beforehand. It was a long bus ride to Claymont. When they got there he took her to his room. She slept on the foldaway bed and he slept on the sofa. She lay down, clothes an all, and fell right to sleep. By 7:00 a.m. Sunday they both were awake. Suddenly Bina felt sorry about leaving her parents. She wondered if she would ever see her parents again. But soon they were off on the bus to see Julia. As they arrived at the back door of Julia's residence, Jerry tapped on the door, and Julia came to the door out of breath. It had to be from the excitement of not seeing her sister for over a year and now meeting her in a different county 3,000 miles away.

She was happy to see Bina and they held hands while Julia told her, "I think if you want the job you will probably get it." They both were happy to see each other, and Julia put on the kettle and they had tea with cookies. After Jerry left, Julia took Bina's things to her room. She asked Bina to stay the night so she could take her for the interview the next day. Bina hoped that the family she hoped to work for, the Babbots of Westover Hills were nice; they came highly recommended by Julia's employers, the Gibsons.

The next day, Julia was given the morning off to help Bina. She and Bina went to a beautiful house. They knocked gently on the front door, which was answered by a lovely woman with an attractive smile. Her teeth were perfect. Julia introduced Bina as her sister. Mrs. Babbot was waiting to hear her accent. Mrs. Babbot shook hands with two hands, a most sincere greeting. They hit it off wonderfully. Mrs. Babbot showed them through the house. They sat in the breakfast nook and talked over a cup of tea, of course. Bina couldn't believe that she would ever be in a house so luxurious.

Mrs. Babbot finally asked Bina if she would come live with them. She told Bina that her hours would be from 7:00 a.m. to 6:00 p.m. Monday through Friday, and Saturdays till 10:30 in the morning. She would have a beautiful furnished room and bath, with not much laundry to do. Mrs. Babbot had two children, Billy, five, and Nancy, four. Bina would be expected to do some light cooking until the kids got a little older, when she might do more cooking and less housework. Her pay would be $16 a week, which would include room and board. She would have an hour for lunch, and one week's paid vacation after the first year. Mrs. Babbot measured for Bina's sizes and would purchase her three black and white maid's outfits, which she expected Bina to keep clean and well ironed.

Bina was so excited; she hardly knew what to say. Mrs. Babbot asked her if she would start the following Monday, and move in Sunday. Mrs. Babbot assured her that she would show her everything and help her learn the family's ways. It seemed it would be easy after a while. Bina met Mr. William Babbot the first morning she started. By the end of the first week she was doing things with ease. Everyone was getting along very well. The children liked it when Bina would play with them, especially when she would sing some of the old Irish songs and play Irish games, like soccer, Billy and Nancy's favorite. Her cooking experience from Ireland would come in handy, especially her soups. She could make everyone soup and a sandwich for lunch that would make them clean their bowls and plates.

One day Mrs. Babbot asked Bina to make them an Irish dinner on Sunday. Bina gave her a list of food she would need to prepare the meal. Mrs. Babbot was excited and couldn't wait for Sunday. Bina told them that dinner was an hour early, at 4:00 instead of 5:00 p.m. They were all sitting around the table waiting for their special Sunday dinner with an Irish flair.

Bina made roast beef with Yorkshire pudding, succotash, and small boiled potatoes peeled and cut in half. The topper was the dark brown gravy she modestly put in a gravy server for them to taste. The roast beef had to be just right, not bloody but medium. Bina was out in the kitchen when Mrs. Babbot came bursting in the kitchen, crying, "Everyone loved the meal and where did you ever learn to make gravy like that?" Mr. Babbot was speechless. He is just sitting looking out the window. Bina told her she had a surprise for dessert. Mrs. Babbot ran like a little girl, saying that Bina has a surprise for us. She had made her mother's famous apple cake. Not a pie, but cake, in a flat pan about an inch deep, with whipped cream on top. The Babbots applauded her and Bina modestly smiled at all this attention she was getting.

Bina heard Mrs. Babbot talking to her friends about the special dinner. She just wanted to tell everyone. It was becoming more popular now to have an Irish girl living in and cooking. Mrs. Babbot started having women over for a light lunch. She would tell Bina to prepare soup and think of some good sandwiches for her friends. Bina made them each a triple-decker roast beef sandwich with horseradish, lettuce, tomatoes, and pickles. She could hear them from the kitchen. The Women were screaming like a bunch of little girls. Because Mrs. Babbot was having Bina do more cooking now, she increased her pay increase to $24 a week, And she had a girl come in to help Bina with the housekeeping two days a week. Now Bina could send home $24 once a month to help her mother out, which was a generous amount (probably around 8 pounds 10 shillings). If Timsey could leave that money alone they could be in good shape. She never said anything to Julia about it, and Julia never mentioned if she was sending money home either. Bina felt bad about leaving home and would mail the money as long as she could; she had opened a savings account and was putting money away too, for a rainy day.

Bina was enjoying her work but nothing else. Julia kept asking her to come to the Irish dances, but Bina didn't want to go. It was over a year before she said she would. Julia told her where to meet and they would all go in together. Right off she saw her old friend from Ireland, Patrick Sullivan, and his Irish girlfriend Bridget. Bina made a lot of friends from the dances, like Tom Tobin and his girlfriend Lilly. She also saw Dan Kelleher, who had lived near her farm in Ireland. It made Bina feel so good to see people that she knew from back home. It was comforting to hear Irish accents again, and to see the weather-beaten faces of the men with their red rosy cheeks.

She saw Jerry dancing and would roll with laughter; it was funny to see him with young girls. Bina was having as much fun as Jerry, who just let it all go; he could keep it up all night. Bina didn't go every Saturday; sometimes the Sullivans would invite her over and talk about old times in Ireland. Sometimes they would make dinner. That was fun, too, because Bina always wanted to help out. Other times she would go out with the Tobins, who introduced her to Jack Fleming and his girlfriend. They all were from County Cork, Ireland; they all had a grand time together.

Julia had made a friend named Alex Davenport. He could really put some booze away. It affected him a lot more quickly than the others. It wouldn't take much for Davenport to start fighting. He was very loud and obnoxious when he was drinking, all the right ingredients for a good fight. Julia kept pestering Bina to go to more dances, but the fall of the stock market and all the depression talk made Bina scared about her job. Mrs. Babbot reassured Bina that everything was going to be all right.

In 1931 Jerry introduced Bina to one of the few people at the dance who was Irish but not born in Ireland. They called him Sonny Jim, his father was gentleman Jim. He was very tall with curly hair parted down the middle. He looked like he was chewing gum, but he wasn't, it was just a nervous thing he would do. Bina was only five foot four inches tall, and Sonny Jim was six feet tall. She was so shy she could hardly look in his eyes. He was nervous, too. What a mix. If he didn't force the conversation Bina was very quiet. He told Bina his name was Jim Toner Jr. He had a way of making people laugh. Bina could hardly breathe after she shook his hand; she felt a little weak in the legs and sat down. He brought her a little punch. Up until then she hadn't had much to do with boys or men. Jim was painting around town with Jack Fleming, Bill Casey, and Tom Tobin. They were starting to make a name for themselves.

Jim used to caddy over at the Wilmington Country Club, just on the edge of Westover Hills. He had a friend there named Porky Oliver. They would play golf all the time, but Porky was too good for him and most anyone else. Porky would win all the money on caddie's day. Eventually Jim concentrated on painting. He made better money and could work year round.

Jim seemed to like what he saw, a nice Irish girl who never drank or smoked. She was just right for some one with honorable intentions. She gave him Mrs. Babbot's phone number, but he didn't have a phone number to give her. His parents hardly had a bed to sleep in, but Bina didn't know that. He lived in a three-story apartment on Pennsylvania Avenue that sat high off the ground, just a three-room dingy little place with shades on the windows that were down all the time. It was all they could afford because when his father was paid, he was determined to drink Wilmington dry. None of the bars would send him home; they kept taking his money. If he wasn't falling down some railroad trestle hill, he would be in a fight in or out of the bar.

Jim's father was well known around the Forty Acres as the guy who had fallen off every railroad bridge or siding in Wilmington. Every one in the Forty Acres knew him as Gentleman Jim because he hadn't worked a day after age 40 because of all his drunken injuries. He was a conductor on the trolley cars and sometimes did blacksmithing. When he was drunk and falling down, he would break something like an arm or leg or hip and was usually hard to rescue. He was spending more time in the Wilmington ambulances than he did at home. He couldn't keep a job. His poor wife had to scrub floors in Wilmington; otherwise they would have been homeless. The only time he had any humility was when he was recuperating from one of his broken bones.

Jim had three sisters who were very nice. Some day Bina would meet them all. Jim's mother should have been canonized because of how she kept things together. What kept her from running away is one of the true mysteries in the last hundred years.

Jim did call Bina. He wanted to go out with her. They would always meet somewhere, always with another couple. Bina felt safe that way. She would have a girl to talk to, usually about work. The guys didn't know how to talk to their dates so they would talk between themselves. Bina was beginning to feel a little more comfortable around Jim, who wanted her to meet his parents. He didn't realize it, but Bina was used to being around the best of everything working in Westover Hills.

When they went to visit his parents, he had to hold her arm walking her up the steep steps, at least 24 steps to the front door. They finally got to the small porch. He lived on the second floor, so they had to walk up another 14 steps to his apartment door. Bina was breathing heavily; she couldn't cover it up. He unlocked the door and walked in with Bina right behind him. His mother was the first to see her. She jumped out of the chair, took Bina's hand and asked her to be seated on the sofa, which was covered with a lot of pillows to cover up the worn spots.

As Jim's mother asked Bina if she would like a cup of tea, everyone heard the toilet flush. The bathroom door opened and a pale, unshaven man stood in the doorway. He was about six feet tall, and they couldn't help but see that his fly was down. He was missing four of his front bottom teeth. He was the older version of James Jr. Bina could see that he was not that old, but the drinking had taken its toll on Gentleman Jim. Sober he was a different man.

Mrs. Toner made Bina feel very comfortable, and kept bringing the tea and cookies. The father sat down at a small desk and turned on a little light. He rolled out a small white towel full of knives and pliers and clamps. He had all the tools to operate on himself if he wanted. Jim asked him what he was doing with all his tools. He said he was going to remove the nail on the ring finger of his left hand. It wasn't long before he had the job done; he was putting peroxide on his finger and had a bandage ready to put on in minutes. Bina couldn't believe how fast he did that. There was never a cry of pain a moan or anything like that. When he covered his finger with the white bandage she could see the blood come through the gauze. He put some white medical tape around his finger. Mr. Toner never said anything after he was introduced to Bina.

Jim was so proud of his Irish girlfriend. He could see that his Mother liked Bina. He knew there wasn't anything his father could say because he didn't know anything to talk about, having never gone to school. It was the mother who spoke to Bina. She had had some education and wanted to treat Bina the same way she would want someone to treat her daughters.

It was pitiful to see Jim's mother dressed the way she was. Her clothes were practically in rags, and her nylons were the thick ones that doubled as trousers. She was so humble that she probably never had her hair done in a beauty parlor. Her clothes had been washed so many times that she had to be careful not to pull to hard on them or they would come apart. She told Bina that Jim Sr. wouldn't do anything to help her, and on Christmas Eve she would ask him to go out and get a tree. After he lugged it up the stairs he would throw it in the corner of the room upright leaning up against the wall. It would stay there undecorated, a bare tree for Christmas. No gifts underneath, just a bowl of fruit on the table that would only be half eaten and then rot.

Jim had told his mother that Bina was a cook for a family in Westover Hills. Bina felt sorry for her when she heard how the mother had to cook a meal from scraps. A small piece of liver and a few potatoes divided between sometimes five or six people. It wasn't hard to be slim in that family because there wasn't anything to eat. Thank God when they all wouldn't show up for dinner. The family didn't have anything to look forward to, except getting out of the house. For the girls, the first good thing that came along would be their way to get out. Junior was Mommy's boy; she knew she had to keep an eye on him. She knew he was drinking and she didn't want him to be like his father. She also knew that the drinkers called it having a great time.

Bina felt bad after seeing his family living in what could only be described as poverty, it made her appreciate the wonderful life she was having and was very happy with the Babbots. They treated her just like family. The kids would make a fuss over her all the time. It made her feel good, but there was a hollow spot in her heart. She missed her mother but couldn't write because it was too painful. She would often lie in bed wondering how her brothers and sisters were doing. Their life styles were so different now. She received a letter from her sister Bridget, who told her that their father would sit on the porch in the summer with her mother looking at the setting sun in the evening sky, saying, "I wonder how the weather is where the children are." That news really upset her. Bina was so caught up with her life in Delaware that her thoughts didn't go to Ireland any more because it was too painful.

Jim asked Bina if she wanted to go to a New Year's Eve Party with him in the Forty Acres to welcome in the New Year, 1932. Lots of people were dancing and drinking, and let's not forget fighting. (Davenport would always have a hand in a good fight.) Bina went and sat with all the other girls talking about work. Bina didn't have to be at work till noon the next day. The good hot Irish music was on, and the loud catcalls began, along with the foot stomping. It was something to see. Jim was chewing his gum like mad, Davenport was loud as hell. She couldn't understand how Julia could put up with him; Julia was a little more advanced in this environment than Bina.

Bina never worried about being under the influence. She never forgot the pledge that she had made on the ship that cold drizzly morning. Her religious beliefs always held her in check. Even if he had been drinking,

Jim didn't have the guts to force Bina into anything. She was the best thing that ever happened to him, and he knew she was determined not to do anything before she was married. Most of the girls felt the same way. Most of the people at the party were passed out and no one was going to risk driving. So Bina curled up in a chair and fell asleep. They all woke up with a headache except Bina and a few girls. Bina looked at her watch and needed a ride to Westover Hills. Pat Sullivan asked his friend to take Bina back to Westover Hills before noon there was plenty of time.

Jim bought an old 1928 Ford. He thought he was a big shot, but it would have been better if he would have given his mother some money. With a car he could see Bina more, mostly on weekends. One evening while sitting outside the Babbots, Jim asked Bina if she would marry him. He told her he was saving up for a ring. Bina was in shock, knowing her whole life would change. Scared, she said yes, and Jim hugged her for the longest time. She opened the door and ran toward the house like a rabbit. As she lay in bed that evening, she wondered about her job, if she could still work. Where would she live? Was Jim still going to make good money painting? She hoped so. What kind of a husband was he going to be? She fell asleep with a lot of questions unanswered. But like all women in love she was blind to her future husband's shortcomings. She knew how his father was, but she never realized the son was a mirror image.

3

On April 20, 1933, a beautiful Saturday afternoon, Bina and Jim were married at Saint Ann's Church. Jim's parents, his sisters, and all their Irish friends were present. Mr. and Mrs. Babbot came with the children. They wouldn't miss it for anything. Bina had a beautiful long white gown, with a veil and all the trimmings. She looked stunning. Tom and Lilly Tobin were the best man and bridesmaid. They only had one picture taken, of the four of them together. Bina paid for the reception, the cake, and the hall rental. Jim used his car expenses as an excuse for not helping out. This should have been a warning of the awful things to come.

Bina wanted to keep working, which delighted the Babbots. She had a week off, and the couple looked for a house or an apartment to rent. They found a furnished one on Pennsylvania Avenue, not far from Jim's parents' apartment. If it weren't for the landlady's furniture, they would have had only their clothes. Jim wasn't tuned in to how to be a husband or provider so that they could buy furniture and all the other things newlyweds need to buy. It frightened him and made him look like he didn't care, but actually he was just in over his head. He became restless and would make up excuses to go out.

When Bina told him she was pregnant, he seemed scared instead of excited, which took the joy out of the occasion. As long as they could have sex he was happy. Bina was determined to work as long as she could, and as long as she was bringing money home Jim never tried to bring home a little more. He didn't have much to contribute. Because she spent so much time on her feet, it was getting harder for Bina to work. Her ankles would swell up, and she would have to come home and put her legs up. In her eighth month she finally told Mrs. Babbot that she couldn't go on. Mrs. Babbot knew it was coming; she could see Bina's ankles at the end of the day.

Mr. Babbot sat with Bina and told her how much the family loved her and to call them if she ever needed help. He gave Bina her pay and another week on top of that. Bina was happy with that, knowing she would need it.

Bina couldn't get over her fear when she wondered why she couldn't rely more on Jim. What was it going to be like now that she had to quit work? She had to go to the doctor by herself; she didn't even know how she was going to get to the hospital. She could hear Mrs. Toner telling her how Jim couldn't be relied on, that he just couldn't handle responsibility, and how it scared him to death.

Bina was relieved when he offered to take her to nearby St. Francis Hospital. After a hard delivery, she gave birth to a little girl, whom she named Theresa, on February 27, 1934. The baby looked a little like Bina's mother, Margaret, without the pipe of course. Jim was asleep in the hospital lounge. The janitor mopping the floor hit his chair and woke him up. A nurse came in and told him that he was the father of a little girl, seven pounds eight ounces. His legs got weak. He sat down to gather his thoughts and then followed the nurse. He held Theresa proudly; he stayed in Bina's room until the staff told him to go home. He could return the next day and be with his wife and baby again.

Four days later Bina was discharged. Jim waited in his car as she and Theresa were brought out in a big, wooden wheel chair. Bina told him she needed diapers, powder, and baby supplies, but Jim was upset because he had to dig into his drinking money. She wanted him to know how important it was to work every day. Theresa was only nine months old when Bina had to go out and scrub floors in a local office building at night. She would rely on him to watch Theresa at night until she got home at 2:00 a.m. She was on her knees for hours and returned home tired and aching. Many times Jim failed to change Theresa's dipper and he would be asleep when Bina would come in from work in the morning. By the time Bina fell asleep she had to be up with Theresa in the morning. Often Jim demanded sex before she could get out of bed.

Jim was not a happy babysitter. On the week ends Jim didn't have to watch Theresa, so he went out drinking with friends. This ate into the rent and food money. It is hard to believe that Bina was cheerful, but she was.

She loved singing little Irish songs to Theresa while she was feeding her. She loved to sing "Twiddle Diddle Dumpling My Son John," bouncing Theresa on her knee and laughing at Theresa's smiling face.

Theresa started walking when she was 13 months old; she was sturdy and had good balance. Bina could see that Theresa was having trouble seeing things, so by the time she was two she had her tested. The doctor said that Theresa would need glasses and Bina didn't know how she was going to keep them on her. But Theresa never had to be scolded about wearing her glasses; she knew how important it was to leave them on.

By then Bina was pregnant again and was expecting to deliver sometime in August. This pregnancy was difficult, and she had to stop working at seven months. She had to stay home and keep her feet up because of her ankles. There was barely enough to live on, and this extra responsibility was making Jim worse. He wanted to be out with the boys, just like his father. Wouldn't you know it, like father like son.

On August 4, 1936, at Bina gave birth to a healthy son, seven pounds, four ounces. She said he looked just like his father so she called him James E. Toner III. To Bina he looked like a little Irish man, so his nickname was Maneen. In Irish that meant little man. Grand mom Toner watched Theresa while Bina was in the hospital. When they brought Maneen home, Theresa wanted to hold him right away, so she sat on the sofa and Maneen was put on her lap. She was speechless. Theresa was a big help to her mother right away. She loved rocking Maneen in his bassinette after his meals. She followed Bina around wherever she went.

Bina's employer understood that when Bina told him she couldn't work every evening. He was very flexible because he knew she was a good worker, honest, and reliable. But soon Bina was pregnant again. The third child would come in August again. Little Theresa would rub her mother's belly and talk to the baby inside. Maneen was still an infant, so Theresa did everything she could for her mother. It was a big help fetching thinks, rocking Maneen. Bina was going to have her hands full with this third one.

With a third child coming, it was clear that the apartment was too small. Julia found a house on Rodney Street. They were able to get it and move in before the baby was born. So at 4:00 p.m. on August 21, 1937, another boy weighed in at eight pounds, six ounces. Mommy told everyone that I just jumped out of her; she could already see that I was rambunctious. Jim was working or saying he was. Bina's brother Jerry was taking an interest in this birth, so she named the baby after Jeremiah

(Jerry) Riordan Jerome Toner. He was so proud that the baby was named after him. He must have told every one over at Bancroft Mills, where he worked.

At the christening, Jerry Riordan and Bridget Sullivan were my godparents. But the priest wrote down the wrong name. Somehow he wrote the name John on the official church register, when it should have been Jerome. So right off the bat I had two names, Jerome and John. Finally Jerry took the birth certificate over to the rectory and made them correct it. Mommy was calling me "Baby," a nickname she loved. When Baby would cry, she simply asked if Baby wanted some candy. She said my eyes would light up and I would stop crying. She would put a tiny piece of candy in my mouth and let me taste it. Then I would suck a little and fall right back to sleep. I didn't start walking until I was fifteen months old, having a hard time with my balance. I liked to hold onto things for a long time in order to reassure myself that it would be safe to stand alone and not fall down. My uncle Jerry had a balancing problem and it looked like it ran in the O'Riordan blood line.

The house on Rodney Street was too costly, so Mommy found a house at 1907 West Fourth Street, where they moved in the spring of 1940. A few months later, their fourth child was born November 19, 1940. Mommy named her Margaret after her mother. Theresa was six years old now and going to attend St. Thomas School on Fourth Street. When ever Mommy sat me and my brother on the front step, eventually we would stand up. Then if no one would say anything we would step down on the sidewalk, it wasn't long after that we would be running around in circles with our new-found freedom. I wanted to call my brother Maneen, but I couldn't pronounce that word so I started calling him Menny.

Mommy could see that her boys were getting antsy, so she bought them both tricycles. We treated them like Jeeps; there was never a dull moment on the sidewalk. We couldn't wait to go out and rain havoc on the side walk of the 1900 block of west Fourth Street. Whenever we had to pee, we would go up to the corner at Fourth and Lincoln and pee on the Colonial Trust Company Bank wall. We would look at the pee run down the sidewalk to the curb; this was only the beginning of the antics we would pull off on Fourth Street.

God help them if a dog would be taking a snooze on the sidewalk while we were on patrol. If we saw a dog, Menny took off first and headed for the poor dog that was asleep on the sidewalk. Screaming rebel yells, pedaling as fast as our little legs could take us; we would ride our three-wheelers right into the dog. Scared, the dog would be yelping as only a injured dog would—it must have been a nightmare for the poor dog.

Mommy was still working nights, so Jim had to stay home and watch the children. He would put the kids to bed early but let six-year-old Theresa stay up after the boys went to bed. One evening he sat her on his lap. He told her to pull on the diaper he had spread over his zipper area; she said that he started to breathe heavy. He asked her to squeeze the lump under the diaper; suddenly she felt the diaper get warm like hot water was in it. She looked at him as if to say, "What was that Daddy?" He told her to go to bed. Poor little Theresa didn't know what she had done. If the first time was hardest time, then this was not going to the last time. Mommy was at work, not knowing this was going on, nor did little Theresa know that something was wrong.

One Saturday morning Theresa and the two boys had bad colds. Bina had to take them to Dr. McKay, a very prominent doctor in Wilmington. She hated going there even though he would never charge her. The price she had to pay was high. He would feel her up every chance he could, for as long as she was in his office. She couldn't say anything and he knew it. She told me he did this for years.

4

War broke out December 7, 1941. Everyone had to have blackout shades on their windows, and if any light could be seen, air-raid wardens knocked on the window and said to cover up the cracks that were letting the light out. Wilmington needed to be pitch black, although it seemed no enemy airplane could get that far inland. During the day there were no restrictions. Due to the war many things were scarce, such as gasoline and rubber, requiring ration coupons. When we went to the store we also had to have ration coupons to shop for food.

Menny always liked to scare me, so when we got outside he would tell me that someone was going to take me away. He would get the biggest laugh out of it, at my expense. A rough-looking man lived across the street from us. Menny would get this man's attention, whether he was walking or sitting on his porch. Menny would yell across at him, "I bet you can't get us." The first time, the neighbor growled and said he was going to come after us. I ran in the house screaming, ran upstairs, hid under the bed, and stayed there until Mommy came to get me. Menny came looking for me, laughing; it was funny to him to see me scared.

Soon after his first scare I started to have dizzy spells and high blood pressure. It didn't matter where I was, I could have a spell sitting on the front step or eating at the dinner table, and when it came it would put me right on the floor, no matter how tight I held on. A few times this madman ran across the street would hold up a burlap bag and gestured that he was going to put me in it. One day he actually ran across the street with the bag, growling fiercely. This was getting out of hand. I would turn white and not want to come out from underneath the bed. Mommy had to forbid Menny from ever teasing me like that again. "Can't you see that your brother is very scared of that man?" she said. He didn't see the damage it was causing me, because he was having to much fun. She could see what it did to my nerves and blood pressure and was going to have an effect on me for years. Baby was a wreck, not sleeping well and having dizzy spells and high blood pressure.

Menny and I continued to ride our three-wheelers around the block. Once we stopped in front of a bar on Lincoln Street. There was a small garage across the street that was turned into a small bakery they made cold tomato bread. That day Menny and I watched the old lady and man making tomato bread with our sad eyes; it didn't take long before they gave us a slice. They scolded us and told us not to cross the street again, but that pie tasted so good and fresh it had to be popular in the neighborhood. It was hard not to go back, so we went back again but had to make it a long time between visits.

On Friday nights Menny and I would ride our bikes around the corner on Lincoln Street to the bar called Dinardo's. We would stand out of the way, just watching, and it wasn't long before two drunks would go at it, ripping each other's clothes and punching the hell out of each other. Menny and I would run out between them pick up their torn shirts; we would look in the pockets for coins or any6thing valuable. We were fearless and couldn't imagine that anything would happen to us. But I was always looking over my shoulder for that madman across the street.

One day a cute little girl down the street asked me to go to the drug store with her. I only remember that her name was Ann. We walked down to the corner of Union Street. Her mother had asked her to pick up a roll of cotton; we came out of the store holding hands. We were crossing back when she disappeared from my hand—a car had hit her and knocked her down in the street but missed me. How could that be? I took off, scared as hell. I could hear her crying. I was home, hiding, out of breath, and terrified. Someone came looking for me to see if I was hurt. I wasn't, but she had a broken leg. They told me a lot of people saw what happened and came running to help her. They couldn't believe that I didn't have a scratch on me. How did this girl get hit and not me? My mother was confused and upset at me that I would cross that street when I was told not to. Ann was in the hospital for a few days and then had her leg in a cast. The For Sale sign went up on her house right away and they moved, never to be heard from again. To this day it's hard to believe I wasn't hit either.

Menny and I used to go to a movie theater on Union Street called the Park Theater. One Saturday, Theresa took us to see a war movie. It was loud and when the bombs went off. I though the movie was blowing up. I was scared to be there and didn't know what to do. The whole theater was lit up with flashes from the bombing and fires everywhere. I thought the theater was being bombed and on fire. I told Menny that I had to go to the "bafroom" and ran into the lobby. It was so quiet there; I didn't realize how long I had been gone until Menny came looking for me. He assured me we were going home soon; the movie was almost over. I told him I wanted to go home now; I was too young for that kind of movie. I was only four years old. The bombs scared me the most.

One day Mommy met a lady named Mrs. Loose, who lived on 29th Street. Mommy had convinced the woman to sell her house to us because with another baby due we needed a bigger home. Mommy had to do all the leg work. Mrs. Loose wanted my father's signature on all the papers. His job, spray painting PT boats, was considered vital to the war effort, keeping him out of the army. He made good money and had to work every day. Mommy knew this was a chance of a lifetime, to own our own house and save extra money.

Mommy's fifth child was born June 2, 1942. She named this girl Nora after her sister in Ireland. Finally my father was making enough that another mouth was no problem. Mommy nicknamed the baby Lovey because as she put it, she was lovely. Now Margaret had someone to play with.

In that summer of 1942, Mommy told us we were going to move to 29th Street. You would think someone had hit the Irish sweepstakes. We were cheering that we were going to have a backyard to play in. My father was moving a little at a time until the house on Fourth Street was almost vacant. One Saturday morning we all piled in the car and headed for the new house. I was very happy to leave Fourth Street and that scary old man across the street, hoping I would never see him again. We turned a corner and Theresa saw the street sign and said, "This is 29th Street!" When the car stopped we all jumped out, as if the car was on fire. We ran up the steps and waited for Mommy to open the door. When she did we rushed around her and the first thing we saw was the oak staircase and fireplace in the living room. Menny and I ran upstairs and down the hallway to the back bedroom. I looked out the window and saw a barn in the backyard with the big doors. Curious what was inside, we ran down the steps but were grabbed by Mommy and were told to slow down. There was plenty of time to see everything. "You don't have to run around out of breath like a wild Indian," she said.

Right after we moved I asked Mommy to stop calling me Baby because the new neighborhood kids would make fun of me. She asked, "How about if I call you 'Babe,' is that OK?" I said yes, so from then on I was called Babe for the rest of my life.

After we moved in, Menny and I got tired of waiting to see what was in the barn, so we went out and walked along a small path in the backyard. We came across a white chalk stone sticking out of the dirt, about a foot high. I thought something was buried under it, so I left it alone. I always thought it was a grave of some kind. It was scary to think about it so we ran to the barn and pulled open the doors. Scaring some pigeons, which flew out the hole in the barn roof? We were expecting to find a treasure like a wooden chest full of gold coins. Menny and I looked everywhere, digging for days. Our total treasure consisted of a tennis ball, an old leather horse collar, a hammer, and a horse whip.

Mommy kept saying how dangerous the barn was, and we were going to have it taken down. Menny and I protested that it was our club house. If we couldn't play in the barn, Menny said he was going to hide in the house and I was to find him. I ran up the back stairs and kept calling, "Where are you?" I could hear him in the back hallway closet that ran practically the length of the house. I went into the closet and saw boxes of all kinds, full of junk, things hanging on nails, even an old baseball glove. There were old paint pots and brushes. I opened one pot and found a dead cat. I dropped it on the floor and ran.

One day I found Theresa standing on the porch talking to a beautiful girl who introduced herself as Alice Ford; she said she had a brother named Billy. He was a lot older than we were and wasn't home because he was working his part-time job. Alice called her parents over to meet us; we were always on our best behavior. We wanted to be the best of friends with them. For several days, Menny and I sat on the front steps after dinner, hoping to meet Billy Ford. We could see the bus stop at the corner, and one evening saw a young man jump off the bus head our way. As soon as he got to our house he said, "You must be the new neighbors." He had a nice smile and put me at ease right away. He asked my name and I told him it was Babe. I told him I was five and would be six in August. Menny told him he was six and would be seven in August. Menny told Billy about all the treasures we found. He asked if they were valuable, and we told him they were. He said he was going in to eat dinner and maybe after that we could go for an ice cream cone down at Tigues Drug Store on 28th and Washington Streets. My eyes lit up at the words ice cream. Boy, he seemed like a really a nice guy, so we waited on the steps until he came out. We finally heard his voice from inside our house and ran down the steps as we heard him say, "Let's go."

I felt safe with Billy as it started to get dark and the street lights came on. As we walked up the street he pointed out all the neighbors' houses, saying the Rayons lived next door and next to them were the Sellers and so on and on. The last house on the corner was the Phelps's, who had two children, Doris and Jon. Billy said, "Their grandfather lives with them, and you'll enjoy meeting him. He's different." We came to idolize Billy a little, but he was too old to play with us. He worked after school, just for a few hours, for pocket money.

At the drug store, Billy ordered our cones. I got chocolate, and Menny and Billy ordered vanilla. Mine was so big I started licking it right away. We thanked Billy. Then I overheard Menny telling Billy how easy it was to scare Babe. We were about halfway up the street when Menny yelled there was man coming after us with a long knife. "Run, Babe, before he gets us!" I took off like a rabbit up the street, still holding on to my ice cream cone. I jumped the hedges on 29th Street and down 29th to our house; I sat on the step waiting for them to show up. I was still licking my ice cream cone. I could hear Menny laughing at how scared I was. He came to me and said no one is coming, I was only fooling. Billy sat next to me and assured me that everything was OK, that Menny was just kidding; Billy made Menny promise he wasn't going to do that any more. I made sure I took my blood pressure medicine after that scare; I had to practically carry it in my pockets the way Menny wanted to scare me all the time. Menny knew that when I was scared I could outrun a dog and no one could catch me.

Another potential new friend was Tommy Farley, whom I first saw standing in front of Waxman's Jewish Deli. I asked him if he wanted to come over to play, he looked up and down the street and ran across to me. He introduced himself and told me his father was a cop. I asked him to come down to my house and play. I told him about the white stone sticking up in my yard and added that someone must be buried under it. When we were standing there a rabbit jumped up and scaring us to death. We both said, "Shit!" and started giggling. Suddenly my nose started bleeding, and I turned around and found my mother standing there. She had heard us cursing and scolded us; Tommy went home scared. I didn't see him again until I started first grade.

Come September, Mommy enrolled Theresa in the third grade and Menny in the first grade at Christ Our King School on 28th and Madison-Monroe St. I was too young to go so I stayed home. Mommy would say to me, "Babe, we are going to have to track your father down and make sure he doesn't waste all of his pay." He was making good money, and if he brought it all home she could pay the mortgage, put food on the table, and clothes on our backs. Jim's painting work was very dangerous. Vacuum lines inside the ships sucked out the fumes while the men sprayed. The fumes could ignite, causing a powerful explosion. This was a big problem and a concern to the painters; it would be a horrible death. The pay was good and everyone knew why because this was the price of war.

My father would say that he went to the local beer garden to rinse the taste of paint from his tongue after work. My thought was what about the smell of beer on your breath? He never did anything about that. He really couldn't hold his liquor, and with the responsibility of providing for five children and making a mortgage payment, his drinking got worse. A beer joint on Maryland Avenue was his favorite watering hole. One Friday after Theresa and Menny came home from school, Mommy told me we were going to go get my father's pay before he drank it all. We took the #4 trolley car over to Maryland Avenue; it was raining so we had to stand under a second story overhang in front of a Chinese laundry. They tell me when given a pile of shirts to wash and iron, this Chinese man's favorite saying was, "Shitty in the shirt tail ten cent extee!"

Mommy kept looking at the bar door waiting to see my Father come out and give us some money so we could have dinner this night. We were still waiting after 6:00; she could see that I was cold and uncomfortable. She took my hand and we walked across the street to the beer garden. Mommy put me in a doorway while she put her head in and asked the closest person to the door to ask Jim Toner to come outside. Mommy came back to me and waited for him to come out; it seemed like an eternity. He finally came out, looking angry. I am sure everyone in the bar could see that his wife was looking for him. He was probably embarrassed in front of his drinking friends.

Mommy told him that he made us wait in the rain for over an hour, and that I was not feeling that well. He asked her what she wanted. She screamed, "What did we want? Its payday, you're not home, and we don't have anything to eat, that's what I want. I want food for these children!"

He was too guilty to look at me. Then he became nervous and squirmy and gave her $12. She told him in a loud voice that $12 is not enough money to put food on the table and pay the mortgage and clothe these kids. He said he had more money but wasn't going to give it to her until he came home. We knew he would be unfit to live with when he came home; we knew we would be awakening by his arguing and fighting. Mommy told me if he came home with his pay, instead of wasting it on beer, we could live very well instead of worrying everyday what was going to happen to us.

I was afraid for my mother because I thought my father would hurt her. I could remember their arguments the loud angry sounds that would jolt us from our sleep especially when he hit mommy and caused her to scream in pain, that night my Mother knew he was going into the girls' room after she would turned him down for sex. I guess he figured if he couldn't have it from my mother he would try Theresa. This night Mommy jumped out of bed and found him tugging on Theresa to join him on the floor. My mother turned the light on and saw him clad in only a white tee shirt. She cried, "You dirty son of a bitch, get out of the room and leave Theresa alone!" He stood up. He had no underwear on; he pulled his tee shirt down to cover himself and walked out of the room as if nothing ever happened. Menny and I were sitting up in bed; we weren't getting the full picture but we could hear the girls crying.

I yelled out for Mommy to tell me what happened, and she came back to our bedroom to say everything was OK. I didn't understand what my father was doing in the girl's bedroom, but Mommy told me not to worry. "Get some sleep," she said. She needed my help the next day to hang the wet clothes on the clothes line. I felt relieved and was able to go right back to sleep; she knew it didn't take much to upset me. She knew my blood pressure was never going to get better with all this going on.

5

On Sundays Mommy walked with us to church at Christ Our King, where Theresa and Menny already went to school. It was a nice church in the basement of a school. The pastor was Father Lynch, who was by himself during the war years. He could be very grumpy, and a lot of times when he talked about his poor mother he would cry. It made us all squirm in our seats.

I started first grade in September 1943. I was just six years old. Not knowing what to expect, I was apprehensive because the nuns and their habits scared me. The first day Mommy took me right into the school to the schoolroom door. I knew Menny was next door and Theresa was there, too, up the hall. I was ok when I saw that Tommy Farley was in my room. I caught his eye and he waved at me. He looked a little apprehensive also.

We had a recess in the morning, then lunch, and a recess in the afternoon. I had a lot of energy and would run all over the school yard like a wild animal. I pulled the girls' pigtails and giggled. I stayed away from the older kids, who seemed rough. We walked to school in the morning, and on trash day Menny hid junk from all the cans in bushes and hedges all the way to school confident it would be there for him after school. He never found anything good in the trash that's why the people put it out to be picked up by the trash man. I thought to myself that Menny was a trash man, but to him it didn't matter; it was the hunt that counted. He might get lucky, but he never did. Some days he would spend so much time in the trash we were almost late for school. Then after school he would start looking for his junk he stashed all along 29th Street. His favorites were broken wooden poles with springs inside them. We would make toys out of the springs. He was becoming a pack rat.

At school we all wore uniforms. Boys wore a white shirt with a brown tie. The girls wore a jumper with a white shirt. I wore knickers in the first grade. Mommy would dress us up in little umpire short brim hats. She was proud of her boys. One day in the school yard Richard McAlter and I were playing and having fun, but suddenly I looked around and couldn't see him any more. Soon after that Sister Francis Genevieve called me from our first grade school window to come to her room right away. I ran up the steps into the school room and saw McAlter standing in the back of the room looking nervous and guilty about something. Sister motioned for me to come to her. She was the most beautiful woman I had ever seen, but she had an angry look on her face.

Holding a 12-inch oak ruler in her hand, tapping it in her palm, Sister asked me to stand in front of her desk. She told me that Master McAlter came to her and said that I had been cursing in the school yard. She was looking at my face and tapping her palm even harder. Without hesitation I said, "No sister, not me." She replied that Master McAlter said that I was, tapping her palm harder and harder. I repeated that I wasn't cursing, but you could see she didn't believe me. She scolded me and told that she better never catch me cursing. She sent me home because all this happened after school. As I turned to leave the room and looked over at McAlter, I saw he was too scared to look at me. He was a coward and wanted the sister to punish me for cursing. Every time I saw him he would avoid looking in my eyes and look down. It took a long time before I had anything to do with him. I was hurt that he would try to get me in trouble just to make himself look like the good guy by turning me in to Sister Genevieve. I am sure that kind of peculiar trait, trying to make others look bad, would prevent him from being successful later on because he could gain no one's trust.

One Friday, with about 30 minutes left in the school day, there was a knock on our classroom door. We all looked up and I saw Theresa walk towards Sister and whisper something in her ear. Sister smiled and told me to go with Theresa, so I stood up and walked out with her. I asked Theresa what she wanted. She said, "I told Sister Francis Letitia you can sing, and I asked if you could come to our classroom and sing to us." I replied, "Theresa I can't sing! Why you are picking me out to sing when I don't know any songs?" Theresa just told me to sing the song I sing at home. When I walked into her classroom they all started clapping and her teacher introduced me to the class as Theresa's little brother, Babe. They started cheering again. Sister said, "Theresa told us you can sing, and how good you are. Would you sing a song for us?" My face turned red; I had to sing a song cold turkey. I looked at the clock in the back of the room and could see that there was plenty of time left before dismissal and thought, "It looks like I have to sing," so I began:

> My girl's a corker she's a New Yorker, I buy her everything
> to keep her in style
> She's got a pair of feet just like two plates of meat, that's
> where my money always go-o-oes.
> My girl's a corker she's a New Yorker, I buy her everything
> to keep her in style
> She's got a pair of knees just like two trunks of trees, that's
> where my money always go-o-oes.
> My girl's a corker she's a New Yorker, I buy her everything
> to keep her in style
> She's got a pair of legs just like two whiskey kegs, that's
> where my money always go-o-oes.
> My girl's a corker she's a New Yorker, I buy her everything
> to keep her I style
> She's got a pair of hips just like two battle ships, that's
> where my money always go-o-oes.
> My girl's a corker she's a New Yorker, I buy her everything
> to keep her in style
> She's got a pair of shoulders just like two giant boulders,
> that's where my money always go-o-oes.
> My girl's a corker she's a New Yorker, I buy her everything
> to keep her in style
> She's got a pair of lips just like two potato chips, that's
> where my money always go-o-oes.
> My girl's a corker she's a New Yorker, I buy her everything
> to keep her in style
> She's got a pair of eyes just like two custard pies, that's
> where my money always go-o-oes.
> My girl's a corker she's a New Yorker, I buy her everything
> to keep her in style

> She's got a head of hair just like a grizzly bear, that's where
> my money always go-o-oes. (I had heard it on the radio
> and remembered all the words.)

I was so nervous, I was glad I was finished. Everyone jumped up and started clapping and cheering. I looked at Theresa and she was crying. I went over and asked her what was wrong, but she grabbed me and gave me a big hug and said nothing. These girls are so emotional, I thought, thank God we guys aren't like that. Sister ran over and gave me a big hug, too. I had those words memorized; otherwise I couldn't have done it. For a six-year-old to sing a song like that with no notice was not an easy thing to do, especially a song that long.

Mommy was happy that Christmas was coming soon, but we didn't have a tree. We had the tinsel and balls, so we all waited up Christmas Eve for my father to bring home a tree. Mommy finally told us to go to bed, he wasn't coming home. Mommy later told us he didn't come home till 5:00 in the morning, and that he came in with the tree and threw it in the corner of the room, (just like his father) leaving my Mother sound asleep on the sofa. She woke up at 6:30 and saw the tree standing against the wall behind a big chair and didn't want the children to come down and see that tree with nothing on it. She tried to put some balls on it and tinsel, and then Theresa came down to help her. Mommy could hear us awaken; we all sounded happy. We wanted to see what Santa brought us. We were looking for Theresa and my mother. Theresa said be patient and we could come down in a few minutes. I found out later that Theresa had wrapped all the Christmas gifts for my mother.

Finally Theresa came up the steps and got us all together, the youngest first in line, and down we went. Our smiles warmed my mother's heart. She was so happy to see our happy faces. We all sat around the beautiful tree, all decorated thanks to their efforts. Theresa was handing out gifts. The girls got stuffed dolls. Menny and I each got a beautiful tin car (I think they were MGs), two-tone green. Theresa got a white blouse, and we all got a bowl of fruit. I loved the tangerines. We were very happy. Mommy was happy that we were so satisfied with our gifts. Thank God we appreciated them; my mother would have died if we didn't like them. Theresa said, "Let's get some more balls and tinsel and put some more on the tree." We all chipped in and made it look more beautiful.

We all got ready for church. We went to 12:00 mass, everyone wearing new clothes. Mommy wasn't happy that my father was still sleeping when we returned from church, but she tried to cover it up. He had no interest in Christmas and didn't care how we felt either. His father had never done anything for them for Christmas because he had drunk up all the money for gifts. Jim had become just like his father, a failure in everything he tried to do.

Menny got sick in February 1943. He had pneumonia during the coldest part of the winter. We had an old furnace that didn't work well, and we were cold at night. Whenever I would look in on Menny he would spit on me. He must have wanted me to get sick too. I would run and tell my mother, "Mommy, Menny is spitting on me again." No matter how many times Mommy told him to stop he kept it up. The school was making some inquiries as to his health and when would he be coming back to school. Mary, the girl next door, was always coming over to visit him. I bet he didn't spit on her. I could hear them giggling the whole time she was there, and Menny wasn't that funny. It must have been something between them, but she hardly ever spoke to me.

I was good friends with her brothers Dean and Leo. Menny was finally better after being sick over 40 days. He could go back to school now. None of the neighbors were missing him on trash day. He missed school 48 days that year, so he was left back and had to do the second grade over again. I wasn't doing that well in school either. The sisters said I was having some trouble comprehending things. I didn't realize it but I was carrying the fears from home, which prevented me from learning anything. I was just getting by; it seemed like I was the dumbest kid in the class. But the other kids never called me names. I was always trying; I didn't know anything about studying. I only knew about surviving.

We never showed Mommy our report cards; Theresa would sign them all. She could write our mother's name better than Mommy could. This was only one of the many adult things Theresa did to help my mother out. I always got D's, no matter how hard I tried.

Every year as Easter closed in; my Mother would get some baby chicks, usually four of them. She would put them in a small box on the center of our gas stove, where the pilot light was. She would have news papers shredded up for them to lie on. They would peep all the time, and when Mommy would go to bed we would look in on them. The mice that lived in the stove would look at us when we would come out in the kitchen at night, through the burner slots. They must have kept the chicks company at night, too. The mice were used to us. They acted like pets, and if we said anything to them they would tilt their heads as if to listen more intently at what we were saying. We had a regular zoo in our kitchen at night; I think it reminded Mommy of her farm back home that she missed so much.

For Easter, Theresa colored some eggs, which were eventually turned into egg salad; nothing was wasted in our house. Easter was fun because we didn't have to rely on our father to get things done, we did it all ourselves. One Saturday after Easter I had a high fever. Mommy made me chicken noodle soup and toast. I started to feel better, but Mommy put a bucket near the sofa and told me that if I felt sick to throw up in the bucket. She told me again that if I felt sick I was to grab the bucket and throw up in it. I was becoming feverish again, getting delirious. I suddenly felt sick to my stomach, grabbed the bucket, pulled it over my head, and threw up, all over myself. I screamed and was making some god-awful noises. Theresa and my mother came running in from the kitchen to see the vomit running all down me everywhere. They were laughing hysterically at me. They said that I must have misunderstood what throwing up in the bucket meant. Mommy had said to lean over and throw up in the bucket, not pull the bucket over my head and throw up. They got me all cleaned up. They were laughing, crying, and wetting their pants all at the same time. It must have been the fever.

Once I heard my mother telling my father we needed a new heater; she told him, "We can't ever spend another cold winter like that again. The children barely got through this one. No hot water, very little heat, and Babe goes to bed with a hat and gloves on. One night he had on ear muffs." Theresa told me it was the funniest thing she ever saw, and I just had to go to bed early so I could get warm.

I remember the day I woke up knowing it was the last day of first grade. We were going to get our report cards and go home. As I was leaving the classroom, Sister asked me to stay behind. She told me she saw how hard I was trying and how much I was struggling. She told me I could go on to the second grade but I would be on probation for 90 days. They wanted to see if I could handle the work. She was going to keep an eye on me, and if I couldn't do the work I would have to come back to the first grade. She also told me that she had already spoken to my mother, who agreed. Menny's news wasn't any better. Because he was going to have to do the second grade over again, we were going to be in the same grade. But that made Mommy happy. But made me very apprehensive as to what way he was going to entertain himself on my behalf, she knew we could keep an eye on each other.

We had the whole summer off. I wanted every day to be great. We played in the barn before it was torn down, we walked the streets, and we met some new kids our age. I met a kid named George H. Booth; he was in my grade in school. His mother had named him after the baseball player George Herman (Babe) Ruth, so she called him George Herman. They called me Babe, but I wasn't named after any baseball player. We would always try to get a game up in the streets such as dodge ball, wire ball, or wall ball. We would play for hours. One neighbor, Mrs. London, would go crazy if our ball landed on her property. She looked out the window all day and screamed at us. Some neighbors would be angry if our ball hit their car. Mrs. London would let her son Abee out and sit him on the steps watching us play. He looked like Lurch of the Munsters. He had some sort of mental problem. He would smile and clap his hands. If he stood up we would all scream and run to our steps; we were scared of him. He was six feet tall with a large head. His mother looked after him and protected him like a guardian angel. She was so overprotective that she never took her eyes off him. Abee had to be ten years older than we were, and he weighed over 200 pounds. Mrs. London made it hard for us to have fun. She banged on her window all day, so she had to be exhausted by the time Mr. London came home. We were never able to understand a word she was saying from inside the house. We were all sitting around one night listening to the radio when Theresa screamed so loud we all jumped out of our skins. She said someone was looking in the window at us. We all ran to the door to see if we could see someone, but there was no one around. Theresa said it was Abee London. It couldn't have been him; he couldn't move that fast. It would have taken him five minutes to get home just across the street.

It wasn't long before a new family, the McMichaels, moved in across the street. They had two kids, Ray and Elaine. One day Elaine came over to see me. We were squirting each other with the hose. She went home and got her bathing suit on and came back. My mother had just bought a new wash tub. It was almost three feet around and at least a foot high. She filled it with water and told Elaine and me to get in. We had a great time that day. The next morning one of the neighbors told us that Elaine had to be taken to the hospital during the night. She had contracted polio, and was crippled. She had to wear braces and walk with crutches for the rest of her life. Elaine's mother blamed me, and our tub and water for giving her daughter polio. Her mother told people if Elaine had never come over to our house to play that day she would not have come down with polio. This was probably the worst thing you could ever accuse someone of, especially a little six-year-old child. I am sure by the time the doctors treated Elaine they were telling Mrs. McMichael that getting in the tub with that little boy had nothing to do with her daughter's getting polio. But Mrs. McMichael became very mean to us; we even noticed Ray wasn't playing with us anymore. They wanted to distribute their pain to us and blame us for their unfortunate medical disaster.

Later Elaine wouldn't look at us or talk to us. She was getting around on crutches. Mrs. McMichael was very upset and found great comfort in blaming us, even when she knew we were not at fault. My mother had me checked head to toe, with blood work and all the tests I could stand, and each one came back negative. That's when my mother asked the doctor how come I didn't get polio. He told her that you carry the germ before it attacks you. It's not contagious; Elaine would have had that germ for awhile. But my mother never got over how badly Mrs. McMichael treated us.

That August we sat out front after dinner every night and played games. Our favorite was hide and seek. We would get very excited about that game. Then suddenly it was my birthday. I was seven, and in just a few more weeks I would have to go back to school.

6

The dreaded first day of second grade arrived, and with Menny in my class, it was a trip. If we weren't shooting spitballs we were sticking long thumbtacks in Dickey Hire's suit coat in the back tail section. When he sat down the tack would stick him in the ass, he would scream, sit down, and it would start all over again until our teacher, Sister Kostka, would come down the aisle and find the thumbtack in his coat tail. She looked around for some guilty faces and hit Menny and me with a yard stick two or three times each. Dickey Hire never said a thing; in fact he was glad we got hit.

In school the smell of urine was everywhere and it took the whole weekend to get the smell of urine out of the school. The eighth graders would piss on the hot radiators, and stink up the whole school. We were all being watched, and the staff was determined to catch someone. The nuns were afraid to tell Father Lynch; he probably would have closed the school down. That's how bad it smelled.

We often went to Mass during the school day, and our church had spring hooks for hats so they wouldn't be sat on or knocked on the floor. The springs were very strong, and if you opened them up all the way and let go, they made a loud noise. You can imagine what it would be like if a number of them went off at the same time, so during recess one day we all agreed that at a throat-clearing signal we would all let go at the same time.

The next time we went to church, our class sat there quietly. I cleared my throat and 40 hooks went off, one after another, like dominoes falling down. Our first grade teacher, Sister Francis Genevieve, came up the aisle, grabbed my hair, brought me upstairs to her classroom, took me into her closet, pulled down my pants, and beat my bare ass. I was so embarrassed. She told me to go back to church and followed behind me all the way. The Mass was just ending when I returned, and everyone wanted to know what happened, so I told them. Menny wanted to know how she picked me out of all of us there. I told Menny I thought she was collecting on an old debt, remembering the cursing episode in the school yard with McAlter. She thought I was lying and wanted to get me for that.

While the weather was still nice, my father went to the lumber yard one Saturday to get supplies to make screens and storm windows. We needed these to keep the house warmer for the winter so the new furnace wouldn't have to work to hard heating the house. He came home to us with his father, who was a complete stranger to us; he seemed like a mean and grumpy old man.

My father decided to do the storm windows first. He had big panes of glass and could cut them to the size he wanted. The wood frame would hold the glass with the molding and putty. As he finished each screen or storm window, he numbered it so it would match the window when it was time to put them in again. Jim sat his father in a chair near the window where he was working so he could keep an eye on him from the outside while he worked.

I think we were getting on Grand Pop's nerves because he was beginning to talk mean to us. He screamed at Menny to get out of the kitchen, and I told him this was our house and he wasn't our father and we weren't going to get out of our kitchen. "You can't tell us what to do, why don't you go home," I added. Well, the look on his face told Menny and me that we better get a move on. He jumped to his feet and started running after us while Menny and I ran up the back steps, down the hall way to Mommy's room, and I dove under the bed. My pants got caught on the springs as he was reaching under the bed trying to grab me. We were screaming; Grand Pop got hold of my leg and was pulling on me to come out.

My father ran into the room and told his father to let go. I think that if Grand Pop could have gotten a hold of me he would have given me a whipping. He returned to the kitchen mumbling about how bad we were. He looked as if he could have used a drink. My father grabbed my shoulder hard enough to get my attention. He asked me if I knew he was his father. I told him I did, but he was mean to us and I didn't like him. He wasn't a nice man. My father looked hurt because he wanted us to like Grand Pop and get along.

One day I saw Mr. Ford out in the yard. He was as white as a ghost and looked drained. I said hello to him, but he said something I didn't understand. It wasn't long before an ambulance came and took Mr. Ford away. We were told later that evening that Mr. Ford was dead. I was in complete shock; I was just talking to him in the yard, how could he be dead?

Now back in those days they had viewings at home. The priest would come and say the rosary. We could hear Father Lynch praying loudly. We kept the door ajar so we could hear the people coming and going. Suddenly there was a knock on our door. Someone came in and asked Mommy if she would let the children come view Mr. Ford. She said OK and pulled out her hanky, wet it, and wiped our faces. Oh god it smelt awful, but her mother did it to her and she was going to pass it on to us. We went out in line on the porch and lined up the oldest to the youngest and went in the house where there was a small aisle to the casket. When Alice saw us she began crying hysterically in the back of the room. I didn't see Billy at all. We all stood in front of the casket where Mr. Ford was lying. When we genuflected one of us cut the loudest fart I ever heard. I didn't know which one of us it was. I couldn't believe the noise.

The whole place started laughing, even Alice Ford. In fact she was the one I heard when I was leaving she was howling and we were like little angels walking out of the house back to our house. When we got to our house we all started laughing. My mother wanted to know what happened, and when we told her she was bent over laughing. When she bent over to pick up her hanky she farted. We were crying with laughter as Mommy ran up the steps, peeing her pants. I am glad Father Lynch wasn't there—he would have never seen the humor in that. The Fords moved soon after the funeral, and we really missed that family. Billy was a good friend to us; I thought he was the greatest.

Around that time I began to steal my father's cigarettes and walk up to the football field at P.S. DuPont School. We always had a group that sat on the beverage pavilion floor and smoked. My father never missed a pack from his carton, and we would hide our cigarettes outside under the porch or in the back kitchen hallway. My father was suspicious sometimes and would say he smelled smoke on us, but we would deny it. It got to the point that we had to keep orange peels outside where we stashed our cigarettes so we could squeeze the orange peel on our fingers to take away the tobacco smell. Even though my father would complain about his cigarettes missing, and at the same time ask why we always smelled like oranges, he never put the two together. We were always one step a head of him; it wasn't that hard to do.

One weekend, one of our school friends, Billy Acton, asked Menny and me if we could stay over at his house. Mommy said we could. I was excited; this was going to be fun. We were going to see Frank Smith and Dave McFarlin on Saturday. On Friday night when we were all going to bed, Menny, Billy, and I were all in the same bed. Billy had five sisters, and all five came in to give Billy a goodnight kiss. Billy told them he wanted them to kiss Menny and me. So each one of them gave Menny and me a big kiss on the cheek. It felt so good and they were so pretty. Come Saturday we found out that Hearn's Food Market was having a grand opening, with all you could eat and drink. We spent most of the day hanging out at the food market eating hot dogs and drinking sodas. We would go away and look for Dave and Frank but always ended back at Hearn's. The sodas were small but the dogs were big. That was a great weekend.

One day Farley, Napolski, Menny, and I were acting up in class, so Sister told us to report to the convent after school. When we showed up it was a little after 3:00. She took us down to the basement to a small room, telling us not to make a sound until she returned. We had more fun running around the basement with no lights on. There was light was coming through the windows, but it started to get darker and darker. Soon only a little pool of light was left in the middle of the room. We could hear the nuns walking across the floor above our heads. Then we heard the phone ring and someone running across the floor. The door opened at the top of the stairs, and Sister Kostka ran down the steps. Shook up, she said, "I forgot you were down here! Please go home—your parents just called looking for you." We didn't mind; we had a good time running around like a bunch of Indians. I wouldn't mind going back.

My favorite candy store, Boles's, was owned by the Napolski's, the parents of my friend Donald. They sold subs and a big selection of candy; I could go in with a nickel and come out with a bag full of candy. One day Donald's mother asked me my name. I told her it was Babe Toner; I was in the same class as her son. This didn't seem to register with her because the next time I went in the store she called me Lucifer. I told her that wasn't my name; she smiled and asked if she could help me, but she never called me anything else but Lucifer from then on.

I was always finding ways to scrape together money for candy. A surprising opportunity presented itself one day in the form of an old man who lived on the corner of my street. We called him old man Phelps. Just to look at him would make you feel real clean. His thick glasses were so dirty it made me wonder how he could see out of them. He hadn't shaved or washed in weeks. His tee shirt was three shades of dirty, with food stains all over it. There were chewing tobacco stains on it, too, and also down his cheeks and chin. He smelled like a toilet and had urine stains on his pants that would probably not wash out. He was pitiful looking, but one day I stopped to say hello to him. He was sitting on the porch trying to spit his tobacco juice in a coffee can; he would rarely hit it, so there was spit everywhere.

Squinting out of his dirty glasses, he asked me if I would cut his toenails. The rest of the kids cried "Ohoooo" and ran off down the street. He said he would give me a quarter to cut his toenails. That could buy a lot of candy and ice cream. He handed me a big toenail cutter. I saw that his feet and toenails were very dirty, but I thought if I didn't help and do this for him, no one would have. He lifted his foot onto a small stool, and I took the clipper and started on his big toe first. It wasn't long before I had one foot done and moved on to the other one. I made sure I didn't breathe through my nose; the second foot was harder because there was dead dry skin all around his nails and tobacco stains on his foot. I kept cutting away and I finally finished; he sincerely thanked me and gave me my quarter. As I started out the door, I took my first breath through my nose and almost gagged from the odor. The kids were waiting for me at my house and asked me how I could do that. This was when Donald nicknamed me Jew Bab. That was what he called me, and his mother still called me Lucifer. I didn't care. I washed my hands—and the quarter—for a long time; I was ready for the candy store.

It was getting to be Christmas time again, and my mother was determined not to have a repeat of last year's Christmas, so she decided to buy the tree and stand herself. She brought it home by herself, and we all decorated it in no time. Theresa was locked in the dining room; I found out later she was wrapping Christmas gifts. I kept insisting too know what she was doing, but she wouldn't say and wouldn't let me in the dining room. Mommy bought some bubble lights, which were the nice touch the tree needed.

Mommy said she wanted our picture taken with Santa. We went to a store called the Wilmington Dry Goods, which was having a Santa, with helpers taking pictures. Behind us was a big sign that read "Say Hello to Santa." A girl took our picture after making sure we were all lined up, and we waited a few minutes for the picture to develop. So when my Mother saw it she laughed out loud, "Hell!" What she meant was that Santa moved his head slightly and blocked out the letter O in Hello so now the picture read "Say Hell to Santa." They wanted to do it over, but Mommy said no, it was priceless. We were going to keep it.

We went to bed Christmas Eve by 9:00 o'clock. I was so excited I could hardly fall asleep. Menny wanted to play Last Hit, one of the stupid games we would play. We kept hitting each other as lightly as we could so the other one couldn't feel it, and whoever got the last hit won. A lot of times it ended up in a fight. We knew better this time, no fighting on Christmas Eve. Theresa was allowed to stay up a little later, helping my mother put out the gifts. My father never gave us anything, not even a card.

On Christmas morning we all woke up at the same time. We asked my mother to get up to see if Santa came. Theresa went down and told us to wait until she came back. She put on the tree lights, and the radio, was tuned to Christmas music. It was just right. Mommy came out of her room and we all followed her down the steps. Together our faces all lit up. Theresa and my mother were very happy with our reaction. We each got two gifts. Menny and I got a sweater and a toy. I got a dump truck and Menny got a motorcycle toy. Margaret and Lovey got clothes. Theresa got a Monopoly game and said she would teach us how to play and that it was a lot of fun. My father was still in bed. Mommy said we were going to have a big turkey with all the trimmings, and eat in the dining room. My father got up in time to join us for a few minutes. He had to go out to see his parents because he had told them he would stop by.

Later on that night we all sat on the floor and played Monopoly. Theresa said we could buy anything we landed on or we could respect what someone else had and not buy an adjoining property of the same color. After an hour we were starting to get the hang of it. Mommy loved drinking her hot cup of tea and eating cookies, and if she could find it fruit cake while sitting on the sofa. Watching Mommy we all got hungry so we stopped and Theresa made us all a turkey sandwich. We all helped. Lovey needed a lot of reassurance from my mother, so she wasn't helping out. She was too young to do that much anyway. Those sandwiches were so good with sweet pickles. You can't beat that combination for a Christmas snack. Turkey sandwiches with mayonnaise and Monopoly.

That night it started snowing, but because our blinds were shut tight because of the blackout regulations, we didn't know it. So when Menny and I went to bed we prayed for snow. We stood at the foot of the bed like the priest at the altar and did some of his moves, hoping God would hear us and help us out. We wanted it to snow real deep, so we could shovel sidewalks and make some money. In the morning we looked out the window and couldn't believe our eyes. It had snowed almost six inches! We hurried, put on our clothes and gloves and hats and ran outside. Using the family's three shovels, Theresa, Menny, and I cleared our sidewalk first and then branched out. Most houses paid 50 or 75 cents and even a dollar. The corner house on 30th and West Street paid $1.50. We made $10 between us. That was a lot of shoveling, but it was going to be worth it to see my mother's face when we handed her our money. I ran from door to door and it paid off. We met on 30th Street and put our money together. Theresa put it in her pocket, and we ran in the door yelling, "Mommy you should see all the money we made!" Theresa handed her $10 dollars in bills and change and we all watched. Mommy's eyes were all filled of tears; she gave us each a quarter.

We were giving her money she needed to keep things going. Three of her children were out-hustling their father. We were praying it would snow every night. We were lucky to have a small store on the corner of 29th and West Streets called Schriber's. The owner was a short fat man, very nice and very Jewish. He would use a big, dark pencil to add up the items on the brown paper bag he put your goods in. He would draw a line for the total. He wanted everyone to know what it cost and how he arrived at it. He didn't use any scratch paper.

Mr. Schriber had two daughters who always peeked through the curtain, looking at us from the back of the store. They were very bashful. We always sat outside his store on his bread box. The bread company would drop off the bread during the night so he would have it fresh early in the morning. Mr. Schriber never yelled at us or treated us mean. You could watch him and see he was slick. Sometimes he would let people run a tab but they had to pay by Friday, and I never heard of him having a problem with anyone.

We had new neighbors moved in next door to us. Their last name was Toskas. They had two girls, Joan and Lisa. Joan was flirtatious, while Lisa was shy and stand-offish. Joan was about four to five years older than I was. She was starting to have a nice figure for her age. She loved teasing me, and Menny was always saying, "Joan, Babe's here." She would pull me against her chest, and it felt so good. My face was as red as a beet. Mrs. Toskas always called me Babes. She was such a great woman, and I got along with her so well. Although Mr. Toskas was never home, he was very nice too. The reason he wasn't home that much was because he was a manager of a restaurant in downtown Wilmington.

One day after school we went out in the yard, and the barn was gone. They took some of the good boards and made a back fence and side fence for about 24 feet. They left us some boards in the corner. Menny and I built a little fort off the fence and called it our club. We called ourselves the Twenty Ninth Street Raiders. We had an old dirty blanket for the door. If anyone wanted to be a Raider, they had to pee through an old vacuum hose that Menny brought home on one of his trash runs. It was easy for us guys, but not so easy for the girls.

After spending all day trying to sign up some future members to our club, we could expect my father would come home in a bad mood. The drinkers in the bar didn't treat each other with any respect. The girls who hung out in the bars were nothing but a bunch of whores. I know that's harsh, but from what I saw they looked like whores to me. My father would come home angry and we didn't know why; we thought it was our fault. Out of nowhere he would go out in the kitchen mad and start throwing silverware through the house. He could have easily hurt one of us. If Theresa said, "What's that about," he would come charging in like a raging bull wanting to hurt anyone in front of him. Theresa was the oldest and the spunkiest, but my mother would put us behind her. She was ready to defend us if he came near enough. When he hit my mother we would scream, "Leave my mother alone!" That seemed to make him worse. As we got older he got worse, but we'll talk about that later.

At this point I don't even remember my father playing with us or even sitting down and talking with us. It never happened. You could plainly see that he had two healthy boys, and if he played with us he might have to show some love. My father never had that in him. His father had never played with him, so what was the problem. We later found out that his mother knew he wasn't being a good father or husband.

In the mornings if it was nice I would go out on the front step and just sing; usually it was loud. I got a lot of relief from singing. Not everyone felt the same way. Especially Mrs. Baylor, Doris Baylor's mother. She didn't like me. They lived in the apartment a few doors down. They were renting and we were buying. That didn't keep her from thinking she was better. Once I was sitting on the front step singing and she came out of her apartment and up the street to me and told me to be quiet because people were trying to sleep. I thought to myself, "At 8:30 in the morning?" That rubbed me the wrong way. I stood up and walked down the steps and stood in front of her and asked her to put up her dukes and fight. She was so angry she stormed off down the street, never having too much to do with me after that. I was friends with Doris, though; she was cute and friendly.

Sometimes to keep myself entertained I would kick over garbage cans or trash cans or throw milk bottles. I also threw wet leaves on cars. My biggest challenge was breaking street lights. I would walk the streets smoking cigarettes. People would tell me I was too young to smoke as I took a big puff. Before I got to the house I had to stash the cigarettes and squeeze the orange peel on my fingers and empty the tobacco out of my pockets and smell my right hand. I was thirty minutes ahead of Sonny Jim and his sniffing.

One evening around supper time a car pulled up in front of the London's house. It looked like someone I had seen before. They were helping Abee out of the car. Abee was in bad shape—he was pale as a sheet and could barely stand up, so they had to help him walk. He looked like a zombie. Mrs. London held the door open for them to get him in the house. It was awhile before we saw Abee again. We found out he had been given shock treatments to help him, but it seemed to have made him worse. When he sat out on his porch he never spoke. If we said hello he never recognized that we spoke to him. He liked being outside even though he couldn't do anything. We never treated him badly. I wish I could say that about his Mother. She had to be missing a few marbles; that must be where his problem had come from.

In the spring Sister Kostka told us we were going to make our First Holy Communion. We practiced almost every day. Mommy was looking for two outfits for us to wear. They had to be all white. She found them and had them in a long bag and hung them up in her closet. Easter came and went just like the chicks. Lovey was outside and stepped on one of the chicks and squashed it all over the place. It made me sick to look at it.

Father Lynch told us one day that it was customary to have a Communion Breakfast and this year it was going to be at the Hotel DuPont, on a Sunday morning at 9:00 o'clock. They wanted everyone to attend. Mommy cried because she wanted Menny and me to go, but we didn't have anyone to take us. The night before, Mommy arranged for our neighbor, Mr. Farley, to pick us up at 8:30. Mr. Farley, a city cop, knew exactly where we lived, having been called there many times on domestic abuse calls. Mr. Farley's nickname was "Jumbo" because he was big. It sure was nice of Mr. Farley to take us while my father slept. Tommy sat up front with his father. He was so proud of his dad. Tommy looked at me and said, "Hey, Babe, how 'bout breakfast at the Hotel DuPont?" When we arrived, we were like angels. By the time we finished we had scrambled eggs, bacon, sausage, toast, and milk. Some of those things were a first for me and to top it all off we had cake and ice cream for dessert. Menny and I were going to burst. Afterward, the ride home with Mr. Farley seemed too short. We thanked him and ran up the steps where Mommy was waiting for us. She asked us what it was like and we told her everything. She said maybe someday we could go there for breakfast.

Menny and I changed our clothes and went to have a catch and find some guys to hit some baseballs down at Eastlake. When we played we would always end up having a catch. I loved to throw things and had a good arm. I could throw hard and long and accurately. I could run at full speed and while running I could pull a stone out of my pocket throw it at full pace and break milk bottles on the porch on the way home, usually at night. I wouldn't do that during the daytime.

The night before the Communion we had to fast. We couldn't have any food or anything to drink after 8:00 p.m. We were so afraid that the next morning we would swallow some water when we brushed our teeth. At my first confession I was scared of what the priest was going to say. We had plenty of training on how to confess if we broke any of the Ten Commandments. I didn't know if my mischievous ways were a sin or not. I was afraid if I confessed any of those things he would probably have me arrested. I started off by telling the priest I had taken the Lord's name in vain. I could hear him gasp. I went on; I still didn't know if raising hell was a sin. I stopped and he told me to say three Our Fathers and three Hail Mary's, to behave myself, and to say an act of contrition. When I left to go to the altar, it was full of people saying their penance.

Mommy got us up and dressed early. Menny and I looked like twins, and a lot of people thought we were. We had to be in our classroom at the school by 8:30. We sat at our desks listening to how quiet our school was. Mass wasn't until 10:00 o'clock. Sister went down to church and came back and said it was full. Then Sister told us to form two lines out in the hallway, boys on one side and girls on the other. I noticed that bags were covering the water fountains.

I was nervous and uncomfortable. As we came down the steps to the church the line stopped at the beginning of the center aisle. Sister Kostka had her little clicker, her way to signal us to do things. She clicked and we started up the aisle. The commotion was unbelievable. The people were acting like they never saw children before. Camera flashes were everywhere. We had practiced how to sit on the altar steps. This was Fr. Lynch's favorite time, and he was moved to tears. He called us little angels sent from heaven. Just before the reading of the gospel Crazy Mary stood up and started saying something. She may have said, "Angels today, devils tomorrow." I am not sure. She stormed out of the church. I don't think she ever finished a Mass. She was always yelling something all the way up the steps and leaving the church. Crazy Mary was a undernourished old lady living in a weather beaten old house that gave me the chills every time I walked by it on 26th. St. It reminded me of a haunted house and she truly looked like a witch. In time it would come to light that she was a nice old lady often looked down upon by the community.

Again Sister Kostka made her clicker noise. We all stood up and made our way to Fr. Lynch. It didn't take long. We had practiced with unblessed wafers, so we knew what the host was going to taste like. When I got to Fr. Lynch I opened my mouth and he put the host in and it was over. I was hungry and Menny and I wanted to eat or drink something. Sister Kostka clicked. We all stood up and walked down the center aisle and up to our classroom. I saw Mommy smiling at us. We all got back to the classroom, where Sister told us how proud she was that we were all good. We had a group picture taken with Fr. Lynch and went outside into the sunny day. Mommy was waiting with the girls. We ran to her and told her we were hungry, so we walked home fast to eat something.

Mommy said she had invited some people over after 1:00 to celebrate with us this fine day. Mommy was afraid Menny and I was going to get our clothes dirty. All of Mommy's friends came: the Sullivans, the Tobins, the Casey's, the Flemings, and lots more. She made a ham, potato salad, and her apple cake for desert. I ate first, and then I curled up in a chair and fell asleep. I woke up to hear Mrs. Sullivan asking where Babe was, and saying I better not be dirty. She asked me if Uncle Jerry had come yet. "You be nice to him," she said. "Your mother named you after him. And when he dies you are going to inherit all his money." Julia came late with Davenport. My father, hearing all the commotion, finally came downstairs to a house full of people.

Finally my mother said we could change our clothes. Jerry did come, but he didn't stay long, just long enough to eat a big dish of food and drink some tea. He slipped me an envelope when he was leaving, patted me on the head, and started toward the bus stop. I don't know what his hurry was; he lived alone.

It wasn't long after that afternoon that the war ended. We couldn't believe it. I had never seen anything like it. People were celebrating all over the city, with horns blowing and fireworks. Everyone was in the streets. I thought this was fun, and a good time to let off steam. Menny and I walked around the streets to see everyone outside raising hell. If they didn't have fireworks, they could beat a pot with big spoons. I thought the celebration would break up quickly, but it didn't. It went on all night and into the next day.

We were happy to have this war over with. For almost a year I had saved three packets of Kool-Aid. Every time I pestered Mommy to let me mix it up, she told me I couldn't because sugar was being rationed and I had to wait until the war was over. Now it was time to make my victory Kool-Aid. My Mother gave me some sugar, and I mixed up a pitcher. I drank a big glass full, we all had a glass, and it was gone. I still had two packs left for another pitcher.

Soon Mr. Baylor came home from the war and so did Dr. Rayon. The Baylor's were hysterical with the anticipation of their father's return. We were sitting on the steps when the cab came down the street. It stopped in front of the apartment and the Baylor's came outside screaming. A short man in uniform and a duffel bag got out of the car. He was attacked before he took one step and practically carried into the apartment. They were very happy. It was good to see all that love.

They were celebrating for a long time. We snuck down to their outside wall and shimmed up it, holding on to the window sill. I pulled up to see in. They were opening gifts. Mrs. Baylor saw me and shushed me away and pulled down all the shades. A few days later Dr. Rayon came home, and it wasn't long before he had his Open for Business sign up on the porch window. He specialized in eyes, ears, nose and throat. He was popular and had a good thriving business going.

A few days later my father gave up his spray painting job. He and some friends—Billy and Buzzy Clough and don't forget Shimmele Finney— started painting on their own. They all thought they were going to strike it rich. But most of the time when they were to be on the job, my father was sleeping. They waited for him to show up if it was his job. Even though they didn't work those hours, they expected to be paid because they were waiting for him to assign the locations to paint. (I maintain that if they knew where they left off the day before then they could start right back in where they left off.) By the time Friday came around, those guys had 10 hours of pay coming just for the hours they sat around waiting for Sonny Jim, but not working. They ended up making more than my father did and it was his job. Eventually this became a problem. He resented having to pay those guys for not working. They showed up where he told them to, but he never thought about getting up early and getting there on time. They did work well together, though, and they all had families and needed the money too.

Fridays were my father's big drinking night. He would be home around 1:00 a.m. or so when we were all in bed asleep. He would be angry at something and would start a fight with my mother. One night he wanted to know who was taking his cigarettes. We were too young to hit, so he would take his index finger and middle finger together and thump our chests until we finally told him to stop. Then he would start on the next person. If my mother or Theresa said to leave them alone that would really set him off.

I remember the night he hit my Mother so hard she reached out for an alarm clock and hit him in the face with it. The clock broke against his head, cutting him, and we were so proud of Mommy as we watched the blood trickle down his face. If there was too much noise, the neighbors would call the police to help us because they didn't know if someone was being killed or not. My father would run out of the house and hide just in time to miss the police. The next day the neighbor children wouldn't be allowed to say anything to us. We were embarrassed but realized we didn't do anything wrong. We had our sad moments, though. For example, when we would knock on the Hitchens' door to see if they wanted to play ball, we would hear Mrs. Hitchens tell her children, "Those Toner boys are at the door. I don't want you to play with them." That really hurt, and we just walked off the porch and went home. Our spirits were only shaken for a few moments, and it wasn't long before the Hitchens kids were looking for us. It was the only time we ever heard anyone talk like that about us. I didn't know what we did for her to say that, I wondered if it was because of my father that we weren't good enough for her children to play with us. Didn't she realize that the cops were being called on my father and not us kids? Some one said that her IQ was showing.

Experiences like that made me feel that if I wanted something, I would have to go get it. I wanted to do well in school, but the trouble at home was stopping me. I was a nervous wreck, jumpy, and with high blood pressure. I acted tough and didn't care if anyone saw me smoking or not. Once two neighbor women bumped into Mommy and asked if she knew her twins were smoking. My mother told them both that if that was the worst thing we ever did, then it was OK. Those women, who I am sure meant well, were shocked to hear that reply from her, as if she didn't care if her children were smoking. We were only seven and eight years old and were smoking in public, but Mommy was glad that we weren't getting in any trouble with the police. I was probably more of an annoyance than anything.

Soon it was the last day of school. Boy, that second grade seemed to go fast. As Sister gave out our last report cards, she asked me to stay after school. There she told me she could see me trying, putting out a lot of effort, but still struggling. She said that she had spoken with my mother, who agreed that I could go on to the third grade, and I would enter my third year as I did my second a 90-day trial period. I would be expected to keep up with the rest of the class. I thanked her and ran out of school as fast as I could. I felt uncomfortable talking to Sister about my stupidity.

I knew I wasn't dumb, but something was blocking me from learning. I had just memorized the twelve times tables, and I could give you the answer to any table as soon as you asked me. It was the other subjects I struggled with. I loved history but couldn't get anything better than a "D." I loved spelling until it was time for the test. I didn't have confidence that the answer I was thinking of was correct. Sister would say to look over our spelling tests and she would retest us later on. Sometimes she would wait two days. I would look it over intently and always did better when I retested.

Because Fr. Lynch needed help, two new priests were assigned to our parish, Fr. Donohue and Fr. Montgomery. They were so different: Fr. Donohue was interested in school activities and Fr. Montgomery was interested in scholastic endeavors. Groups of girls were always giggling and flirting with Fr. Montgomery, whose face would get red. Whenever they saw him blushing, they would try to keep him blushing, which I thought was mean. This was probably sex to these girls, mind sex.

One day we were out playing in the school yard during lunch. The head nun rang the bell and announced that Fr. Lynch had been made a Monsignor. They didn't disrupt our lunch recess but we could see the tables being put up during lunch break in our school yard. A big Borden's ice cream truck pulled up and started unloading some ice cream on the tables. We were all looking to see what was coming next. A group of women were dipping ice cream cones for at least four hundred of us students. Mother Superior kept telling us, as if we hadn't heard, that Fr. Lynch was named

Monsignor and we were going to celebrate and take the rest of the day off. I loved that news. Sister reminded us that it was Father Lynch who founded Christ Our King Church and raised the money for the school and convent. He used the best of building materials; both buildings were made of stone. He even had a piece of land next to the convent where he planned some day to build a new church. His promotion was long overdue.

I was determined to have a full summer, planning to get up every morning and play ball all day. I heard all about the park on 30th St. I walked up to take a look to see what was going on there. I met Mrs. Lemon, who was in charge of all the park activities. She showed me how to make these round and square bracelets out of four strands of plastic gimp. She was very nice and dedicated helping all of us children to have a great summer. Mommy bought Menny and me each a new pair of Keds sneakers. With them on, I was ready for anything. We had a good time playing dodge ball, even though some guys used the game as a way to bully and show superiority, throwing the ball too hard at the little kids and hurting them.

We played softball and horseshoes, too. Mrs. Lemon signed out the equipment. We had the most fun with softball, after which we would play horseshoes for the rest of the day. Tommy Farley was the one to beat. When Mrs. Lemon would turn on the showers in the afternoon I would get in for the longest time. I would take off my shirt and go in with my shorts on. So did every one else; there was so much water coming out of those pipes it was like being under a waterfall—it was wonderful. Some kids would bring a bar of soap and use that time to take a bath. It didn't bother me when they put down the bar of soap I would use it. A store on the corner across the street from the park had the best Nehi orange sodas I ever tasted. They were only a nickel, and I had one every day when I was up at the park.

I cut my hair short during the summer; I really never knew what I wanted my hair to look like. Short was cheap and easy to cut. My father's money wasn't going too far, so Mommy decided to take in wash, and starch and stretch sheer curtains. Mommy said we had to do something or we would lose our house because my father was so irresponsible I wondered why a man like him had ever wanted to get married. The last thing you could call him was a husband or a father; he must have just wanted a guaranteed piece of ass.

He never explained why women called all the time and asked for him. If I answered I would say, "No, he isn't here and don't call here again."

When Mommy answered calls from other women, she would call them the bar whores and tell them he was married and had five children. Then she would hang up on them. Can you imagine this father and husband giving these women his phone number?

It wasn't that he didn't try, he was just a nonachiever; it just never worked out for him, leaving him frustrated. He never planned anything; he couldn't see that the drinking was causing all his disappointments. Not getting out of bed in the morning was probably caused by the drinking, the guys he worked with didn't even respect him, but I don't know of anyone that would have any respect for a man the way he treated his family. He wasn't a visible drunk, but he just couldn't hold his liquor, which make him mean to his vulnerable family. He didn't realize that he was less than a man in beating up his wife and children?

Still, lots of people thought he was a nice guy. Of course none of them were living with him. When he wasn't drinking he was a nice guy, but when he was drinking he was a chip off the old block. Even though I was only going to be eight in August, I knew enough that I never wanted to be like him. I can honestly say I have no recollection of him ever showing me any love. Not even a hug, nothing. And I can tell you I don't remember ever feeling any love for him in return. He beat the love out of us. When the other kids spoke proudly of their fathers, Menny and I felt bad when we heard them. There was nothing we were proud of him for.

Mommy wanted to have a garden in the back yard, so Menny and I would have to dig it. Having a garden brought back a lot of memories for Mommy. We soon had a few rows of corn, tomatoes, beans, carrots, and rhubarb. Mommy made us weed; weeding around the rhubarb was the worst. Garden snakes hid under the leaves, and they scared me so much I would kill them. We had a cherry tree and a pear tree, but you couldn't eat the pears because they were too hard. They were good for throwing, though, and I could throw them a long way. Mommy was afraid to ask me to cut the grass in the back yard because I would mow down everything that the mower could be pushed over.

There were a lot of nights that I would go up to Boles's and get a sub if I was hungry. For dinner we often had liver and potatoes with onions, which didn't stay with us long, so I would have a sub some nights. One night I was walking home from the store and noticed that my ass was hurting when I coughed. My ass began hurting me more and more, especially if I would laugh or cough, but I was afraid to say anything. I just hoped it would go away. One evening when Mrs. Sullivan was visiting, she saw me wince when I got up from the sofa she asked me what was wrong. When I told her my ass hurt, she took me to the bathroom and told me to pull down my pants. She bent me over and could see that my right cheek was swollen and red. She went downstairs and told my mother I should be taken to a doctor the first thing in the morning. Mommy took me to Dr C.C. Neece, who found that I had a tear in my rectum, and a fissure. He said that I had to be operated on right away. He explained that it was a weakness that I had since birth and didn't help if I would be forcing a bowel movement, she asked me if I did that and I said yes, sometimes.

What an operation! I remember them wheeling me into the operating room. They put tape over my eyes and stuck it to my forehead and cheeks. I was so scared I couldn't speak, and my mouth was real dry. Mommy left Theresa with the kids and waited at the hospital for me. When we got back to the room after surgery I was beginning to come around from the ether. The nurse was talking loud to me and asked me if I felt alright. I told her to get the hell out of the room and leave me the hell alone. She must have told every nurse on the floor what I said because whenever a nurse came in the room, they wanted to see the little boy that was cursing. Of course I denied it. I didn't know that I had said anything like that. To tell you the truth the nurses thought that was funny. I can tell you what wasn't funny and that was when I had my first bowel movement. I told you I was throwing stones at the milk bottles on porches. I thought I was starting to pass them; it felt like broken bottles going through me. I screamed that hospital wing down, it was that painful. Mommy was at home and came in that afternoon. I made sure I was pouting and told her how I was by myself, so she wanted to make it up to me and asked me what I wanted. I told her I wanted a pair of cowboy boots. The next day when she came in she had the box under her arm. I got better fast after that.

That operation took up a little of my summer. I had to be careful, so I stayed around the house and played Cowboys and Indians, which I loved the most. In a few weeks I was up at the park just like old times. Forty days were left before school started. At that time my mother was taking care of five children, taking in wash, and starching and stretching sheers. It didn't bother my father at all. He still couldn't get out of bed in the early morning, which has to be the first step in being successful. The neighbors could hear us three to four times a week screaming, so they had to know that we children had to be scared to death. A lot of times when we went out to play we must have looked that way too. Plenty of times Mrs. Toskas saw me by myself and told me she heard the ruckus last night, and asked if I was OK. I told her my father hit my mother for no reason and hurt her, but he didn't hurt me, so I was OK. She sometimes got choked up and told me if I wanted her to help me all I had to do was ask. What a great person to have as a neighbor. Her daughter Joan was nice to me, too. Always hugging me and putting my head between her breasts. She said she was going to teach me how to kiss. I was a little young to know how to kiss, so she was going to wait till I got a little older. From the look on her face and breathing she wanted me to grow up quickly.

Mommy made an apple cake for my birthday that year, just for us kids, and we ate it up. I loved it with milk. Because my father wasn't there to play with us, she would take us in the back yard and have a catch. She wasn't that good at it, but we loved it anyway, because she would laugh the whole time. These were times I would never forget. Mommy felt a strong feeling that she was going to give us two boys what we weren't getting from our father. She was bonding with us she loved us that much.

On the last day before school started I got up early and was out all day, jumping fences; the higher the better even having a few smokes. Then we had to get a bath and Mommy said to me, "Babe, if you don't get in that bathtub soon I'm going to give you a bath." I didn't want that so I ran up the stairs as fast as I could. I ran my own water, got in the tub, and grabbed my wash cloth. I was bashful and so afraid she would see me naked. I think she knew it.

7

All my school chums showed up the first day of third grade, neatly dressed up; we didn't have to wear our uniforms the first couple of days. Our third grade teacher was Sister Genevieve, who had the same last name as our first grade teacher. She was very nice, and happy to see us and get back to work. These teaching nuns were very young—in their twenties— and devoted to God and the teachings of Christ. Sister Genevieve loved to teach religion. You could tell our catechism class was her favorite; she loved to tell religious stories to children on our age level. She would keep us on the edge of our seats and tried to get everyone involved.

We had to memorize all our prayers, even how to say the rosary and Sister was working with us to name the twelve Apostles. It wasn't easy but I knew I had to do it. I could listen to songs on the radio and didn't have any trouble remembering the words, so I figured I could handle this. Sister told us of the nine first Fridays. She said that if we went to mass the first Friday of each month for nine months in a row, we would be guaranteed a place in heaven. Each first Friday of the month, Theresa, Menny, and I faithfully got up for 7:00 Mass, running to church to be there on time. When we got home we only had 15 minutes to get back to school. I loved the Stations of the Cross, which were long but very exciting because I could revisit those moments in Christ's life.

Mischief Night, the night before Halloween, was something to experience in our neighborhood. We would talk about that night for weeks. I would stick pins in doorbells, to keep them ringing until someone would pull out the pin. Soaping windows and screens was another trick. We would also soak a brown paper bag with lighter fluid, put dog shit in it, find a porch, lay the bag down, light it, bang on the door, stand back in the dark, and watch the person run out onto the porch and start stamping on the lit bag of dog shit. They would get the shit all over the porch and shoes or slippers. We had to see it or it wasn't any fun, so the person banging on the door had to run fast and stay out of sight.

We had so many other tricks up our sleeves. We always traveled in packs, but we were not the only pack out there. We broke out the street lights, and the older boys went behind the trolley cars and pulled the pole off the electric line (one pole off the line would stop the bus from going). We cut all the clothes lines from the back alleys; sometimes when you cut the lines the clothes poles would fall against the house. I loved to throw things; I made sure I had plenty of tomatoes and pears on hand. (It wasn't surprising that you couldn't find a milk bottle on Mischief Night.) I threw them at anything that moved: cars, buses, and motorcycle police. I made sure those motorcycle police were far away before I threw anything and then run like hell.

The most fun was going on our corn run. We would get a group of about eight people and go up to the Blue Ball Farm across from the reservoir on Rt. 202 and steal dried corn. The farm was marked by a blue ball on a white round post near the road, a target for all kinds of tricksters, and by the end of the evening, someone would paint the blue ball red. Causing such a commotion that it would make the newspaper's front page with pictures: "The Famous Blue Ball Had Been Painted Red." It was hard to believe, all the fuss that was being made over this blue ball. There were people wanting to be the first to paint it a different color than blue.

It wouldn't take us long, less than five minutes, to fill our knapsacks with about 10 ears of corn each and run back across Rt. 202 and home. We always kept an eye out for the farmer, who never knew what hit him. If somehow the farmer found us, he would have had to be a track star to catch me. We were all safe by the time we got to the stony road that ran from the golf course all the way down to the railroad tract. Now the tough part was to get those kernels off. We didn't know any better, so we used our thumbs. That hurt after a while and we all got blisters. When we finished we had a lot of corn and corn cobs to throw. When the corn hit the windows of someone's house it would scare the people inside. I would throw the cobs as I imagined soldiers threw hand grenades. That's how we spent Mischief Night at eight years old.

We couldn't wait for Halloween to come. With just a little charcoal on my face I would work five city blocks and get enough candy and fruit to fill a shopping bag. I would jump the railings and fences and go house to house. I would finish around 8:30 p.m. and go home to have a look see what I got. My mother would make us empty our bags out in front of her so she could check out everything. She picked out anything that she thought was bad for us. My candy hoard would last me for months.

As fast as Halloween went by, Thanksgiving came in just as quickly. Mommy made a turkey, mashed potatoes, and of course corn. I loved it, with plenty of gravy on everything and bread to clean up our plates. That night, Theresa wanted to play Monopoly. We all agreed not to play cutthroat (where everyone bought the other players' outstanding property, which made it no fun). Halfway through we would call time out and make turkey sandwiches with all the trimmings. Something about that turkey sandwich break was wonderful. Mommy enjoyed watching her children having such a good time.

I don't know where my father was on these holiday evenings. He wasn't with us, probably gone to see his parents, but I doubt it he wasn't that thoughtful, and couldn't sit with them for any length of time because he had never done that when he was growing up. This was a ploy on his part meaning that he couldn't be comfortable with his wife and children that he had just terrorized and beat up. We were a lot happier when he wasn't around. When we went to bed, we had no idea what we had in store for us. We all hoped he wasn't drinking. If someone else was giving him a hard time, we would catch hell. I was so affected by all the tension I would walk down the hall in the middle of the night, past the bathroom and into my mother's closet, where I would pee on a cardboard box. I was awake but asleep. It seemed like I knew what I was doing, but I guess I didn't. I think they called it sleep walking.

One day, we went down to see if Donald Morice could come out to play. When we opened the apartment building entrance door, you could see down into the basement. There was Donald's brother, Chubby Morice, working on a contraption that was an exact copy of an electric chair. Chubby was a lot older than us and didn't treat us with any respect. He would make fun of us. I stood there that day when he was being mean and I told him I was sorry for him and that he acted like a man who drank. He apologized and was sorry he didn't realize he was coming off that way.

He was happy trying to scare us all the time, but he knew that if he tried to scare me, I would get even. I am sure Donald told him of our antics. Their father was sick in bed, so I know he didn't want any trouble. One night I dumped three apple baskets of wet leaves against their apartment door. I saw him cleaning that up when I walked by a short time later. I am sure Chubby had a good idea that I had done that and didn't want more payback. To keep everything on an even keel, we just didn't go into the basement.

That year Theresa told Menny and me that there wasn't any Santa Claus, and that she was the one who was wrapping all the Christmas gifts. Menny believed her but I didn't. I loved Santa and that was that. We got our Christmas tree and decorated it all in the same day. I found the tree stand from last year and made sure the tree stand was straight. We put it in the corner of the right front window. Theresa got the balls of tinsel we had saved from last year and we hung carefully strand by strand. We put the bubbly lights on for the finishing touch.

I loved Christmas. Come Christmas morning Menny and I were the first ones up and woke the girls. Mommy and Theresa made us all stay upstairs until she got the downstairs just right for us. She came to the bottom of the step and said it was OK to come down. I was first because I wanted to see what Santa brought. There were more gifts than last year. We all sat in a whole circle while Mommy sat on the sofa with her usual cup of tea and a couple slices of toast, watching our response after opening the gifts. We mostly got clothes and one toy. I got a big construction dump truck and Menny got a bulldozer. Together we could move mountains. We played our usual Monopoly after dinner; it helped pass the time until we could have out turkey sandwiches. My father ate dinner with us but left right after that and didn't say where he was going. All the beer gardens were closed. We felt safe that he wasn't going to come back in a drunken rage.

Julia was pestering my mother to have an Irish dance at our house for New Years. Julia asked if they could invite a few dancers and also some drinking. My mother gave in, but we had to go upstairs at 9:00. The party started off slow and wasn't that noisy at first. By midnight none of us were asleep but we were sitting on the steps watching the partygoers stamping their feet in unison. Julia's friend Davenport was loud as hell and staggering drunk. Julia was having a great time, a little tipsy herself. Mommy, always remembering her promise not to drink or smoke, was having a good time with out it. My father was chewing gum. He really thought he was a real ladies man. When they ran out of booze after 2:00 a.m., the cigarette smoke was everywhere, even upstairs in our bedrooms. That's when the party broke up. Julia and Davenport were asleep in two chairs. When he woke up he was his usual loud self, which annoyed Julia; she got up and went to make a cup of tea. We found out that when she referred to her sister's children she called us tinkers. In Ireland, tinkers were low-lifers or gypsies. I remember my mother saying that when a person spoke badly of us, they were leaving someone else alone. She knew that Julia would say those mean things for no apparent reason. My mother told me one day, "Just because you cook and clean for a rich man and live in his house doesn't make you rich or righteous. Julia should not be passing judgment on others especially if they're children."

Jerry had been at the party, too. He was not a drinker; he only sipped on a beer. He had made his usual trip over after Christmas and had given me five dollars, making sure that no one else knew about it. He thought my being named after him was the best thing that ever happened to him. He was proud to see me grow and later become a man.

When Jerry visited, I usually sat with him in the kitchen and had a cup of tea. He would tell me stories, usually about crazy things he did on the job and after work. One day he told me one story that has always stuck in my head. He and a friend had a scheme to go to a local restaurant and order a big meal with all the trimmings. The plan was that Jerry's friend would have a bad look on his face and when the server came to the table, Jerry would tell him that his friend was sick and was going to throw all over the restaurant. Jerry would say it must be the steak. The server excitedly told Jerry to get his friend outside before he threw up in here, and that maybe some fresh air would make him feel better. Jerry took his friend outside. To other customers, it looked like his friend was drunk. When they got outside they would run away. They had a free meal, in this case a steak dinner. He said they did this all over Wilmington. There were plenty of restaurants around to do this sting for a long time.

At home I was a nosey son of a gun; I was always snooping around to see what I could find. Theresa was 12 now, so she could iron and help Mommy with the wash. One evening Theresa was ironing and Mommy was sitting on the sofa chatting with Theresa and drinking her warm cup of tea. Meanwhile I was up stairs looking in the hamper and came across a pair of girl's panties with blood all over them. "Oh my God someone is hurt," was my first reaction. I picked them out with my fingers, holding them where there was no blood, and started down the hallway. I started saying out loud, "Mommy someone cut themselves and is bleeding bad. You should see the blood, Mom," holding the bloody panties up. I got half way down the steps and hung them over the railing for my mother to see. I was out of breath with fright. I looked at Theresa, but she never lifted her head and just kept on ironing. I said again, "Mom, can't you hear me? We need to find out who's bleeding and take her to the hospital real soon."

My mother told me to put the panties back in the hamper, but I kept asking why no one was upset about this. Theresa finally stopped ironing looked up at me and told me to shut up. That's all I needed; I told her to shut up, too. We were going at it pretty strong when my mother stepped in and sent me to my room for fighting. I put the bloody underwear back in the hamper an was in my room for the longest time before my mother came and got me. She thanked me for being concerned but said everything was fine.

One weekend Theresa called my cousin Kitty Ford to come over. I think my mother had an inkling that my father was going to be acting up. Kitty came and we had fun playing cards and telling stories. Finally we all went to bed around 11:00 p.m. My father didn't know that Kitty was staying over. Kitty said that about 1:00 o'clock, my father was lying on the floor in their bedroom pulling at Theresa's pajamas, telling her to come down on the floor with him. He didn't know it but Theresa was pinching Kitty under the blankets. Kitty woke up and sat up and could hear him pleading with Theresa. Kitty turned on the light and said in a loud voice, loud enough to wake up the whole house, "Uncle James, what are you doing down there on the floor? Why can't you leave Theresa alone?"

He stood up and only had on his tee shirt; he wrapped it under his balls and left the room with his balls in his hand. We talked about it the next day and told kitty she was our hero. She had heard all our stories but couldn't believe them. This was not the last time Kitty came to Theresa's rescue. Kitty's mother, Eleanor, was my father's sister and he didn't want anything to get back to her. She had her hands full too.

This type of incident was not good for my sleepwalking or my blood pressure. Neither were the times Menny and I saw our father beat our mother and knock our sister down on the floor. We would tell him to leave them alone, and he would come charging at us like a mad man, pushing his fingers into our chests and asking if we wanted a punch in the mouth. When we put our arms up to block him from digging into our chests, it would make him worse. As a result of this stress, I would feel worse, and my mother would take me out of school to see the doctor who was treating me for my blood pressure. He kept me on that pink peppermint-tasting medicine. It a wonder the way Menny was entertaining himself by scaring me every chance he got, that I wasn't walking around with a drip attached to my arm.

All my father's problems were brought on by the booze. He was a total failure. His wife and children had no love or respect for him, and we honestly didn't care if he came home or not, preferring that he didn't. Margaret and Lovey were never involved in any of this. They would go in the bathroom and pray through the length of the attacks, but their prayers were never answered.

The day after an incident that ended in screaming or my father's running out before the police came was always the worst. Menny and I were OK, and would have a smoke the next day. I would always hope that the Rayons wouldn't hear the commotion; our neighbors the Bakers across the street were very nice to us. Mr. Baker worked for the DuPont Company. They had the most beautiful cat I ever saw, with long silver hair. They called him Silver. They didn't have any children, and Mr. Baker was very nice to us kids. Mrs. Baker would ask us to do small things so she could give us something for helping her. She asked me to put some books in the garage or carry some trash out of the yard, but the house was off limits. We never did any mischief to them or Mrs. Toskas.

We had heard this story going around about a talking parrot. The owner would talk to him all the time. The parrot couldn't get enough of talking; she even taught him to pray. She trained him to say the Our Father if you pulled his right leg and the Hail Mary if you pulled his left leg. She called the rectory and spoke to Fr. Donohue and told him that her parrot could pray. She said he would be right there to see this praying bird. When he arrived He rang her bell and she let him in. He said, "OK, show me." So he stood in front of the parrot and Fr. Donohue said, "Let me get this straight. If you pull the right leg he will say the Our Father, and if you pull the left leg he will say the Hail Mary." She agreed. Looking right in the parrot's face he asked, "What will happen if I pull both legs?" Just then the parrot squawked, "What the hell do you think Father? I'll fall on my ass!" With that he left.

Fr. Donohue, one of the new priests, could only deal with families that didn't need any help, so my mother didn't trust him. Like a lot of Irish in those days she relied on the church for help. I heard her ask Fr. Donohue for help because of my father's physical abuse of her and us children, and his attempts to have sex with his oldest daughter. Fr. Donohue never tried to help. (I guess the priest had heard all the horror stories that I know must have been circulating around the parish about my father's drinking sprees.)

His resolution of our nightmare was to find us a place to live in an area of the city known as Eastlake, a very low-life housing community for the down and outs. We might have been down but we weren't out. This was his brainchild on how to solve the cruelty of a man physically abusing his family almost every night. We weren't the lowlifes; it was my father who was lowlife. My mother was shocked that this priest felt the answer to our problems was for us to be in another parish and out of his hair and his guilt-ridden mind. He didn't have any training on how to handle this kind of a problem. He never mentioned to her one word about my father and his brutality. I am sure he didn't want us to be a burden to Christ Our King. It's hard to believe that God would have approved his plan. He probably never asked God for guidance.

Mommy called us all together one evening after dinner and told us how Fr. Donohue wanted to resolve our problem with my father; by moving us all to Eastlake. We all objected and said that we weren't going to live in Eastlake. I told Mommy I wasn't going; she could put me in a home. We would be safer there. Menny and I knew first-hand how life was in that rundown housing community, having played ball at the Prices Run Ball Field. We didn't deserve this kind of resolution. Mommy was just playing the hand she was dealt.

Poor Theresa had it the worst, with a father who wanted to abuse her sexually when he was drinking. She was constantly helping my mother with us kids, doing the wash, and ironing and some babysitting. All of this made her bitter because she really didn't have a life. When she was out with us kids she was ready for a fight at the drop of a hat. This scared a lot of the other girls, so they stayed away from her.

Theresa could whip any girl's ass in the neighborhood and some of the guys too. She was definitely affected by all her treatment at home; she was a walking time bomb who could explode with just a look in the wrong way. She could grab people by their shirts, and they would collapse in fear. I know she loved Menny and me, but it didn't stop her from having big knock down fights with us. You could only blame this on my father's treatment of his kids.

It was only Mrs. Toskas, our next door neighbor, who ever extended her hand to help us. She would always ask me if I was OK. As I have mentioned, her daughter Joan liked to see me blush. She was starting to fill out and was sometimes all over me. One night Menny and I went out in the back yard to have a smoke. As we turned around toward the back of our house and Joan's house, her bedroom light went on. We saw Joan unbutton her shirt and pull it off, leaving her in her bra. Then she reached around her back and did something because her bra was off. Suddenly my legs got weak. There she stood bare-chested, with a beautiful pair of tits standing out erect like the healthy girl she was. I knew I would blush the next time she rubbed those beauties on me again. Whenever her mother would go into Wilmington to the market, Joan would sit on the step or the railing. She would make sexy gestures at me. Menny thought it was funny; he loved it when she would act sexy like that and grab me and say, "Come here Babe, I want to kiss you." I would be shaking in my pants.

Menny would say, "Joan why don't you wrestle Babe," and she would pull me in the living room. We were on our knees; that's how she wanted to wrestle me so no one would get hurt. This was not about getting hurt, but was about having fun touching her. After seeing those beautiful tits from her bedroom window I knew I was going to hang on to those beauties through the entire match. They were a nice handful. She laughed the whole time. Menny was egging her on, and she rolled me on the floor, but no matter what she did I never let go of those beauties. If that wasn't enough, she kissed me all over my face. She put her tongue in my mouth and moved her lips all over mine. If this was wrestling I wanted to be a wrestler.

Joan was a hot chick; I couldn't ask for anything more than that. In fact I didn't ask for anything, it just came my way. But she wouldn't do anything if her mother was home. Now that Menny and I knew she would undress in her room with the shades up and the light on, we would defiantly grab a smoke more often in the yard at night. We weren't successful all the time just sometimes we were rewarded.

At this time my mother was not only taking in wash, but she had also decided to take a little girl into our house as a boarder. Her father was a sharp-looking airline pilot in his thirties. When he came to interview with my mother, neatly dressed, he didn't say anything about his wife, but later Mommy told me he was divorced and had custody of the child. One day after school when we came home she was there. Her name was Brook and she looked just like Shirley Temple. She was cute and very well mannered. I think that Brook's father was happy that Mommy had five other children; he could trust my mother with Brook. She stayed with us for a year. Whenever my father acted up, the girls would take Brook to the farthest part of the house. She was very protected, in fact, overprotected from the wild man. We took Brook everywhere, and she never seemed to miss her father. She was fine as far as we could see, and Mommy asked us to look for signs such as crying. We treated her just like a little sister, and there were too many of us for her to be lonely. She was a hit everywhere we went with her because of her curly blond hair. I don't know her last name; I wish I did. I miss her, and maybe some day she'll find me.

My mother was constantly trying to keep from losing the house she loved so much. My father could have cared less. He didn't want any responsibility, but only to drink with his loser friends in his off hours. Up to this point he had given little guidance to his children. It was too soon for us to know what we wanted to do anyway. I was determined to make something of myself. I wanted to be rich and live in a big house. I never told anyone because I was afraid they would have laughed at me, so I kept it to myself. Even though I was eight years old I knew what I wanted. I had the desire and the hunger to have something, to be somebody. I never lost the hunger.

In the spring, Sister Genevieve started to talk about the May procession, when we honored the Blessed Mother. The first grade through the eighth grade would all dress in white. We would walk two abreast around the entire school blocks and end up at the church for Mass, where we would place flowers in front of the Madonna's statue. There were candles all around her. It was beautiful. So was the May queen, who had to look like the best Christ our King had to offer. She would put flowers in front of Mary, say a short prayer, and walk away. Lots of relatives took pictures in and out of church. Mommy stayed outside with the smaller kids and Brook.

After the procession, Mommy went home to cook a big dinner for us: meatloaf, mashed potatoes, and a corn, a vegetable that we would all eat, applesauce, and strawberry shortcake. When I finished that, I was full. We changed into our old clothes, jeans and our lumberjack plaid shirts. With a full stomach I wanted to do something. Menny and I got our gloves and had a baseball catch.

On the last day of school, Sister Genevieve gave out the report cards. She asked me to stay behind. After school she told me she was going to let me go to the fourth grade, but they wanted to see if I was going to struggle doing the work. She said I would be on probation for 90 days while they kept an eye on me. Suddenly this was familiar; it was the third year in a row now I would be on probation. But I never got sent back. I couldn't wait to get outside where Menny was waiting. I told him about my promotion and probation. Then we celebrated, we had three months off and decided to make the best of it.

Menny said we should go up to Rock Manor golf course and caddy. I said I would give my money that I made to Mommy. We didn't know anything about caddying, but we expected the golfers to show us what we needed to know. The next morning we woke up, got dressed and took off for Rock Manor, known as "The Rock." It was a very long walk. When we got there we saw a bunch of older guys standing around smoking, so Menny and I lit one up too. We asked one guy who looked friendly how we could get a caddy job. He said, "See that old man? Tell him that you want to caddy. When you're finished with that come back here and wait."

Boy did we wait. The Caddy Master was an old grumpy bastard. We just sat around on some benches as caddies were called one by one. He called out Menny as James Toner and told him to caddy for Bill Street, who came up to Menny and shook his hand and told him to call him Bill. We could tell these loud men had been drinking. We could hear them talking about the night before, how much they had to drink and how they hadn't been home yet from the night before.

Then I was by myself and didn't know anyone or what to do. Out of nowhere I heard Grumpy call "Babe Toner" so I put my hand up. He didn't see me, so he kept calling "Toner." I jumped the wall and came to him out of breath from running. He told me I was to caddy for a man named Oscar, standing over there holding his bag. Somehow Oscar seemed out of place. I told him that I never caddied before, but he told me not to worry, just find his ball and hold the pin on the green. He would tell me what to do and when to do it. "You can't beat that," I thought, I was determined to be a good caddy.

Oscar couldn't hit his ball very far, so it wasn't hard to find. He asked me where I lived, where I went to school, and so on. I could tell he wasn't going to give me any more than the one dollar caddy fee, but I had fun. He taught me a lot, naming the clubs for me—driver, spoon, mashie, and putter. Oscar kept his own score. After we finished and were walking toward the club house, I put his bag down; he reached in his pocket and pulled out a dollar. No tip, no lunch, just good bye. The word in the caddy shack was don't caddy for Oscar; he is too cheap to tip or buy lunch. I would hear the other guys refuse to caddy for him. Menny got two dollars and lunch. But Grumpy took advantage of my niceness and asked me if I would caddy for him. That meant my day was ruined for a stinking dollar.

It leaked out that if we caddied Saturday and Sunday we could play golf free on Monday, which was caddies day, as long as we could tee off before 9:00 a.m. We showed up early Monday at 8:00 and told the Caddy Master, old Grumpy, we wanted to play. Can you imagine showing up to play golf with no clubs or balls? You should have seen the look on his face—he wanted to run us off. He couldn't, though, because we had caddied on the weekend and they were his own rules. I went in the clubhouse and saw Luther, the caretaker, and told him we didn't have any clubs. He went and got Menny and me two sets of clubs, as nice as the ones I saw when I caddied. It was nice of Luther to do that for us.

Grumpy was out there throwing a fit that so many caddies showed up; he told us not to hold anyone up or he would come out and get us. He said no cursing, club throwing; or laying the bags on the green. After all those threats Menny and I were ready to play our first round of golf. Grumpy put Kautz and Napolski with us and we were off on our own. Boy could we slice deep into the woods. Donald and Kautz would be in the woods looking for their ball and all of a sudden they would yell "Fore!" and this beautiful shot would come through the trees over the trap and land on the green, 12 feet from the pin. You could see those two throwing the ball from the woods, but if it was good for them it was good for me. We totaled up our scores and I shot 134. We all shot within in two or three of each other. Menny had better balls than I had because he had taken them from the bag of the guy he was caddying for. I was afraid to do that, even though he told me how easy it was.

I was hooked on golf after our first round. I really enjoyed it. I used to study the pictures of Ben Hogan hitting a golf ball that hung in the pro shop for a long time. Mr. Douglas, the pro, would see me looking at the pictures for a long time and told me, "Son, you picked a good guy to copy." Mr. Douglas was a real pro and always treated me well.

We caddied as much as we could all summer. Sometimes I would go on my own, Menny didn't want to but I did because I wanted to play on caddie's day. By the end of the summer I had my score down to 114, which included the cheating. I was improving. I had a hard time hitting my long irons, so I kept looking at the Ben Hogan's still pictures. He made it look easy. Every now and then I would luck out and get a good caddy job. I got Bill Street when Menny didn't show; he was funny and a real nice guy. One day he hit his ball near a tree on the reservoir hole and didn't want to take a penalty. I told him to be careful before he took the shot, but he didn't listen. He swung hard and broke his five iron on the tree root that was hidden just under the dirt. He looked over at me and I was laughing so he started laughing. He told me he could get it fixed, no problem. Later he gave me two dollars and bought my lunch and soda. I told Menny that I caddied for Bill Street, and boy did he get pissed off at me. Just to make him mad, I told him that Bill might like me better. I had to hide from Oscar so I could get Bill Street. I felt bad for Oscar because no one liked him, I can't say they didn't like him, he was a tightwad and he had to pay the price for that. When he couldn't get a caddy, he would put his bag on his shoulder like you would carry a small log. It was sad.

That summer my mother collected little baskets in the back kitchen and finally told us what they were for. She found out that alongside of the P.S. DuPont High School football field were tons of blueberry bushes. She wanted to be the first to get them. We walked about eight blocks to the school, and when we got there the blueberries were everywhere. Mommy was so excited with our find. We had picked almost more than we could carry. She was overjoyed. We all had purple fingers and lips and laughed to see each other's purple tongues. By the time we got home we were dead tired. Mommy cleaned the berries in two big wash tubs down in the basement. Needless to say we were either eating blueberry pie or blueberry jam for a long time.

When I wasn't helping my mother, caddying, or playing golf, I was playing baseball or softball at the 30th Street Park, or wherever I could find a game. I wanted to throw something, anything. Imagine being able at my age to throw an apple, tomato, or pear half a city block. I would be gone in a flash by the time it hit the ground. When boys were practicing for the upcoming season at P.S. DuPont High School football field, I would go on the field and have a catch with some of them. One nice-looking guy threw me the ball and I caught it. He looked surprised that I could throw it back. In fact he couldn't believe it. After a while he walked down to me and asked me my name, I told him I was Babe Toner, and he said that figures. "You have a good arm, kid," he said. He called over another guy and said, "This is my brother, Junie Eisman, and I am Herbie Eisman." They said they played in the backfield. Then he told his brother, "You should see this kid throw a football." Every chance I got I went up to see if I could catch them practicing.

During the home games I would stand near the gate, and the Eismans would sneak me in under their big coats that they would wear to keep them warm. Who was going to stop a ball player with a kid under his coat? I never paid to get in any game, which was lucky because I had given Mommy all my money. She needed it. I was still finding more ways to make money when I wasn't caddying. I took orders at the A&P store on 28th and Market Street, shoveled snow, and ran errands. The only money I kept was from clipping Mr. Phelps's toenails, which was too hard earned to give up. I wish I could tell you that with my help, Mr. Phelps got cleaner. He didn't.

8

Every year, my birthday also meant it was almost time to go back to school. I was now in the fourth grade, on probation again. The first thing sister Francis Letitia said to me was, "I remember you, you sang in my class room one day. Your sister brought you to us." Sister was very good to me and made me feel very comfortable. It didn't stop me from misbehaving, though. When I wasn't in school we could play golf and smoke for hours with no one lecturing me. We didn't carry cigarettes to school because we didn't want the nuns to catch us and take them away.

One night Theresa said when Mommy came home we were going to sit her on the sofa and show her how we saw her in our eyes. Each one of us was going to put on a skit imitating Mommy. Theresa would do Mommy first. When Mommy came in we told her to sit on the sofa. Theresa started right in doing Mommy with the vacuum cord wrapped around Theresa's throat asking her to beg for her life. Mommy is howling with laughter and saying she was going to wet her pants. She could see herself through our imitations. We had a lot of fun doing that. On my turn, I imitated my mother also knocking Theresa to the floor and using the vacuum cleaner hose, with one foot on her chest telling Theresa to beg for her life as well. The funny part was that we knew she would never hurt us. Mommy was crying with laughter. Theresa added to my imitation about how it felt. Theresa had thought she was a goner that day after talking back to Mommy about vacuuming. Mommy used as much force as necessary to get the job done or get the point over.

Menny and I needed a break from all that funny stuff, so we went out in the backyard to have a smoke and see if we could see Joan undressing. We wondered if she could see us out there puffing on our cigarettes, but I don't think she could. She looked so neat taking off her clothes like that. When she took off her bra our mouths dropped open. We didn't want Mommy or Theresa looking for us, so we would see what she wanted and go right in, giggling like two dummies. Menny kept saying how he wanted to tell all the guys, but I insisted on not telling them. They would come and ruin it. I was real strong on that point and was able to convince Menny I was right.

On fall and winter Saturdays we would go in turn to the movies at the Grand Theater to see Roy Rogers, Trigger, and Gabby Hayes. I loved the cartoons and the Three Stooges. One Saturday some bums in front of us were drinking loudly and smelling up the place. In the glow of the small aisle lights I watched them put their bottles on the sloping floor. We reached under the seats, grabbed the bottles, and poured the beer on the floor under their seats. Then we threw the bottles between their feet, bouncing them off the metal seats supports and making a lot of noise. The smell was awful. We called out for the usher and said that they pissed on the floor and threw beer all over the place. It was too dark for the men to recognize us. The usher went outside and got a policeman who came back with a policeman, who threw them all out and told them not to come back. The whole theater smelled of beer, so we moved to the balcony to watch our movie and cartoon.

We never had money for candy at the movies. Once Menny told me he would be back in a few minutes. I heard a big bang and Menny came back with his shirt full of candy bars, laughing so much he could hardly talk. He must have had ten candy bars in his lap. He had put a fire cracker in the candy machine, and when it went off the shelves collapsed and the candy came out. Menny was able to leave the scene before anyone knew what happened.

Mommy got Menny and me some used bikes with fat tires. Mine had a motorcycle seat on it. One time as we went down a hill my brakes failed, and I ran right into the side of a moving car and fell on the ground. I looked hurt but I wasn't. The car had a dent in it and my bike tire and rim were bent out of shape. Menny went home to get Mommy, who came running to see if I was hurt. The driver was a wreck. He was sweating and assured my mother that he was going to replace the bike. I kept saying, "Mommy my bike is ruined!" I was playing up this accident that was really my fault because I could see that the driver was going to make restitution. He asked my mother for her address and said he would bring a bike back the next day after work. He kept his word and showed up with a beautiful bike with a light and a horn. He was pleased that I was happy and he was even happier to leave. I had a better bike; I really made out on that deal.

That October there was a lot of talk about getting some corn for Mischief Night. We all agreed to go back to the Blue Ball Farm. We all had bikes and rode them to the reservoir. Leaving them behind some big bushes, we ran across Route 202 to the corn field. We had a couple of girls with us, so we had to keep an eye on them. We were picking those big ears of corn off as fast as we could; someone yelled that we better go. That was enough for me. A girl named Judy was in front of me, out of no where I could see the farmer appear and went to grab her, but I tripped him, I grabbed her hand, and we were gone across Rt. 202 before he could get his footing. What an old fart, trying to pick on girls.

Judy was grateful that I saved her life. She had dropped her bag, so I gave her half of my corn. We had an extra shopping bag, so she put them in that. Judy rode alongside me the whole way home. Every time I would look over at her she was smiling at me. We had to be a lot more careful the next time we went for corn. Someone in the group heard the farmer yell that he was going to shoot us with rock salt, but that didn't scare us. We still would go back. To us it wasn't stealing. To some people it was, but the thrill was too much to pass up. We didn't have any sympathy for that farmer. He wasn't taking care of the place, and each year it looked even worse. I couldn't think what was so valuable about 60 ears of dried corn that were about 25% bigger than any corn that I ever saw. There's got to be something to that. Why were those ears 25% bigger than any other ears of corn around? It was a rumor that this farm was owned by a chemical company and they had experimented with plants, especially food-bearing plants, but it was just a rumor mind you. The blue ball was intact, but it definitely was going to get a new paint job on Mischief Night. When I saw Judy in school she ran over to me and thanked me again for saving her. I wondered what she would do if she got me alone and thanked me. I'll never know, but she did have a look in her eye that gave me ideas.

We had a lot of mischief stored up in us, so Mischief Night was a big release. There were police everywhere so I would pelt their cars with tomatoes. It was so bad they had to clean them up because people were laughing at them. Throwing tomatoes was a big release for me. No one could catch us because they didn't know the backyards like we did. We would kick over garbage cans or dump them down their back steps to their basements. What a mess that was. The night was young and I had plenty of cigarettes to last me.

Throwing corn was becoming a girl thing. I ended up giving some of my corn to some kids in the neighborhood. I was more interested in throwing tomatoes and pears. The cops wanted to catch someone, but not too interested in some girls throwing corn. They wanted the tomato throwers—someone to blame for hitting a cop. We actually felt like on this night that doing mischief was OK; we didn't break any windows or do serious damage.

Actually, every night was Mischief Night to me. I would always be up to something. I could sweat easily, so I always looked sweaty when I was doing things. My main focus was not to get caught. Maybe that's where Donald Napolski's mother got the name Lucifer. Donald probably told her of my hell-raising adventures.

Halloween came and went. I dressed like a bum. It wasn't hard with our old clothes. Menny dressed like a witch, with a long hat and a long black wig. He looked good. You could imagine living in the city how much candy you had to have on hand to give out. When you could fill half a shopping bag up with candy, you had something. The candy bars were a meal on their own.

Our boarder, Brook, stayed close to the house. When her father telephoned, it would really lift her spirits. He would tell her they would be together soon—maybe by the summer—and she jumped for joy. He always spoke to my mother, who probably knew more than Brook did. He would always pay my mother by mail, never missing a payment. With his income, he could well afford to pay for her care. He had told Mommy that he couldn't hold a full-time job and care for Brook. Mommy might have been Brook's only contact with a mother relationship. Brook's father divorced brooks mother early in her life and no matter how devoted her father was, she needed a mother's love. Brook probably didn't remember much about her mother, and she never said anything. She loved sitting out on the front step with us, playing hopscotch, and skipping rope. We took her everywhere, and I noticed that Mommy always held Brook's hand. Mommy loved that little girl and she loved us right back.

I always wondered why Julia and Jerry never come around to help out. They stayed away, knowing that things were real bad at our house. They weren't the aunt and uncle to stand up to my father. Maybe if they had, he might have changed. (That was a real stretch of my imagination.) Julia and Jerry took the easy way and treated him well. It was like they didn't believe the stories.

When Julia would visit our house, she never seemed to visit us children, just our house. We just happened to be there. She would walk around in her slip, sipping a cup of tea. But she was our Aunt Julia; we loved her and were happy to see her. We would run up and surround her and make a fuss. She would become very nervous and give us curt answers, so everyone would just walk away. But I would sit with her and have a cup of tea. She loved that one-on-one and I was the only one who didn't threaten her. I don't mean with violence, but with issues. I liked Julia and Julia liked me, but she never gave us a single gift or any sign of affection, like a hug. Theresa always asked Julia for money, which turned Julia against her. She never liked Theresa and she would not hold back in showing it. She would call me Babe with her little Irish accent. It sounded nice, but she really wasn't. She even talked about us behind our backs to other people.

Jerry didn't have anything to do with anyone in the family but me. I was his godson and nephew and that was all there was to that. Whenever we sat together, I could always make him laugh. When he laughed, he was so cute with his little mustache. When he walked, he swung his arms just like a soldier marching, digging those heels in hard. But neither Uncle Jerry nor Aunt Julia ever gave my mother one cent, not that she was looking for handouts either. Theresa, Menny, and I would give my mother all our money to help out. Sometimes we would hold back a quarter. She was proud that her children would help her out like that.

When Jerry and I would sit around and talk, it would always go back to Ireland. He would always come down to my age level and tell me great stories about some funny things he had done in Ireland. One funny story he told me was the one where he would lock the outhouse door so when one of the girls would need to use it they couldn't get it to open. They would stand around jumping up and down having to keep from wetting themselves. Jerry thought that was funny and would do a lot of little pranks like that around the house. His mother would say to him in Gaelic, "Ta fabharin ifream." (There's favor in hell and the biggest devil gets it.)

He rarely talked about his brothers and sisters, just his mother and father. He said his father was strict and would knock him to the ground if he ever got out of hand or missed a chore. Jerry didn't like that. He felt restricted and wanted to branch out, to get more out of life. When we sat on the sofa with Mommy, she would show us pictures of her father and mother. I remember one picture of her mother smoking a pipe. We were very proud to be Irish, thanks to Mommy. She never pushed it on us, but we wanted that heritage of hers. I think she used to write to someone back in Ireland, but I don't know who.

Sometimes Julia asked my mother if she had anything to send back to Ireland. She told Mommy she was going to send some things and she could throw Mommy's things in with hers. What she didn't tell my mother was that she told the people in Ireland that it was all coming from her. She did this for years. Mommy had strong suspicions because no one ever wrote to her, it was always to Julia to say thank you.

One day in school, Harold, who sat to my right in class, he leaned over to me and told me he was going to write f-u-c-k on the top right corner of his spelling test paper. I told him he better not, he wouldn't put anything over on Sister Letitia. She would see it and get him for it. He said he could write it small and use a newly sharpened pencil. I was insisting he better not; why he was doing this was beyond me.

On Friday morning, it was time for our ten-word spelling test. Sister handed out all the test papers, just narrow strips. We would write our name at the top and write down the ten words as Sister read them. I looked over and saw Harold writing on the right top corner. His face was only three inches from the paper. I saw him look over at me and look back and bang his hand down and write FUCK as small as he could. I didn't see it. It couldn't have been that small. Sister called out the words for us to spell; it seemed like an eternity by the time number ten came around. We passed the papers up front to be collected, and the bell rang for recess. While we were out in the school yard, Sister was correcting them.

We did everything in our 15-minute recess that any group of children could think of. Our favorite pastime was to kick a half-inflated round ball around. I saw Harold, who said he had changed his mind about his prank. Boy was I relieved to hear that. Sister rang the bell and we all got in line by grades, eight lines in all. We returned to the room and sat at our desks. Sister stood up and started down the aisle between the seats, handing out the spelling tests results. Anything marked in red was wrong, and she would spell the correct word alongside the misspelled one. I only got three wrong on this test. I was happy. She kept going down the aisle until she came to Harold. She slapped him full force across his face, knocking him out of his desk and onto the floor on one knee.

I knew his FUCK wasn't small enough. She definitely saw it. Everyone wanted to know what happened and by lunch time Harold was telling everyone that someone squealed on him. He kept saying, "No one could read that, it was too small." I told him, "Just because nuns wear glasses doesn't mean that they can't see, and besides you told me you didn't do it. As you can tell, they can see fine." They would see me and catch me when I was ornery. I felt that the nuns would release their frustrations on us; how else can you explain the yardstick beatings?

Sister Letitia was also keeping an eye on me. She would often stop at my desk. Ballpoint pens were just starting to come out. Menny and I took them apart and wet some paper and rolled it around the refill. When it dried, we would remove the refill and the paper tube became a blow gun. Those shooters were accurate and perfect for shooting spit balls made out of gum. If you hit someone in the back of the head, it stung. You could see people rubbing the backs of their heads. One day I didn't know that Sister was watching me. She snuck up behind me and grabbed my ear. I thought I was shot. She slapped my hands with a yard stick, but I didn't think she actually saw our blow gun because she didn't take it away. Menny hit Dickey Hire in the bare neck. He screamed out and Sister beat the shit out of Menny.

At home, Menny and I were still stealing cigarettes from my father's carton. He still couldn't catch us. He would search us, empty our pockets, and smell our fingers and our breath. He never once found anything. It was simple. We were smarter than he was; I think he had only completed the fifth grade. I think my father must have watched his own father like a hawk because he became a mirror image for everything his father had done wrong. If his father hadn't drunk up all their money, they probably could have owned a house. Likewise my father had no motivation and didn't want the responsibility of being a father.

My father would pick up any pig in the bar, probably with some disease, have sex with her, and come home to beat on his wife and three of his five children. He would probably try to have sex with my mother too. It's only a miracle that my mother didn't get a disease. He had no scruples about wanting to have sex with his 12-year-old daughter. I don't think that anyone could have planned to destroy a family any better then he was doing. He would have been better off being single, but then he wouldn't have had anyone to beat up on.

It was to a point now that we were in a survival mode. This treatment from him caused us to fight among ourselves. Mommy got us under control by reminding us who we were acting like, which was the last thing we wanted to hear. She was right and we would stop. We were able to respect each other better through my mother's guidance. She didn't what any of us to be like him, and with the examples he was setting; there was no chance that any of us would turn out like him.

At this point in my life, aged nine, I was still under a doctor's care for high blood pressure. Why didn't the doctor turn in my father to the family court, knowing that this child was a nervous wreck from his treatment at home? I was afraid of the nuns who were trying to help and afraid to go to asleep at night, but ready to step in to help my mother and sister if need be.

My father never gave me a solid hit. He would poke us with his fingers hard in to our chests and dare us to swing at him. He was trying to provoke a fight with eight and nine-year-old boys, knowing we weren't strong enough to take him on. The look on his face and in his eyes was that of a madman. Unhappy, frustrated, and unfulfilled, he had his family scared for their lives. He never took the time to figure out that no child could ever anger a father to this rage, to wreck the interior of the house, kicking chairs over, throwing the phone. All because one of us would try to get him to stop hitting one of us. His answer would be, "You know what you did, do you think you can fool me?" He would say, "Do you think you can talk to me that way? You better be quiet." Whoever was the defender was going to get hurt. It's a good thing my mother could scream. That would stop him. He knew the police would be coming soon.

Fr. Donohue from Christ Our King turned his back on our family because he didn't know how to solve our problems. How could he, a single man with no children? Trying to help families was totally the opposite of his understanding of life. We kids were the ones going to church, saying the rosary, making nine first Fridays in a row for nine months and sometimes, for four or five years, helping out when asked around the church school or convent and rectory. We were the ones doing all that, not my father. Yet he walked scot-free. There were a lot of people who liked him, yet we suffered. Maybe some people found it hard to believe we were victims of abuse. I want to assure you that I am not bitter, although I know I might sound like it. I just want you to feel the pain we experienced. We were let down both by relatives and religious people who took the easy way out.

Christmas was coming, and Menny kept telling me that there wasn't any Santa Claus. I kept telling him to leave me alone. He wanted to stay up Christmas Eve with Theresa and Mommy and was willing to use me to get what he wanted. Mommy saw right through him and that behavior and made him go to bed with me. He told Mommy that I wanted to get more gifts. Whenever it came up, Menny would try to embarrass me and say, "Babe still believes in Santa Claus." Theresa knew that I preferred to believe. She thought it was funny and never embarrassed me over it.

We loved Christmas, and Mommy loved to see us decorate the tree. This year seemed like the best. We got the tree off of the porch; I was in charge of the stand and to get in straight. It always went in the same corner. We had the lights on and we just stood there looking at it. When I was putting the stand on the tree out on the porch, Joan came out and asked me to come to her, as only Joan could do. Somehow I think she wanted me to grow up fast. When I came over to her she gave me a big kiss, and put her tongue in my mouth, the only way Joan could do. She would hold me against her tight; there was no mistake she was all girl. She told me that was my Christmas gift. What was I going to give her? I told her I didn't have any money. She said just wrestling with her was good enough; she was waiting for the opportunity. Menny kept saying, "Babe she really likes you, I hope you know that." I was beginning to believe it too. I was beginning to feel more comfortable with her. She liked me being bashful, it added flavor to the catch.

I stumbled upon Theresa wrapping gifts in the dining room. I was dumbfounded and asked who all this stuff was for. I never got an answer. Menny wanted me to confess that I didn't believe so we could stay up. I told him I still believed in Santa Claus and that's all there is to it. Mommy told him to go to bed with his brother on Christmas Eve; I was so excited to see what I was going to get the next day. Menny wanted so much to be elevated up to Theresa's status of staying up Christmas Eve and dumb Babe should be made to go to bed and he should stay up with the adults. Mommy could see right through him.

On Christmas morning, Theresa called us from the living room to come down, that Santa had come. "Come on and see what he brought." We let the little ones go first. Theresa gave out the gifts; it looked like there was more than last year. I got a white shirt for school, some socks, and a pair of dark gray slacks. Menny and I got a wind-up train that ran in a three-foot circle. We ran it every way we could; we put up barriers made out of paper and broke through them with ease. It was practically worn out by noon. My father didn't get up with us again. When he did get up he left quickly, saying he had to see someone. When the door closed a peaceful feeling came over all us, even though it was hard to see that he didn't give a hoot about Christmas or his children and how he should celebrate Christmas with us.

Mommy was a great cook and had Christmas dinner ready by 4:00. We had it all: turkey, mashed potatoes and her great gravy, biscuits, and succotash. We played Monopoly later and took our usual sandwich break and went right back to the game. It was a tough game with five people playing, but I always did well. One of these days I was going to win. I watched Mommy sitting on the sofa, trying on her red leather gloves with fur trim and eating a slice of fruit cake with her usual cup of tea.

Mommy was always knitting a sweater for someone and trying to teach Theresa how to knit, but Theresa wasn't interested. Sweaters were fine, but if we could only get Mommy to turn up the heat, I could feel warmer and not have to wear my clothes to bed some nights. Theresa loved to bring people up to see me sleeping in my clothes, the blanket pulled up to my neck, wearing a stocking hat and ear muffs and gloves. I knew one thing no heat and no hot water was tough living.

There was some talk of a snowstorm after New Year's. Menny and I prayed, and again it snowed eight inches overnight. Our prayers were answered: no school and we could make a lot of money. When we woke up and saw that snow, we ran around the house for boots and gloves. I was first out of the house. I started on West Street and made two fast dollars. I was still going strong. I came across Menny doing two houses. I was able to get the house on 30th and West Street. That was another two dollars. The deeper the snow, the more money. I stayed on 30th Street and shoveled some small sidewalks for a dollar a piece. There was a big house on 31st Street. We agreed on two dollars. I made eight dollars made by 10:00 a.m.

Everybody was out shoveling, but the secret was to get out early like I did. Theresa and Menny were getting lots of jobs too. I turned down Washington St., knocked on a few doors, and got one job for a dollar. That gave me nine dollars; we decided to go home for a hot cup of soup. Mommy was waiting for us with hot soup ready. Our faces were red from the cold; you could tell it was rough out there. I took the wet money out of my pocket and gave it to Mommy. We three made $25, which was a lot of money—more than my father had given her last week. She gave us a dollar each to spend on ourselves. We prayed for snow all the time so we could help Mommy.

My mother knew we would be losing our boarder, Brook, and a source of income, soon. She saw an add in the newspaper for an opportunity to start a soft ice cream store. She jumped at the chance and made an appointment to discuss the business. We were told to be on our best behavior when the owner came to the house. My father never showed up;

it was just my mother and the ice cream man. He stayed about an hour, took some information, and told Mommy he would get back to her. About a week later I came home from school and found my mother crying in the kitchen. I asked her what was wrong. She said the ice cream man told her that he was going to let another family have the business because my father had bad credit and didn't seem interested enough to show up for the meeting. He told her that to finance the business, my father would have to qualify, too. He could see how much this meant to her and said he was awfully sorry.

This really tore my mother up. She needed a way to make some money, and Sonny Jim wasn't interested enough to show up for the meeting of a lifetime. I know it was an opportunity to have our own soft ice-cream business and be one of the first in Wilmington to have that franchise. Mommy felt we would have been set for life. We could hear how disappointed she was when she told a neighbor that her children could only do so much and that they were supporting the family more than their father was.

On one of Menny's trash runs, he and I found some trains and some track. We needed a transformer, so we went to talk to the guy at Knowles Hobby Shop in Wilmington. He practically gave us a transformer and explained that it could run more than one train. We hurried home to the basement and hooked up the transformer to the trains. After placing pieces of wood around at the end of the table, we laid one of my father's old drop cloths over the sticks and made a mountain, with all the paint splashes looking like snow. We had hills and valleys and a smaller mountain as well. It was perfect. We were constantly adding to our train landscape. We put everything on a ping pong table so we had enough room to walk around it. To save space, we pushed the narrow end against the wall. The wall was white washed and uneven, and standing back; it looked like a snow-covered mountain.

It was hard for me to get the transformer away from Menny. I could tell by the way he talked to me that he was going to be in charge, and if anything, I was going to be in the way, he didn't have any respect for me and never tried to cover it up. He would tell me after he was finished using the transformer that it was too hot for me to use so I better wait and let it cool off. It didn't feel hot to me, so I used it anyway. After a few minutes, Menny would say again, "Babe, that's enough now, you better stop." I couldn't get over how worried he was for me and how lucky I was to have such a caring brother.

Every chance we got we would go in town to Knowles. Their display had coal around the tracks, so we bought some bags of coal for our tracks. We finally agreed that it was time to show it to Mommy. We were proud of what we did with junk. She couldn't believe that all that work was done from the scraps and old trains and track that no one wanted. It wasn't long before we started building little towns and villages. A lot of the things we had were broken, and we had to spend time fixing them. What wasn't fixable, we would set around in strategic places. We had cattle cars with tiny cattle, loading docks, street cars, even milk cars with small milk containers. But even with our success, I was never comfortable in the basement by myself. To me it was scary. The ceiling light was the only light, and if the heater kicked on while I was down there by myself, the hair on my neck would stick out with chills because the heater made soft noises and breathing sounds.

One night we took a break from the trains and went out in the backyard to smoke. Joan wasn't going to bed or her light would be on. We did see her the next day, and she had that look in her eye. She said "Hello Jim, Hi Babe." This time she asked if I wanted to wrestle her. She said that her mother was out shopping. She took my hand and walked me in to the house. Menny came along for the show. She kissed me on the mouth. She asked me how I was doing with my kissing. I told her didn't know; she was the only one I was kissing. She put her tongue in my mouth. Menny wanted to know whether we were going to wrestle or not. We got on our knees. She grabbed my shoulders and was going for a fast pin. I went immediately to the tits, where her nipples were standing out nicely. I held onto her for dear life. This went on for five minutes, then I let her pin me. She was laughing the whole time. She sure was nice to hold onto. The more shy and embarrassed I was the more Joan wanted me. I think she got her jolly off wrestling with me. I didn't know of anyone who was getting this kind of treatment. Menny kept saying, "Babe, she likes you a lot." She knew she was safe with me. We never touched each other anywhere else. She was just developing her skills; someone had to be the student. Some young man was going to be very lucky to have Joan at the controls.

Speaking about brushing up on skills, a bunch of us at school were talking about branching out. We walked down Washington Street to Matson Run, about 12 blocks away. We came across a lot full of little trees about three inches in diameter. We decided to go home and get some hand saws. We all met back about an hour later with carpenter saws. We started right in on the trees yelling TIMBER and all that. We tied a rope around the tree we were going to cut down. One guy would cut and one would pull. It wasn't long before there were downed trees everywhere. We had no idea we were making a mess out of someone's building lot. In fact, this woman from across the street came over and asked us if we had permission to cut down trees on this private property. I told this woman we weren't hurting anyone and turned away from her. She stormed away, pissed off at this young boy talking to her that way. It got dark early, so we went home, smoking all the way. We went back one other time but decided we had made such a mess that we should stay away before we got into trouble.

One of our classmates, Nancy Kebles, invited Menny and me to her ninth birthday party. We all sat around acting stupid when Nancy said, "Let's play Spin the Bottle." We all sat in a circle. If a girl spun the bottle, she had to kiss the boy the bottle pointed to. None of the girls kissed like Joan did, but I was having fun anyway. This kissing must have set off some of these nice girls' magic buttons because Nancy said, "Let's play Post Office." This is when a girl would take a boy or a boy would take a girl in a closet and kiss. One person would stay in, and everyone was assigned a number. If your number was called, you had to go into the closet. These girls kissed differently in the closet than they did playing spin the bottle. They would hold on tight and press themselves against me. I opened my mouth a little and they did the same. The longer you stayed in there, the ones outside would cheer and heckle you when you came out. None of these girls had the equipment Joan had. Nevertheless I was happy to be invited. The next day in the schoolyard, when I walked past a group of girls, one of them said, "Hey Babe, I heard you were a good kisser." I didn't pay any attention to them; they were just having fun. There weren't any secrets in our classroom, but no one ever threw anything up to us about our father. The only person was Mrs. Hansen telling her children not to play with us.

When I said I was happy to be invited to Keble's Birthday party, it should be understood that this seemed like a special treat because we didn't have a good self image. People didn't say hello or ask how we were doing, including the nuns. It would have been hard if someone would have walk up to us and said, "I heard you guys last night. Boy, your mother sure can scream. Did you get hit?" The Bakers across the street and the Toskas family next door were the only ones to take an interest. Mrs. Toskas was our guardian angel with big wings. She was like a second mother. Later on she would even make me dinner. That woman could cook Italian food, the best I have ever eaten. When she would hand us the dinner plate she would say. "When you're finished, bring back the plate clean. Babes, make sure you clean it good." Most of the time my mother never knew she had fed us.

The other neighbors either loved me or wondered what the hell I was up to. I guess I was a pain in the ass. They knew if they yelled at me or told me to stop doing something, holy hell would rain on them, either right away or in a few nights. I knew everyone's nationality. We knew the difference between the Italians, Jews, and so on. The nuns told us that the Jews killed Christ, so we disliked Jews, only because of these teachings. We were too young to know any better. Some nights, we would do mischief to Jewish homes, like soaping their screens, which were the hardest thing to clean off. Other times we knocked over garbage cans, cut clotheslines or threw wooden clothes poles like javelins. If you could jump fences and run through backyards and not get caught up on clotheslines, you could get away. It was nothing to see some boy in the schoolyard with a red line on his neck. You know he got caught up running full force. That clothesline would burn your neck, which would take a few weeks to heal. I think that Donald's mother would see me running up and down the street just like a devil; that's where my nickname Lucifer came from.

The next birthday party Menny and I were invited to Margaret Wagel's. She had a big house on 18th Street near Monkey Hill. I thought I was in a mansion and couldn't stop looking around. Margaret was a gracious hostess. Margaret had a beautiful birthday cake which I helped to devour. Then we played pin the tail on the donkey, and some kissing games, which I dearly loved. I wonder if the girls wanted to play kissing games as much as the boys did. It was good for Menny and me to be invited out like that. It helped strengthened our confidence because we felt inferior. We walked home with Farley and smoked a few cigarettes. I think Farley had a crush on Margaret, but we didn't know how she felt. A lot of these girls didn't telegraph their feelings; Joan was the only one who made it loud and clear.

The day finally came when Brook was going to leave. I asked her if she would miss us, and her eyes teared up. We all gave her a hug. She was happy holding her dad's hand when they left. He said they were going out west. Mommy was wiping the tears away. I knew Mommy would have taken care of her for nothing. They got in his car and pulled away from the house, they turned down West Street; Brook was gone, never to be seen or heard from again. The next thing you know, we had another little girl as a boarder. We called her Penny. She was different, waking up in the morning, rocking in her bed and saying, "Mat da vence" all the time and smiling at us. She only did this in bed, in the morning, and stopped when we took her out of bed. She was cute, but she didn't stay long. There was something wrong with her.

One day a short woman brought three little girls for Mommy to take care of. This woman was not a happy trooper. I didn't like the way she looked. The youngest child was Alice. The next girl, Barby, was three, and the oldest, Lee, was almost five. I couldn't tell how my father felt about it. He was hard to get a read on this one. He had to be embarrassed that his wife had to take in boarders to keep the house, and his children had to hustle up jobs for money. The embarrassment didn't improve his job outlook, though. He had to know Mommy was going to do well enough to keep the house.

My fourth grade teacher had decided to call on me in class so I would study and pay more attention. It helped a lot, but I still had a way to go. We had to do book reports, sometimes on books an inch thick. There had to be a better way. The word got out that Classic Comics put out a short version of books. What a lifesaver. It made it a lot easier for me. I don't think that Sister knew about Classic Comics yet.

I was becoming apprehensive about the end of the school year. Sister said that final exams were coming soon. My handwriting was OK if I took my time, but I didn't do well on tests unless I knew the subject cold. Whenever I read the question, I always read more into it than I should have. The first day of the exams, which usually lasted three to four days, I was a wreck. Then the final report card. I dreaded that day because I knew the drill. Sure enough, Sister Letitia asked me to stay after school, where she told me that she was going to let me go on to fifth grade but I would be on probation for ninety days. At least I had the summer off. I was very happy now.

My goal was to get up early every morning. Kautz always climbed our back shed, walked up the roof, pushed up our unlocked bedroom window, and came in and woke us up. We would plan our day right then. The three of us might do something or Menny and he would do something. I always had somewhere to go, or I could jump on my bike and go up to the Rock to see what was happening. One day I went up the Rock and saw some very dirty-looking bums sitting on the curb just outside the back door of the snack bar-pro shop. They were eating hot dogs with so much relish and onions that it was impossible to fit them in their mouths. I must have looked at them hard, because the ugly one asked me what I was looking at, and I told him nothing much. He didn't like that and neither did I. He didn't know that when I told him nothing much, he scared me with his ugly distorted face. I felt I would have to get even for his little muscle flexing in front of his hobo friend.

I never went golf ball hawking by myself. Ball hawking was when we would stand near the out of bounds or where there was a probability that the golf ball would go out of bounds and if it did go out of bounds, we would find it and offer it back to its owner and sometimes get up to a quarter for retrieving it. But sometimes you would run into those bums. Menny, Kautz and I were out ball hawking this day when we came across Ugly in the woods. He tried to tell us this was his spot and we three told him that it was ours also. We were cutting into his liquor money, but we knew he couldn't do anything about it. Three against one was definitely not good for him, and he knew it.

The bums slept in the woods at night. The bad weather, thunderstorms, and mosquitoes must have been a nightmare. The worst weather brought them to our caddy lean-tos, either that or be swept away by flooding. They weren't allowed to come in to our lean-to unless they were caddying, but they couldn't get any caddy jobs because they were dirty and you couldn't trust them. After lying out in the rain all night and all the mud splashing up on them, they were more camouflaged than a snipe would look. A lot of times they were soaking wet and shivering, and very humble because we ten caddies would kick the shit out of them given half a chance. They knew that fighting with the caddies would have them barred from The Rock.

When Menny or I got a caddy job, we waited on the curve of the tenth hole for the other one to finish. We had to sneak down because Grumpy didn't want a lot of us down there. There was a three-foot stone wall all around the curve and down the hill toward the green. Most golfers would try to hit over it. That's where we came in. Most of the time they would hit their ball out of bounds. If it didn't get over the wall we would find it, and give it back for as much as a quarter. You could make some money fast. We could spend four hours caddying for Oscar for one dollar or hawk balls at the curve and make four dollars in three hours, plus find some balls that couldn't be found before. Grumpy knew it was good down there, so he often sent a messenger telling us to come up.

One time I asked Grumpy why I wasn't allowed down there, and that he seemed to be playing favorites. I told him I had already caddied 18 holes. "What is wrong with me going down there after I have fulfilled my obligations?" I asked, "I am waiting for my brother to get in." At first he went into a rage but later agreed that after we caddied 18 holes we could go down, along as there was no fighting. The older guys didn't want us down because we were chipping away at their gold mine.

Menny came down to meet me it was just after 2:00 o'clock. He said, "Let's walk the course and find some balls. We need some good ones for caddie's day." We came across that Ugly bum's burnt-out hollow log where he slept at night. It was about three feet around and about six feet long. He had a piece of cardboard inside, which we pissed all over and called it a christening. Boy could we piss a lot. If we ever found the log vacant and no one around we would take a leak again. But seeing these bums gave us the inspiration not to grow up and be like them.

When the bums got hungry, they would come to the snack bar by way of the back door for coffee and a hot dog or donut. One morning when we came up to caddy a bum was lying in our caddy shack. He was very sick and moaning, so someone called an ambulance to come get him. They put him on stretcher and whisked him away. I never saw him again. Grumpy came over to see what was going on. I asked why he let the bums hawk balls; they scared the decent golfers to death. Golfers would hit a ball in the woods where the bums might be standing and would be too afraid to go over after it. The bum would keep it and sell it later. When I asked why he didn't say something to the bums, he looked me in the face and said, "They don't caddy and that's when it would become an issue." He spun around and walked back to his chair and sat down.

On caddies day we knew not show up after 9:00 because Grumpy wouldn't let us go out. He would run around screaming about the 9:00 o'clock cut-off. He didn't want the caddies playing behind the people who paid to play. "I know what you guys do out there," he yelled, "throwing clubs and cursing. We can hear you all over the golf course." He was a very unhappy camper and definitely didn't like us young men and boys being boys. I thought a lot of times about letting the air out of his car tires. I wanted to but I thought it over and figured it would only make him worse.

Grumpy didn't even like us practicing on the putting green. He didn't like us gambling either. We had gotten to the point where we wouldn't play unless it was for money. It was hard to gamble with all the cheating going on. I didn't know who was worse, Menny or Kautz, who expected to win all the time and with his hand mashie (his hand, no club) he had a good chance.

No matter what caddies did at Rock Manor, we were second-class citizens. But we didn't care; we were on a mission to earn money for

Mommy and have cigarettes when we wanted them. I stopped smoking Camels and started smoking Lucky Strikes. All of a sudden my father had cigarettes. His carton was lasting him longer lately. I didn't care about him finding my cigarettes; they were mine, not his.

I did one thing to his cigarettes that he never forgot. One day after caddying I came home and sat at the dinning room table. I found a razor and some scotch tape. I took a pack of my father's cigarettes, slit the cellophane on the bottom open so it would fold open, and carefully slipped the cellophane off the pack and put it aside. I then took the state seal off the aluminum foil by steaming it just long enough for it to slip off. I opened the tin foil, exposing the heads of all 20 cigarettes. I then got a big comb, broke off 15 teeth, and pushed each one into a cigarette so they couldn't be seen. It was a long and careful process. I had to make sure that the ends with the comb teeth were on the bottom of the pack, so that end wouldn't go in my father's mouth. That took the most time. I put some wooden match heads into five of the cigarettes so when the flame hit the match head, it would explode in his face. I then folded the aluminum foil back and re-glued the seal, making sure it stuck to the foil. Then I pulled the cellophane over the pack, taking my time not to tear it. When the cellophane was back on, I had to do was to use a minimum of scotch tape on the cellophane and he would never be the wiser. I didn't tell anyone else, but I was so excited I was sweating, hoping we would hear about it later.

It wasn't long before the shit hit the fan. He must have stunk up the bar. He told us that when you get a bad pack of cigarettes the smell made you sick and the taste was awful. He had a bad sore throat and was going to sue the tobacco company for making cigarettes that smelled so bad. He said that they kicked him out of the bar. He ended up throwing the last pack in the carton away. That means he smoked most of them. I wanted to hear about the five wooden match heads. I didn't think they would burn his nose, but I was hoping they would. He did get mad about that and said that cigarettes would blow up out of nowhere. But with his short memory span he had forgotten about it in a few days.

I couldn't wait to tell Menny what I had done. We were laughing so hard we were almost throwing up. I started to lose my breath. I told Menny, "Imagine Sonny Jim in the bar—Mr. Big Shot—stinking up the place, and just before they kicked him out, one of his cigarettes blew up in his face, almost singeing his nose hairs. What a night he must have had." Thank God he didn't come home and take it out on us. He wasn't able to drink with the sore throat; I saw him look at Menny and me as if we had something to do with this. He never kept his cigarettes on top of the china closet again. It was a good idea because I probably would have come up with some more ideas.

On the way home after caddying at The Rock, I often stopped by the 30th Street Park to see if the showers were on. Those showers were like being under a waterfall. So much water came out of those ten heads and the water built up so fast that it had a hard time going down the drain. I didn't know of any other park that had showers like that. I would take off my shirt and shoes and go in. It was wonderful. The wind dried my hair on the way home. It was always a mess, and each one of my hair cuts was different. I was so cheap I got my hair cut at the barber school. When I got home to change out of my wet clothes, Menny would be looking at dirty pictures of naked girls that he kept in our bureau. Everywhere we turned we saw seven-page sexual comic books. People sold them to us kids for 50 cents.

Everyone we caddied for wore golf shoes, but we didn't have any, so we always looked in the club trash for golf attire. We would find plenty of gloves, but no shoes. I was getting hooked on golf. It definitely was a gentleman's game. Like the time I was caddying for a real nice man, about six feet tall, who was a good golfer. We got to the sixth tee where they sold sodas. He asked me if I would like something to drink, and I said I would like an orange drink. He said he was the president of the Coca-Cola Company and that I could have a Coke. You never knew who you were caddying for. Rock Manor was famous for its golf course and the celebrities who came there. The clubhouse was beautiful, all stone and brick with stone columns. It was one of the better golf courses in the surrounding three states, but it was also public and cheap to play. It drew a lot of players, but it also attracted a lot of gamblers and drinkers who never went home to their families. I would never caddy for them.

The caretaker at The Rock, Luther, was responsible for the care and maintenance of the club house. He also lived there. Luther had full dentures, both upper and lower, and he often took his teeth out and made funny faces for us. Sometimes he let some of the oversexed Hollywood types take women upstairs. Luther was always nice to me. He told me he liked to go out on the golf course at 5:00 a.m. with a towel around him, walk to a stream that ran through the course, find a good place where it was deep, and sit in the cold water and soak for half an hour. He said the best feeling in the world was walking in the cool summer air early in the morning. Luther was always busy, but I think that is what he wanted. The only break he got was sitting in the cold stream before the course opened or when everyone went home. Luther worked there until he retired many years later. One day I asked him what he did on his day off. He said he was married, that his wife's name was Maud, and sometimes he would visit his sister in Wilmington. He only got one day off and that was during the week. It was hard for him to leave the club. He loved it so much; it was his home. Rock Manor was owned by the city of Wilmington, so I guess he was a city employee. I hope he was taken care of in his retirement. He deserved the best; after all, he gave his best.

On the way back from The Rock I often stopped at Boles's. Their subs were so good; I made sure I had one as often as I could. If I wasn't eating a sub I was eating a half pint of ice cream. If you went into the store around 11:00 a.m., you could see at least five big egg boxes full of at least 250 subs. Businesses would call in orders early so they could be ready for pickup. Mr. Napolski, "Boles," did this five days a week for years. When I came in the store Mrs. Napolski would smile and say, "What can I do for you today Lucifer?" She knew I didn't like that but it didn't stop her from saying it anyway.

I only lived about a block away from Boles's, but sometimes on the way home, the older guys would try to rough me up and threaten me to get off the street, but they were only tough when they had you out numbered. I never paid any attention to them, so they basically left me alone. I think I was too unpredictable; they wouldn't pick on anyone who would fight back. If people saw that you couldn't go to a store on your own street, the police would get involved, and these guys wouldn't like that.

One day Mommy bought a used lawn mower and asked me to cut the grass in the back yard. I got it started and my motto was that if it was green and sticking out of the dirt I was going to mow it down. I didn't know anything about lilies of the valley or peonies. When Mommy came out to look she almost had a heart attack. She cried, "Babe, you cut down all my flowers!" I said, "What flowers?" and she replied, "That's right; what flowers, they're all gone." She was heaping mad. I told her I didn't know they were flowers because they weren't blooming. What a dumb reason. We also had three fruit trees; apple, cherry, and pear. Sadly, we couldn't eat any of the fruit because the cherries were sour, the pears were too hard, and the apples were too small. You had to be very hungry to eat that fruit.

Mrs. Toskas had a cherry tree and an Indian cigar tree, at least that's what we called it. There were hundreds of little "cigars" on it. They were about a foot long and flat; we cut one ends off and lit the other end. They tasted strong and rough on the lungs; it's a wonder I tree. We picked them and dried them out and tried to smoke the have any lungs left. They would make us sick if we smoked one more than half way.

I realized as the summer was draining away that it would be time for school soon, so I tried to cram a month of fun into a week. I could probably get some more caddying in so I could play caddies day. I was starting to hit the ball good, but my long shots needed some work. Even if I hit a long iron off the tee I still would dub it; some people said I swung too hard. My goal was to break 100, but with my cut balls and trash can clubs it was going to be hard. The balls would cut easily, so when we were on the putting green, a really badly cut ball would go straight until it slowed down. Then it started acting funny, sometimes in your favor and sometimes not. Most of the time we marked our balls and replaced them with a good ball that was only used for putting. Even though that was not the correct thing to do, we had our own rules.

I needed to practice; I had my confidence but didn't have the time. I still always looked at those still pictures of Ben Hogan swinging. Menny and I really thought we were hot stuff on caddies' day; when I walked to the first tee I wanted to look good and take a couple of practice swings. Then Grumpy would say, "Come on, Babe, hit the ball!" I wanted to perform good in front of Grumpy. If I didn't hit a good shot I would look over at Grumpy; his head would be down like he didn't see me hit a bad tee shot. He really did have a soft spot for me.

I was fiercely competitive; I never wanted to three put, and be out of a hole I wanted to win, making par was rare for me. I wasn't accurate enough. When I hit the green my ball would be too far away to have a realistic chance for a birdie. But nothing could stop me from trying. Sometimes Menny and I would sneak on the course and play three or four holes when the marshal would go home. That would satisfy us, and we could either hawk balls or caddy.

The first very cool night, the bums would go into Wilmington and live in some boarding house in the bad section of town. They didn't have much of a life, just drinking wine or beer all the time. You could see how it destroyed them; it affected their whole appearance, skin color, and hair. They looked really old. It didn't stop them from drinking. I hated liquor so much I wanted it to disappear off the face of the earth. I hated what it did to people's lives and innocent families. I couldn't understand the popularity of it; I know it gave a lot of people false courage to go on, and in some cases physically hurt people.

Just before we went back to school, I could tell that Ballsey was overdue for one of his terrorist encounters. One night after midnight we heard Theresa calling out to leave her alone. We all ran down the hallway toward Theresa's room. Mommy reached for the light and turned it on. My father was on his knees with no underwear and his penis sticking out. Mommy was yelling at him to leave her alone; she's your daughter. Theresa had her face buried in her pillow; she didn't want to see anything. Margaret was in another room with Nora; you could hear them praying. Menny and I were looking through the doorway at him; he had to be embarrassed. He had folded his tee shirt under his balls and held it with one hand. Mommy ran up to him and cried, "Get out of the bedroom, you son of a bitch!" He couldn't handle that so he hit her in the face, breaking her glasses and cutting her nose. Menny and me ran to him and told him he'd better leave Mommy alone. He was still holding his balls. He wanted to hurt Menny and me, but he got caught and was reacting to the embarrassment of that.

Mommy picked up the phone to call the police; he grabbed the phone and pulled it out of the wall. He left the room as if to say, "I'll quiet down and you quiet down." How could we be so lucky to have a father like that? God must have had a good reason for this torture because he made it our hell on earth. We all went downstairs to sit with Mommy and Theresa. Mommy was crying and holding a towel to her head. We tried to reassure the both of them that we would stay with them. I looked in on the boarders, and they were all right. We all had a cup of tea and got our blankets and pillows. We slept on the sofa and chairs. They both had the sniffles, so we kept a small light on all night.

We never heard about divorce; we thought that Catholics played the hand they were dealt. I kept thinking that if my father could be honest with himself, he must feel bad, with not one ounce of courage to do something about it. He had to know he was giving in to his evil thoughts and deeds. He was existing as a nobody and would die as a nobody. In time it would be as if he never lived.

It was hard to be religious with all this hell going on around me, but we never missed Mass on Sunday. We never missed Communion, Benediction, Stations of the Cross, nine First Fridays, or all the Holy Days of Obligation, and prayed to God on our knees every night for help of any kind. It never came; in fact it got worse. I prayed so much to the Virgin Mary for intercession that I was sure she would send a Messenger. I know when she finally sees me in Heaven she would say, "Hi, Babe, it is nice to finally meet you."

I knew that this experience someday was going to make me a better man; it was my goal to get a kick out of life and not let life kick me. If I could survive in this environment, there wasn't anything I would have to face in my life that would be worse than this experience.

As if beating his wife and children wasn't enough, my father was starting to use the money set aside for our house expenses, putting us in jeopardy. He never had enough money to pay it back and had no money to start the next paint job that required a deposit. He could always raid our house money with the promise to pay it back Friday. As a result, Friday was one of our worst days of the week because when he paid the men who worked for him, he would only have $20 or less left over for himself. Then he would have a beer with them, they would go home to their families, and he would stay at the bar. Then he would keep drinking, pissed off about only having $20. He would be drinking with this misery, and that would spell trouble for us.

Eventually a lot of painters wouldn't work with him anymore. They made excuses that they had jobs they had to finish. He got to the point that he started diluting the paint. He thought he was cutting his cost, but in fact he was cutting his own throat. The paint was too thin to cover, so it would lose some of its color and he would have to paint another coat, increasing the amount of paint he had to buy. Some of his customers asked him to paint over wallpaper they didn't know that he had cut the paint, it had too much water in it, and so it would bubble up and peel the wallpaper. Then the customer would blame him, and he had to spend more money and time to finish a job. It took him a long time to take the wallpaper off the walls (in those days it was messy). You can imagine, at the end of three weeks on what he thought would be a one-week job, hitting the bar with that frustration and no money, and drinking the money that was to start the next job. The thought of taking care of a wife and five children, a house and all that was something he couldn't handle. No one can drink away that frustration.

In the end the liquor fueled his anger, and by 12:30 or 1:00 a.m. he just had time to catch the last bus. Heaven forbid if he should miss the last bus, because he would have felt every step of the walk home. He was not a staggering drunk, just an angry one. My father wasn't a dumb man. The fact that he quit school when he was twelve had nothing to do with his intelligence. He quit school because he didn't see any value in an education. I guess you can say that's dumb. He was just able to get by, but everyone who came in contact with him liked him. I had seen him come down the street with a roll of nickels in his hand, giving them out to all the kids on our street, which of course made him popular. But when he got to us sitting on the steps and I asked him for one, he told me to go in the house. When he came in he started sticking his fingers in my chest telling me not to embarrass him like that again. Somehow things were backwards; I should have been the one poking my fingers in his chest, telling him not to embarrass me like that again.

He had the nerve to tell me not to embarrass him one afternoon when Theresa had some relatives over and one of our neighbor's girls. I walked in the living room and all of the girls were giggling. I asked myself what could be so funny. There was my father sitting in the corner chair with a towel on his lap with a spoon on it. He had his head down and didn't even know I was there. The girls were still giggling, and then I realized what he was doing. He was making that spoon jump around on the towel by flexing his penis. He would do anything to make people laugh, and this was one of those anything's. I was disgusted to see how far he would go to get a laugh. He told them that he was a magician. I couldn't watch this any longer; I remember getting my cousin's attention and motioned her to come out in the kitchen with me. I told her that he was no magician. My cousin went back in the living room and lured the other girls away from him by saying, "Let's go out in the back yard with Babe; it's too nice to be indoors." Thank God they listened to her and I was able to get them away from him. I didn't know where this was going and felt safe that I had rescued them. Can't you imagine if one of those girls would have told her parents about this incident, there would be hell to pay? I could see that sex was playing a part in his life, was going to be a problem for him; if he should keep it up he might get himself in trouble some day.

I remember once meeting a woman whose house he painted, both inside and out. He did this job by him self, so it must have lasted forever. The woman would make him lunch and a cold drink and sometimes she invited him to stay for dinner with her and her husband. She had him painting the trash cans and the address number of the house at the cement edge of the porch. Then she asked if he would paint an extra coat of paint on the porch floor if he had any paint left over. She also asked him to paint two sets of Venetian blinds, He had to take them apart and paint each slat on both sides. All this work was extra, and not included in the price he gave her for the original job. She never gave him a penny for spending all those hours doing all the extras.

I was lucky enough to meet this woman one day. She looked at me and told me how lucky I was to have a father like him; He had her and her husband laughing all the time. In fact she said she would invite him to their parties; he was a big hit, and they laughed all night from his funny stories and facial expressions that he would make to emphasize the story he was telling. I looked at this woman straight in her eyes and told her, "While you were laughing with my father, my mother and her children were home crying. We had no heat, no hot water, no food, and no money to speak of. My mother had to take in boarders, and take in wash just so we could survive. My sister, brother and I had to hustle up money from caddying or carrying groceries out of the food market that were to heavy for some women to carry, we would do this all day. Trying to survive was uppermost on our minds, not to mention all the terror he put his family through probably after one of your funny parties. Sometimes we couldn't make our house payment because he would spend all of the money my Mother had put away, money his children had earned practically begging, he was drinking and making people like you laugh." The woman started crying; she said she was sorry and walked away.

My cousin Kitty told me that this woman came to her house, which was only a few blocks away. She wanted to talk to Kitty's mother (my father's sister). Kitty told her that her mother wouldn't be home until after midnight, at least another six hours. Kitty could see the woman was fighting back tears. She told Kitty that she had met me in a paint store, and heard the salesman call out the name Toner, so she immediately wanted to see if he was Jim's son or any relation. When she was sure it was me, she told Kitty how I informed her of all the abuse that went on, about how Jim's wife and children were treated by him. She couldn't believe how such a nice man like Jim Toner would do such a thing. Kitty agreed that it was hard to believe, and if she hadn't seen it with her own eyes she would have never believed it either. She went on to say to her, "One thing Babe didn't tell you is that when I stayed over some nights, I saw him trying to pull his 13-year-old daughter out of bed onto the floor to have sex with her, kneeling on the floor along side the bed with nothing on but a big hard-on. His own mother had shaken her finger at him and told him shame on you for the way you are treating your family." Kitty could see that my father's former employer was sad and could never see him in the same light again. The woman thanked Kitty and assured her that she and her husband would never tell anyone of this, for fear it might get back to him and what he might do to his family.

9

After so much caddying and playing golf, I had a nice tan when I went back to school, that fall of 1948. Everyone wanted to know what I did over the summer to get so brown. None of them had a summer like me; every vacation day had been exciting. I had learned so much, especially about golf. Our fifth grade teacher was Sister Margaret Xavier, who seemed to be all about school work. She probably spent the summer getting prepared for us. Sounding like someone leading a pep rally, she told us she expected that all the work had to be turned in neatly and on time, with no cheating. I looked around at the girls, but their uniforms were too loose to see if any of them were blossoming out front.

A couple of days after school started, I saw Joan on her porch talking to Menny. I had only seen her but a few times that summer. I started up the steps when I heard Menny telling Joan, "Babe's here." She asked me to come over and talk to her. She wasn't interested in talking to me. I sat on the porch railing; she pushed my legs apart and got real close. She asked me as sexily as she could if I saw any nice girls like her in school. I said never. She loved to hear that, but I was trying not to blush because this would drive her to be even sexier. I knew she was going to give me more kissing lessons, which were fine because they made me better for the other girls to enjoy.

It was every man's dream to have a young healthy goddess all over him, but I was always too nervous to really enjoy the moment, thank God I was being successful in not allowing her to arouse me. Menny wouldn't stop telling her to wrestle me. "Joan, you can beat him," he said. When Joan said she didn't know when her mother would be home, Menny offered to be the lookout. That's all she needed to hear; she opened the door and told me to come in. As I stepped over the threshold she had her shirt off and was down to her tee shirt. Those tits were big and firm. Her nipples stood out like door knobs. We both had shorts on. We got on our knees; she knew that when she grabbed me I would grab her tits. She probably wanted me to do more, but I was too dumb and scared around girls. The most I did was to give her nipples a small pinch, just enough to see a wild look on her face. She kept trying to pin me and she had her crotch rubbing up and down my leg, laughing the whole time.

Joan, who was five years older than me, never did anything with anyone else, so my bashfulness must have turned her on. I wasn't turning any other girls on, at least, to my knowledge. She was definitely going to make some young man very happy; even though I was too immature and scared, I didn't mind her teaching me what girls had to offer. When we were finished her tee shirt was pulled up almost up to her tits. She lay on me and French kissed me for the longest time. When I went to birthday parties and played Spin the Bottle, I had to pretend I didn't know about all that tongue because I had no idea how those girls would react. Joan was wearing me down, but she never laid a hand on me. She knew I was too young for that. An older boy would have put his hands in her panties, looking for some action. I never saw anyone dating her, so I am sure the house rules were strict. In the mean time Menny was going to make sure she would have all the contact she wanted with me. He was always looking in those little plastic viewers that had naked girls in them, and he also had plenty of magazines in our top drawer of our bureau. No wonder we wanted to see her undress in her window.

I was still enough of a boy to be interested in toys. The word got out that some Hawaiian guy was coming around selling yoyos at 27th and Washington Street. He showed us how to use the yoyo and told us to practice because he would be back in one week for a contest. The person who did the most loop-the-loops would win an emerald-studded yoyo. I finally had enough money to buy one, and the Hawaiian carved some palm tress on it for me. Everywhere you turned guys were doing yoyo tricks.

I was having trouble with the loop-the-loops. After 10 the string got loose. The Hawaiian would come around Thursdays around 4:00 p.m., just in time for practice after school. I saw other guys do over 50 loop-the-loops every week and saw it was important to keep the string tight.

It's hard to believe that a little thing like a yoyo could hold the attention of so many guys.

The competition was tough, which is what made it so much fun. Thursday in the school yard was quite a sight to see. The yoyos were everywhere, but only about a dozen of us would be in the contests. The Hawaiian didn't charge an entry fee; sometimes he would give a demonstration and sometimes he wouldn't. This guy could make his yoyo dance and when he was finished he would make it jump in his pocket. He had boxes of yoyos, some carved, some plain, and some studded. I was determined to win one.

At the same time the word was out that altar boys were needed and there would be a meeting after lunch. A whole bunch of us showed up. Fr. Donahue said that they only needed about 10 boys to replace the eighth graders who had left. He gave a test on the Mass, including Latin. As usual I was nervous and I didn't expect to do well on the test. When we met again a week later, Fr. Donahue surprised me by announcing my name and asking if I wanted to do Benedictions in the early evening. I said I would. Menny signed up for Masses, so sometimes he had to be at church at 5:30 a.m. for 6:00 Mass. A schedule was always posted in case anyone wanted to change times and days. Two boys served at each Mass, seven days a week. It was a circus keeping track of that schedule; everyone wanted the weekends off to go somewhere. Menny and I never had a problem because we weren't going anywhere.

We went to training classes, which Fr. Lynch did not attend, but he expected us to be perfect at Mass. He often lost his temper and threw things at the altar boys, who sometimes quit because of him. It wasn't a nice picture for parents to see their son embarrassed in front of 400 people, but many people realized Fr. Lynch had sudden mood swings. They knew he could do anything, including bringing his black standard poodle into church and walking with him while he took up the collection.

Every now and then, while taking up the collection, Fr. Lynch would tell someone to leave. I saw him kick people out of the church because they weren't Catholic. It wasn't embarrassing enough that he would kick them out, he would scream at them all the way out. Even though he did a lot of good, Fr. Lynch seemed to ruin things with his antics. But he never treated me badly when I was on the altar with him. Sometimes he would walk up the center aisle towards the altar and started talking to the congregation. He would talk about his dead mother and how he thought she was a saint, and how scantily the women were dressing in the summer. He would say,

"I see you; you better not come to church with those shorts on because I'll throw you out!" Then the priest at the altar had to finish up to ensure that the next Mass started on time.

I did Benedictions with Fr. Lynch, and he showed me how to light the charcoal, so when he put the incense on the hot charcoal it would smoke really well. He must have taken a liking to me; I hoped I wouldn't give him a reason to yell at me. At one Benediction I couldn't tell if the charcoal was hot or not. I wasn't going to touch it so I put a sprinkle of incense on it. That filled the sacristy with smoke. Fr. Lynch walked in, and you would have thought the church was on fire, but he didn't scream at me. He just told me in very strong terms that it was his job to put the incense on the charcoal, not mine. He just said, "Don't do that again."

Another time I put two big pieces of charcoal in the censer, filled the incense cup with incense, and heated the big pieces of charcoal red hot, so when Fr. Lynch put the incense on the charcoal it smoked just right. The sun was shining through the stained glass windows and it was beautiful. You could see the smoke, and I made sure no one could see me put more incense in on the coals. I carefully pulled the shaker up and down, and the smoke got so bad the ushers were opening the windows. Fr. Lynch shook it again for the last time, with the windows open and the smoke gushing out. A woman passing by saw the smoke, ran home, and called the fire company to come at once, thinking the church was on fire. There was no fire; it was just me.

With the windows open you could faintly hear the fire sirens from far away, getting closer just as we finished. The entire block and the school parking lot were full of fire engines—eight fire engines and one hook and ladder—and traffic was blocked for blocks around. Fr. Lynch started walking toward the fire chief at the back of the church and I quickly ran up the front steps to the bathroom and dumped everything from the censer into the toilet and flushed two or three times. When he was through talking to the fire chief, Fr. Lynch wanted to inspect the censer, I told him I had emptied it in the toilet to put out the smoke. He commended me for my quick thinking but was scratching his head, saying he didn't realize he had put so much incense on those coals. He probably would have choked me to death if he knew what really happened. I told him I wanted to help him out by dumping the charcoal down the toilet; it was our business, not the nosey fire departments. He put his arm around me and thanked me for thinking of his welfare.

I was putting my robes away and saw him looking at the censer and the incense holder trying to piece together this puzzling mishap that I could see clearly was bothering him. He was satisfied that all was as it should be, but I must have put three quarters of a cup of incense on those coals. I was glad I was one step ahead of him, and he never did figure it out what had happened. I went outside. I never saw so many people in all my life; they were standing around watching the firemen rolling up the hoses. Menny called out to me and asked me what happened. We had had a conversation a while ago about what would happen if you put a lot of incense on a big piece of charcoal, and he looked at me and started laughing. We both bent over laughing and he said, "Babe, you didn't?" He was smoking a cigarette at the time and the more he dragged on it, the more he choked, laughing at the same time. When we got home, I exploded, laughing about what happened. I told him about Fr. Lynch trying to figure it all out and putting his arm around me, thanking me for looking out for his welfare. Menny said we had some more years to go as altar boys and he didn't think we could top that. But we would see.

I had lots of other things to do to keep me busy after school until bed time. If I wasn't in the street I would be in the school yard, playing cops and robbers or cowboys and Indians, using broom handles as rifles. There wasn't a fence I couldn't get over or a garage I couldn't climb or jump off. I just liked to run and hide. Most of the time the other kids gave up trying to find me and called out that they quit. I had to come out of hiding to keep the game going.

I usually found Menny in the basement, playing with the trains that he thought were his. We had one stool by the transformer, so I was always sitting on the cellar steps looking at what I thought was half mine. When I finally got to play, Menny would say he was tired and was going upstairs, leaving me all alone down there scared to death. It wasn't long before I would come running up the steps, thinking someone was behind me. I had goose bumps all over me, especially my neck where my hair stood straight out. I reached for the door knob. Once I had it in my hand, it only opened one way. I only had a few feet to go before I was in the kitchen, and I didn't want to turn the knob the wrong way and slow me down. I pushed the door open and fell onto the kitchen floor, out of breath and pale white. I looked back down the steps; although no one was there, I still had the feeling that someone or something was down there.

When we took our baths, Menny and I would take them separately because we were too big to fit in the tub together. We always got into a fight anyway. Mommy would have to come in and break it up. We always played cards after our baths, and if no one wanted to play I would build a house of cards and see how high I could go. If I got the whole deck out I was good. We had a checker set, and I loved to play Kings, when I made six kings and jumped them forward or backwards and sideways. I was hard to beat. We also played marbles and card games with baseball cards.

The most fun was imitating Mommy. She would laugh and scream. Theresa could really do her well because we were more inhibited It was fun to see my mother howl with laughter; I guess it was fun to see herself through the eyes of others. We did short skits as if Mommy was a movie star and we were comedians imitating her. It was good clean fun.

We loved it when Mommy told stories about Ireland and the farm. She said her father would take a drink at the pub down the road even though he was a farmer and couldn't stay out all night. He had to be on his feet at 5:00 a.m., just in time for the rooster to crow, usually with a dry mouth. Mommy said she was expected to help out; it would take two men to lift those heavy milk cans up on the platform for morning pickup before they would take a break. Breakfast was the favorite meal; it had to get them through the day. There were plenty of eggs, bacon, and fried bread, which was so hard you could use it as a shovel. With the excess drippings spread on it and a hot cup of tea to top it all off, it was a lot for them to look forward to. I think she missed that hard toast because her face would really light up talking about it.

Mommy said her brothers and sisters all got along well, but Jerry was a little different. He got along well too, but at times he was a little serious He had a little mustache and when he laughed you would laugh with him. I know he took a lot of razzing about that little mustache. He seemed to be cheaper and more secretive than Julia, and I think I was the only one he trusted or confided in. After all I was named after him. Jerry was an adult but had a young mind, and later on he would rely on me a lot.

Julia, on the other hand, was different. She was working for a very rich man who would later become a very famous rich man. Not long after that, she thought she was rich and acted rich when it suited her. But she never went after her driver's license and neither did Jerry.

She never offered my mother a penny. She could have paid off our house and my mother could have paid her back. Julia had to know all about my father, how Mommy was struggling to make ends meet, and that the children were bringing more money home than their father. Julia never let my father know that she didn't like what he was doing to his wife and children. I don't think anyone did.

Julia liked me, and I always got along well with her. I always offered to make her a cup of tea and put a few cookies on her plate, which she loved. Someone was waiting on her now. She would say, "Oh, Babe, thank you very much, you are turning out to be a very nice boy." I figured it was better to be on her good side than on her bad side like Theresa. Julia and Theresa clashed very badly. Theresa was hurt by that and could never make it better. Whenever she would try to do something nice like I did, Julia would snap at her and, as Theresa put it, "hiss like a snake." That drove Theresa crazy; she would fold her hand into a tight fist and wanted to punch Julia. We told her to forget it. I guess Theresa asked Julia for money one time too many. Mommy only tolerated Julia, who never treated Mommy as a sister, never calling to say hello or asking about the children's health. While we children were always happy to see Aunt Julia on her day off, once or twice a year for an hour, I never got the feeling she felt the same way.

My mother loved to cook, so for Thanksgiving she could really put out a spread. She knew how to get the most for her money. A fresh turkey wasn't that expensive. Theresa helped her make the gravy. My theory was that if the gravy was good, the meal was good. We always had mashed potatoes without a lump in them, and when I poured the gravy on those potatoes my legs would get weak. Theresa picked up the gravy-making skill fast, and it wasn't long before Mommy gave her full responsibility for that part of the meal.

My father left early on Thanksgiving to go see his mother and father. He never said goodbye when he left. I am sure he had a lot of guilt because he couldn't sit and have Thanksgiving dinner with his own wife and children. We were probably strangers to him with the little time that he had spent with us. When he left no one looked up or cared, but I felt relieved. The only way we knew he had left was when we heard the door close. When we told Mommy he left, she said, "Goodbye." She was like the big hen looking after her chicks.

That year Fr. Donahue wanted to have a Christmas party for all the altar boys at the Hotel DuPont and just rent a small room and enjoy a small meal together. There were about twenty of us, and I knew he never considered me an altar boy because I was only able to do Benediction. When the time came for a head count, no one asked me if I was going, even though I felt I was on the altar more than any of the alter boys. Menny didn't go because he didn't remember being asked, and I didn't want to go to a celebration and be treated like a second-class altar boy. Could you imagine the look on his face if Menny and I would have walked in before they served dinner? Fr. Donohue would have been so shook up he would have made the mistake and said, "What are you two doing here?" Of course we would have told him that we were altar boys too. Wasn't this for altar boys? He would have died. Menny and I never asked anyone how it went or who went; we knew that Fr. Donahue had his favorites; it was hard to believe that an ordained priest could treat some children differently from others. I am sure that God will have to talk to him about this kind of treatment. It all boiled down to the haves and the have-nots. You should have seen him asking the "haves" if they were interested in becoming priests. It was obvious he didn't want Menny or me or anyone like us to be priests because we would be dependent on the parish for funds. He only recruited the ones whose families could pay for their schooling. But when the priests wanted their cars washed, they asked us have nots. It didn't take a genius to see who they could rely on for hard work around the rectory.

Theresa started asking everyone what they wanted for Christmas. Menny and I both wanted a BB guns. We knew we were going to get clothes because that's what we needed the most. In school, Sister felt out the class to see who believed in Santa Claus and who didn't, so she could stay away from certain subjects. I was the only one who believed. It was embarrassing, but nevertheless I thought I would get more gifts by believing.

After the first snow, Menny and I went sledding at Prices Run, where all the hills were. When we got home Mommy was in the kitchen with Theresa waiting for us to come back to her. She had heard on the radio that some kid was run over trying to hop on a car for a ride. She had a brown horse whip that Menny and I had found out in the barn in her hand and asked us where we were. We told her we were down at Prices Run, sledding. She jumped up and started swinging the whip at us, missing on purpose and eventually laughing and hitting the chairs and table with the whip.

She wanted to know who was going first for a horsewhipping. I said Menny should since he was the oldest. That broke Mommy up. I wanted to know what we did wrong; we were only sledding, not hopping cars. She was happy to hear that, so she put the whip away. She had made her point and scared us badly. We had to promise to never go down there sledding again. That was easy. We didn't want to; the hills were small and there were too many people.

Mommy had wanted to put the fear of God in us. Instead we went to Monkey Hill, which had oak trees 20 feet in diameter, steeper hills, and countless rocks. It was definitely dangerous. A lot of people got hurt but never got on the radio. But we were fearless—the more risk the more fun. We would even hop cars all the way back to 29ᵗʰ Street. When I said I was fearless, I was not as fearless as Dickey Hire, my classmate. I have never seen anyone swing from trees like he could. He was tall and thin and would go limb to limb and in some cases jump from limb to limb. He wasn't five feet off the ground; he was 40 feet off the ground. If he had fallen, I don't think he would have survived, but I am sure it never entered his head.

Right before Christmas, Theresa was locked in the dining room again wrapping gifts. Menny and I bought Mommy some powder and a powder puff, and Theresa wrapped them for us. I really was waiting to see what we got for Christmas. Mommy made us go to bed early, saying that an early bedtime showed that we wanted Santa to come. This annoyed Menny, who wanted to stay up again. Our bedroom was so cold I ended up wearing a sweater and a hat that Mommy knitted me. I put my hand on the radiator and it was freezing. I knew now the heater wouldn't turn on until the morning. I woke hearing Theresa say, "Babe, aren't you going to see what Santa brought you?" That's all I needed to hear. Cold or not, I jumped out of bed and put on my long socks and I was ready to go. Menny was a little sluggish that morning but he soon snapped out of it when he heard all the whooping downstairs. At first we thought all our gifts were clothes, but then I spotted a thin box with my name on it marked Daisy Rifle. We couldn't believe we had our own BB guns, but we didn't have any BB's; I guess everyone else was glad about that. This meant we had to wait until the stores opened to buy some BB's.

We were thrilled to move up the popularity chain with BB guns. I had something to play cowboys and Indians with, and the guns looked real. Right away I put my name on my gun and box so there wouldn't be any problems with Menny.

Theresa had taken it for granted that we all would play Monopoly. I did but my heart wasn't in it. I was hoping my pain didn't show, but it did. Eventually I told Mommy that when I had a bowel movement my backside hurt. She took me to the doctor's office the next morning. He told her I needed an operation right away to relieve my hemorrhoids. I wouldn't wish that operation on anyone. Before the operation, they scotch-taped my eyes closed. I don't know why I didn't put up a fight, but I didn't want to curse the nurses again either.

I woke up to see Mommy staring at me. She was worried this was my second operation in three years. "Why me?" I thought. I guessed it was my payback for all the hell I was raising. The good part was looking at the nurses, who were all starched up and beautiful. I loved it when they made a fuss over me. They would flirt with me a little and I would turn red, especially if they had to look at my ass. Before I went home, the nurse said I had to take a sitz bath. She took me to the bathtub and told me to sit in the hot water on an inflatable "donut."

I don't know what happened but the ring burst and my ass hit the tub. It was like a tidal wave with the water going up and down the tub. The nurse ran in and pulled me out and got a towel for me and dried me off. When Mommy came in I told her what happened. She laughed, but asked the nurses why no one was with me at all times. I didn't want Mommy to make the nurses mad at me because I liked them all. They treated me well and hugged me and said good night to me every night. They would check in on me every 30 minutes.

I went home the next day, happy to be walking out of Memorial Hospital, I only missed one day of school, and it wasn't long before I was my naughty old self again. I went to the hardware store on 24th and Washington Street, ready to buy some BB's. Menny was broke so I gave him a dollar to get some. We bought six tubes each, which should last us for a long while. I shot at any target I could find, even setting up a target on a cardboard box so there wouldn't be any ricochet and I could recover some of the BB's.

I stayed out in the yard in the cold or heat and tried to shoot birds, with no success. You could see the BB go straight and then suddenly dive. I was developing an eye and could actually see the BB in flight. I loved to shoot at those big blackbirds. Some of the other kids got BB guns also. You knew we were going to have a good time; we would play all day long from yard to yard, but no shooting at each other. Every now and then you could hear a BB go by or hit a tree nearby. I wasn't going to be anyone's target, so I let a few go back. Eventually I said I wasn't going to play if anyone took potshots at me. So we all agreed not to shoot each other. Someone was going to get hurt and I didn't want it to be me.

Jerry didn't come over the day after Christmas, the first one he missed in years. He found out I had an operation and stayed away while I was recuperating. He came over a month later and gave me five dollars. He said he was happy to see me and we had our usual cup of tea together and our usual small talk. He told me a lot about work and he said that the fumes were bad and so was the pay. He could barely live off the wages. He was renting a room on Lancaster Avenue for five dollars a week, plus meals. Jerry saved a lot of his pay. He worked along the Brandywine at Bancroft

Mills; Julia's boyfriend Davenport was working there too. It was hard to understand him; he was always under the influence. His voice was rough and deep, which put you right on the defensive. Jerry was different. He was easygoing and would pull his lips tight and laugh without showing his teeth. He had told me that he had to leave Ireland because he had shot someone, and I must have gotten him real relaxed because he described everything in detail. I had no way of knowing whether he was telling the truth or not, but I did know he couldn't get anything out of lying to me. I was more interested in what he had done with the gun. He described in detail everything he did and how he disposed of it. I asked him if he was ever going back to Ireland and look for that gun he hid. He said no, he was never going to go back to look for anything.

The next day the mother of our three boarders came to the house. It was raining so we all stayed in while she packed all her children's clothes. In less than an hour they were gone, without a goodbye. Mommy was a wreck, and she had a scared look on her face. My father was up, but he stayed in his bedroom. Two men in suits drove up in an unmarked police car and knocked on the door. Mommy let them in, and the three of them went upstairs. They were up stairs for at least an hour. They came down with my mother behind them. She was pale and shaking. When the men left, we all asked her who they were, and she said it was about getting a license to take in boarders. That sounded good so we left it alone.

I went out into the kitchen and sat with Mommy. I told her about the boarders not saying goodbye and how mean their mother was to us while she was getting the children ready to leave. "Mom," I said, "she was sneaky looking. How could she even leave her children with anyone?" I pulled on my mother's arm and told her those two men were policemen. I'd seen them around before in that car. Mommy looked over my shoulder to see if anyone was listening or coming into the kitchen. She said quietly that the boarders' mother had gone to the police and filed a complaint against my father. He had done something to the five-year-old. The poor little girl couldn't explain what it was, and her mother asked the detective to talk to my father about it. Even if they scared him and he never did anything like that again, she could still file charges against him for a couple of years.

My father was only spared because the little girl was a wreck, too scared to go through any type of trial. They checked Mommy out as to what kind of a mother she was, and had a good report on her. That helped him. My father stayed up in his room all day. I saw him through the crack in the door, just sitting fully dressed on the bed. He was a pitiful sight. He was very lucky; he could have gotten 20 years. When he finally came down, chewing his gum, he was very nervous. He went to the closet and got his coat and went out. I hoped it would dawn on him that he had just gotten away with murder that day. You can bet he didn't come home fighting that night.

That winter was so cold that we ran not walked, home from school. It was even too cold to go out for recess. I looked forward to our 15-minute breaks in the morning and afternoon. We were allowed to stand up and move around but not make any noise or leave the room. At home it was cold enough to wear my sweater and long socks to bed. Someone was always trying to get out of going to school, but Mommy was too smart for that. Everyone went, even if she had to drag you there kicking and screaming, which was not an experience we wanted to repeat. Every morning she gave us a tablespoon of cod liver oil from a bottle that looked like a fish. She said it was good for us.

One day a woman came and begged my mother to take care of her two girls for a little while until she got back on her feet. The two girls were Bonnie and Mikey. Mikey had freckles and Bonnie looked like her mother. They fit right in. They were too young for school and happy to be with us. Mommy needed the money. She was determined not to lose our home. It wasn't long before the girls felt just like family. Every time their mother would come see them, her leaving was the worst part. She would cry hysterically. I thought it was a bad way to leave her children; I don't know why she had to leave those girls with us in the first place. There had to be something wrong with her life. I was too young to know what it was, but I think her boyfriend didn't want them around. She was pretty and looked like Lana Turner and unlucky enough to have the same problem with an abusive boyfriend.

Mommy didn't want any problems with Menny or me, either. It must have been a miracle that Menny and I never got in trouble, with the year-round mischief and throwing all those bottles and tomatoes and apples. You would think that we would have gotten into trouble, but maybe we were only a pain in the ass. Maybe Jimmy Farley was right when he told me I was "the most ornery son of a bitch he ever met." I think I was releasing tension from my home life. But I always made sure I didn't hurt anyone, just rained havoc.

In spite of my orneriness, Mommy relied on me to make the right decisions. You could say that Menny and I were bringing ourselves up. I came home whenever I wanted to. I was never asked where I was going or where I was, but I never abused that trust. It was up to me to take a bath or shower. It was up to me to do well in school. Mommy never saw our report cards either. She knew Theresa was signing them and relied on us kids to do the right thing.

It was also up to me to bring home money Mommy needed. A lot of people say, "I had to quit school to help out my parents." That's a bunch of bull. They used that as an excuse to quit school. If that's the case, then we all should have quit school to help Mommy out. But she didn't want us to, and we didn't want to. I did have to be discrete about my smoking, not walking around with a cigarette hanging out of my mouth. I always cupped my cigarette whenever I took a drag. It was less noticeable. People still walked up to me and said, "Does your mother know you smoke?" I always replied, "Yes, she does." Mommy knew a lot of things.

Theresa was in the eighth grade now. She was only getting C's and D's. She was very angry. She had a chip on her shoulder that was as big as a railroad tie. It wouldn't take much to start something; just a bad look would do it. Sometimes she and Menny and I would do things together. She even taught me how to iron. Other times she fought with Menny and me a lot, usually over nothing. She had my father's fight moves in her. She would hit us with anything she could get her hands on and was determined not to lose.

All the girls in the neighborhood would stay away from her. There wasn't any way they would play with her—she was too strung out. We had to import our relatives to play with her. She didn't drink or do drugs, she just smoked. It's hard to believe, but it's true. I could see then that no man would ever dominate her. I asked her where she was going to school after Christ our King. She wasn't sure but was thinking of going to Wilmington High School, on Delaware Avenue, across from the graveyard. I told her she could go to P. S. DuPont, but she said she wanted to go where her girlfriend Betty Dueling was going. I asked her, "Why doesn't Betty go where you go?" (To P. S. DuPont). She could walk to and from school, with no buses to catch. In the end, though, she went to Wilmington High with Betty.

In early spring, the weather started to change. It was still chilly out, so we went up to the A.I. football field, practically surrounded buy eight-foot-high grass that we called African grass for some reason. This place had an upper field and a lower field, which had bleachers and a shower room that we never used because it was always locked up tight. We all took our BB guns along for something extra to do after playing football. When we finished playing football, we walked through the high grass. We were very adventurous and found an opening in the grass that let to a big pond with a wall around it. I called it DuPont Lake. It was fun watching our BB's hit the water. The pond was full of cattails. If I shot a cattail, it exploded, and hundreds of little "parachutes" floated down to the ground. We spent a lot of time up there.

The older guys would get us in a football game and then beat the living shit out of us. I had to take myself out of some games so I wouldn't be crippled for life. The older guys were brutal. They must have had a lot of enjoyment out of watching us limp off the field. Eventually, we stopped playing with them. Only one of us, Tuffy Pabst, could play against them. He could fake them out. They couldn't tackle him if he was on a leash. He was too slick and could fake them out of their pants. They dove after him but he would be gone. This kid had asthma and was only five feet four inches tall, but he was a far better athlete than we were. Whether on the field, or in the street, he raised hell with us.

One day I found a wagon in the trash; the body and wheels were good. The handle was bent so I straightened it out and put a couple of pieces of cardboard in the bottom. I didn't know how long it would last, but I had an idea to go down to the A&P store on 28th and Market Streets and help the women with their groceries. I would do that in place of snow shoveling. I hustled. I stood at the check-out line and watched the paper bags fill up with food. That was my cue to ask the women if I could help them with their groceries. Most of the time, they said yes. I put their bags in my wagon and walked along with them and usually talked all the way to their houses. They asked about school and where I lived. When we got to the house, I helped them carry their bags to the porch, and waited for my tip. They usually gave me a quarter, rarely more and rarely less. I would turn my wagon around and run like hell back to the store. Sometimes there was a line of other kids, eager to help, but I felt it was my idea. When I put on my sad face, the women never turned me down.

The rule among us kids was that the line was kept neat and when we got an offer, we stepped out of line and let the other kids get up front. There were at least five or six checkers, so that line would move fast. Some days were good, like Friday and Saturday. Making money gave me a lot of pleasure. Even on a bad day, I could make $2.50, and on a good day you could make four or five dollars in at least as many hours. It was a lot of money for me. Even though we could have more fun at the Rock, this was a good fill-in. Sometime I would just carry the shopping bag to the car and get a dime. I never turned anyone down. The women would come as far as three blocks because they knew someone would be there to assist them. If you think about it, we were helping the A&P out for getting these people in and out of their store as fast as possible.

Sometimes we would go around the corner of the A&P store and pitch nickels. Throwing was big for me, so I won a lot of nickels. I knew how that coin was going to react when it hit the cement. The older guys didn't like me winning all the time. I even played 500 Rummy for a penny a point and made a few dollars.

After a busy day at the A&P, I had Benediction that same night. Sometimes when I showed up to serve I was scruffy as hell. Some of those people sitting in the pews must have said, "There's that kid who smokes and is always running around the street." Fr. Donahue made sure to tell me to make the charcoal hot and not to put any incense on it. He never seemed happy; he never smiled. I loved doing Benedictions because it was easy and fun. If anyone asked me to fill in I would be right there, and I can assure you I wasn't getting a cut from the collections. I did love the smell of the incense; it made me feel holy.

The altar boys who served at Mass were always looking for someone to switch with them. In the summer they wanted to go to the beach or on vacation and would pay money to switch. God help them if they missed; with no replacement they would have to have a good excuse. If it wasn't good enough they would get the worst schedule that Fr. Donahue could give out. Mass at 6:00 a.m. and 12:00 were the worst. They had to be careful if the punishment was too hard. They could just drop out and wouldn't be missed, except by the other altar boys.

One day when I came home a gray cat was hanging around our porch. We started giving it food and milk, which was a big mistake. Once you feed them there yours. I was uneasy and uncomfortable around cats, but we played with him so much he would hide from us, just for a rest. What we called playing he would probably saw as teasing. We had a yellow flag with a rattlesnake painted on both sides. If we held it in the cat's face and spun it between our fingers, the flag flipped and the snakes really looked as if they were going to jump off the flag. The cat screamed and jumped backwards, his hair standing out straight, as only a cat can do. After that I noticed the cat starting to act funny. When I let him out, I was hoping he would leave. He didn't. He stayed around for the good food.

One Saturday morning, early, I could hear the cat meowing. He jumped up on our bed, walked across Menny, walked up my chest, squatted, and pissed in my face. I sat up yelling, "The cat just pissed in my face!" I jumped out of bed and was looking to kill him. I had piss all over me. Menny was howling on the floor. The cat took off and I took off after him. Theresa was standing at the front door and quickly opened it. The cat ran out and we never saw him again. I could only guess that he literally wanted to piss me off before he left. I went back to bed, but my pillow was wet and smelly, so I asked Menny if I could sleep on his pillow with him. He said, "No, sleep on your own pillow." He was always good to me like that; somehow I knew he cared for me he just never showed me that he did. I hope I can find that cat someday. Maybe I'll piss on his face.

That spring, Easter was a big excuse for Mommy to get some baby chicks. Oh did she love those chicks. She put them in a shoe box in the center of the stovetop above the pilot light. We put shredded paper in the box as well to keep them warm. With the chickens on the stove and the mice peeking out from their hiding places, and the black roaches on the floor, we had a regular zoo going on. We could hear the mice behind the walls, racing around all night. I always thought they were playing hide and seek, like we did. We had plenty of entertainment. Wilmington must have been roach infested because everyone had them. Whenever I walked out in the kitchen, I jumped from chair to chair to get to the light switch. If you ever stepped on a big, black roach you would never forget it. They were as big as your thumb. When you stepped on them, all of these white guts would gush out on your shoe or bare feet, causing you to scream in disgust, and then you had to clean the floor, your shoes, or feet. We hated roaches. We would buy roach spray and spray everywhere. In the back closet, down the basement, and all the walls and beams. We didn't realize it, but this would drive them over to the Toskas'. When Mrs. Toskas would spray they would be right back to us a week later. This would go on continuously. When she saw me, Mrs. Toskas would ask, "Babes, were you spraying your roaches?" I always said yes. She replied that she had roaches everywhere and that she was going to spray too.

As the weather improved, we spent more time in the schoolyard. It was about three-quarters of a city block square of blacktop. Just after the Easter holidays, some men drove in to our yard with trucks and started laying out a lot of lines. They had some big post-hole diggers, like the phone company hole digger, which could dig a 12-inch round hole. They drilled at least six deep holes and slid six-foot poles in the holes. When Fr. Donahue came over to see the work, we asked him what they were doing. He said it would be a full-sized basketball court for the boys and a half court for the girls. The men came back later with the backboards and rims. They looked high to me.

I had never played basketball before, and it looked like it was going to be a challenge. Fr. Donahue put in a waterproof box away from the court against the iron fence to store the new basketballs. When the balls came out, that's all you could hear day and night. I even played at dusk, but not pitch dark. Everybody wanted to play; even the girls were getting hooked. I could see that my smoking hurt me because I breathed heavily and gagged. Running up and down the court, I was clearly struggling. I kept it going because I wanted to be a part of this new sport. We would choose up sides for some crazy games.

The older kids dominated the court: the games, and everything. They were good, and I was only eleven and still learning. Boy could they run fast. I realized that if the older guys let you in the game, your job was to pass the ball to them, get rebounds, and do the best you could. If older guys showed up, we younger kids got yanked. I was never dumb enough to get under the boards with those bullies. You would be elbowed black and blue for getting in their way. The school yard became known all over the city as "The Yard," a good place to get up a game.

When we went out to recess at school, we got the balls out of the box and gunned them up for 15 minutes. But no matter what, the girls had to have a ball, too. Sometimes if a ball bounced just right, it would land on the fence spikes and burst. Sometimes you could patch them and sometimes you couldn't. Fr. Donahue didn't always replace the balls as fast as we would have liked, so some kids would bring their own and take them home after they were finished.

The yard was beginning to play a big part in our lives. Fr. Lynch didn't want anyone playing on Sundays before 1:00 p.m. Some days when he got a wild hair growing, he would come out on his porch and yell and wave for us to stop playing. Sometimes if we didn't pay attention to him, he would come off that porch like a wild man. Then we would run because we would definitely not want him to get hold of us. We couldn't understand why he wanted us to stop, especially on Saturdays. I wasn't going to ask him why either. Maybe he wanted us to go to Confession.

Speaking of Confession, some people went in and talked so loud, you could hear them as clear as a bell while standing in line. After Confession one Saturday, a man was standing outside the church recruiting kids to try out for the Christ Our King basketball team starting in September. I was going to wait because I thought I wasn't good enough to play against those eighth graders. But I could watch and see what he expected of them. He never yelled at anyone. He looked like a nice guy, a good coach. You could tell he knew what he was doing. This guy was so good he had five different ways to put the ball in play from out of bounds, and they worked every time.

We had awhile before school was over, so one Saturday morning, even though it was April; I went up to the Rock to see if there were any caddy jobs. I saw that president of Coca-Cola man that I caddied for before, but he had a caddy. I lucked out and got with a group who had been out all night drinking and ended up at the Rock. Usually they were good tippers, and if I got a good tip I would take their bags to their cars. We finished around 2:30. One guy bought me lunch and soda and gave me two dollars. The dollar bills had "Hawaii" stamped on them in big letters. I had never seen that before. He said that during the war, money was kept in caves and this is how they kept track of where it came from. I bet some day they would be worth money.

The course was wet that day. Walking was tough on the wet ground. My feet stayed wet, so by the time I took my sneakers and wet socks off that night it made my athlete's foot worse. This kind of neglect took a toll on my feet, which itched so badly they bled. Mommy took me to the foot doctor, who put my feet in little pans of water. He had some wire connected to them and would turn on a small dose of current, just enough to curl my feet out of contortion. He kept that up for about five minutes, saying it would strengthen my muscles. To this day I have never been able to make my feet do what those electric shocks did. Then the doctor put some purple chemicals on my toes and put them under an ultraviolet light. It only worked for a few weeks because my hygiene wasn't good enough to get rid of athlete's foot. We later found out that the way to get rid of athlete's foot is to boil your socks. With Menny and I were wearing each other's socks, so we were giving it back and forth to each other.

One day when I went up to caddy, Old Grumpy was sick, so nobody was going to threaten us. For the first time in a year I didn't see any bums around or on the course. I snuck down to the corner that was out of bounds. I didn't have to worry about Grumpy, so if a ball came out of bounds we would pick it up and wait for that person to claim their ball. A lot of the people were mean, like one guy who told me to show him where I had found his ball. I laid it down for him to see in the high grass about a foot out of bounds. This man was livid and accused me of picking up his ball inbounds, and that I should have waited until he got here and decided what was in and out of bounds. He had blood in his eyes, and needless to say he refused to give me a tip for his ball. His partner, however, said not to treat me that way and to give me a tip. The first man said, "I wouldn't give that little son of a bitch anything, he just cost me two strokes." I walked away because I knew that there would be a day that he would have to pay for yelling at me. Somehow I would get him.

The next day Grumpy was still sick. I wanted to caddy, and I saw that bastard who had yelled at me the day before. He was getting some balls out of his bag to practice putting on the putting green; so I saw which bag was his. Down on the putting green some guys were clowning around and getting everyone's attention, so I quickly took a cup out of the trash can and quickly scooped up some real soft dog shit near the big oak tree and quickly dumped it down his golf bag, sliding down his shafts to the bottom of his bag on his grips. It smelled awful. Eventually everything died down on the putting green, and everyone was concentrating on the first tee. I sat on the green metal chairs far enough away to see what would happen next. Grumpy would never have let us sit on those chairs. I saw my victim look at his putter, and then push it in his bag, right in the soft smelly shit. The new starter called out "Next," and his foursome picked up their bags and walked up to the first tee. Keep in mind that the first hole required a driver.

My hot-tempered friend pulled out his driver, put it in his hand with dog shit all over the grip, he looked at the glove, and ran back to the bag and started pulling all of the clubs out of the bag. Just then he yelled, "I have dog shit all over my clubs!" His buddies couldn't believe it; he also had shit on his hands, and it smelled terrible. They couldn't start so the starter made them go to the back of the line. It would be over an hour before they could tee off. He was frantically trying to find some wet towels to clean his clubs off, but his bag was not to be cleaned because he couldn't get the shit out of the bottom. He went into the pro shop, bought a new bag for at least $40.00, and threw his old bag in the 50-gallon trash can outside. For some reason the smell was still really bad. His buddies were not happy about losing over an hour. They all had made plans, but he not only lost his tee time and had to buy a new golf bag, his attitude now made matters worse.

That guy raised so much hell that everyone would remember him as "the man with the dog shit in his bag." After a long time he finally got his clubs cleaned up. I think that in his frame of mind, he couldn't play golf that day. I got a caddy job and was out on the course before he teed off. The group I was caddying for were laughing and imitating him, yelling, "I have dog shit on my hands." Someone said he jumped on the starter, wanting to know how this could happen. "Aren't you supposed to be responsible for what is going on around here, how could you allow this to happen?"

When I came in after nine holes, everyone was laughing, saying he dubbed his drive, and on his second shot he still wasn't over the road, which wasn't that hard to do. When he missed his third shot, they said he picked up his ball and bag and stormed off the golf course, mumbling something all the way to his car. Maybe he learned not to yell at young boys for nothing. I never saw him again; maybe he was too embarrassed to come back. I didn't have the nerve to tell anyone that I got that bastard back; the fewer people who knew it the better.

The Rock was going to have some changes made to it. A new tee was to be added at the par three near the reservoir that ran parallel to Route 202. That's where they had a soda stand, so instead of caddying you could sell sodas. One hot day no one wanted to go out and sell sodas. They felt that stopping after the ninth hole and getting something to eat and drink would prevent them from getting a soda on the 14th tee. I was counting on the hot weather to change that. So I took the job, and ended up making $4.50 from 10:00 a.m. to 4:00 p.m. They said that no one ever sold that many drinks before. I had the Irish gift of the gab; it just came naturally for me.

I was glad to get home; Menny was playing with the trains but it was to nice out to be in the basement, so I took a nap in the chair and had a nice dinner when I woke up. I wanted a cigarette so I went out back for a smoke. I looked at Joan's room and just then the light went on, and I saw her. She must have had a friend over because they both started to take off their blouses, looking at each other and laughing. Then Joan took off her bra. Joan was faster at undressing than her guest was. I only saw Joan this evening; her guest must have been standing somewhere else in the room. I ran in to tell Menny what I saw, but by the time we got back outside her light was out and they were gone. He ran in and accused me of luring him away from the trains. I never thought of that, but it was a good idea. The next day Joan and her friend Hannah, from North East, Maryland, were standing on the porch when I came out.

Joan immediately said hi and pulled me to her and gave me a big kiss. She introduced me to Hannah as her secret boyfriend. My face was getting red because Hannah was flirting too, so I was blushing. I was so conscious of my face that I could hardly smile. They were having a good time with me, but that was OK—it was clean fun. Joan wasn't going to hurt me, or allow me to get hurt.

I was more relaxed about school now that the fifth grade was a little easier. With a month to go I started to get excited. I loved my summers off; I was trying to keep my nose clean. No more pissing on the hot radiator in school (which was hard to do with the nuns looking in the door all the time). It was the worst smell; I guess you would say that it was equal to a skunk. Just because I wasn't pissing on the radiator doesn't mean it wasn't being done. One day that they had to turn the heat off in those smelly bathrooms. Then they had radiator covers made to stop the pissing, but it was only a setback because young men can piss long and hard.

Once when we got home, Abee London was sitting on his steps, and we were still afraid of him. He had no equilibrium; the poor guy just staggered around. His mother watched us through the front door curtain and would pounce on anything or anyone if they disrupted his sitting time. It was not a nice thing to see him walking around looking like a zombie. Sometimes he smiled, and he had never done that before. It wasn't bad for a guy who didn't have anything to smile about; his older brother came around with a new car and nice clothes. He never stayed long, but he looked like he had money and probably helped Abee out if he needed it. Abee was interested in our caddying at the Rock, but he would have to walk better than he did to caddy for 18 holes. I don't know if they would be ready for him either. He could barely put one foot in front of the other. How could he take the long walk to the Rock, a long walk caddying, and a long walk home? God help him. I knew he couldn't do that; we could hardly do it.

I'd seen Abbe's mother take him to the Jewish deli on the corner of 29th Street to get a few things. Waxman's Deli really smelled good, and I loved those big Jewish pickles. The owners were always nice to me, and their food was fresh. It didn't take me long to believe that Jews had money. In just one or two blocks we had three Jewish stores: Schriber's, Waxman's, and the kosher meat market on 28th and Washington Streets. Our Jewish neighbors kept to themselves, making sure people didn't get too close. Sometimes we were mean to the Jewish people, but I knew we would grow out of that. It all started in the Catholic teachings at that time. We would call them some nasty names, but they were smart, they never acted like they heard us. They took a lot of grief from us kids.

I felt sorry for the Jewish kids because everyone celebrated Christmas except them. Sometimes I saw a Jewish father sneak a Christmas tree in at night. I heard they would open gifts too for their Hanukkah. On occasions like this I felt that having money doesn't help if you're out of step. I didn't want the Jewish kids to be hurt, but just because we played in the street didn't mean that the Jewish kids were going to get in with us.

Some of the Jewish homes were targets. We would dump their garbage cans over the back yard, cut their clothes lines, or tie their front door to their storm door. Then the house door wouldn't open because the storm door opened out and the house door opened in. They would have to come around front and cut the rope, but they never chased after us or called the police on anyone. They knew it would have gotten worse. We mainly left them alone because they weren't any fun. The fun was in being chased and screamed at. Besides we knew every alley, every garage, and every hiding place in our neighborhood and surrounding streets. To me every night was Mischief Night.

Old Man Phelps must have gotten someone else to cut his dirty smelly toenails, and I was making too much money to go back to that. We would never see him outside until the summer. Someone probably put him outside to disinfect the house. He still had on the same urine-stained pants and his white tee shirt with tobacco and food stains that was so dirty it was gray except for the black ring around the neck. When he laughed you couldn't help but laugh at him or laugh with him. You could see the chewing tobacco stuck on his teeth, which were so stained that they couldn't be cleaned. His tongue was black, too. Jon and Doris had their hands full with him missing the coffee can with his spit. Can you imagine what it must have been like to be in an enclosed room with him?

By the day before school was out, the weather was nice, and we were going to get our final report card the next day. I can tell you I was scared. Fr. Donahue was giving out the report cards in our class, and I was afraid he would hand me my card as if I had a contagious disease. I told Theresa I was nervous, but she told me not to worry, that I would pass. She said, "You're not dumb, you're just having trouble with tests. They evaluate you on what you demonstrate as well."

In the morning I woke up, and the next thing I knew we were walking to school. Everyone was singing, "No more pencils, no more books, and no more Sisters' dirty looks." Sister asked us to clean out our desks while we were waiting for Fr. Donahue to show up. Of course he handed me my report card last. Sister asked me to stay behind, but this time she told me she was proud of me for trying as hard as I did, and being a altar boy and always eager to help out. However, I would again be on probation for 90 days. She also asked if I was going to be around that summer. I told her I would, so she asked me to do her a favor and water the plants on the back porch. She would leave the water on, and the watering can on the porch for me to use. She was so nice and told me she picked me ahead of everyone else to help her. What a sales job. I told her she could count on me. I was only too happy to prove she had made the right decision.

I made my usual decision to be up early during the summer and do something; golf was first on my mind, caddying, practicing basketball, and trying out for the park softball team. For some reason they didn't play baseball. I was going to keep busy. I wanted to play golf every Monday, so that meant I had to caddy the weekends. I wanted to caddy at least three times a week plus hawk balls so I would have some good balls to play with. Grumpy made sure to tell us that the minimum caddy fee for 18 holes was now $1.50. Menny and I were glad to hear that.

My first caddy job was with a happy group. I thought they had been partying all night because they were talking about breakfast at the diner on Route 202. I was assigned to Bill Street, who said he worked for DuPont. He was really nice; I had caddied for him before. He took an interest in me and always walked with me when I carried his bag. We always talked about school and work. When everyone was on the green I helped the other players if they left their clubs behind; maybe I could be lucky and get a tip from those guys. After the last hole Mr. Street gave me two dollars and bought me lunch and a soda, and the other three guys flipped me half a dollar each. They all shook my hand and said we would meet again.

Ed Kautz, Tuffy Pabst, and Donald Napolski were caddying, and sometimes Tommy Farley. Monday we were up early with plenty of good balls in our pockets, plenty of tees, and plenty of money for gambling if we played teams we didn't ask for strokes. The number one player would have to play with the number four player and two and three would play together. All the caddies had a favorite to play with, but Pabst never showed up, so Kautz, Donald, Menny, and I played as a foursome. Grumpy, our old caddy master, also known as the starter, gave us his usual "I am in command" speech, before we teed off. He said that people last week were complaining about our loud playing and throwing clubs. I told him my clubs were too old to throw—they would probably break upon impact to the ground,

I wouldn't throw my clubs; I would only have to go after them. When we caddied and a person threw a club, we were expected to go get it. One low-lifer I was caddying for threw his club up a tree and had the nerve to tell me to go get it, not asking me please. I told him the tree had snakes in it, and I wasn't going to get bitten by a snake. He looked at me and the tree he just lost a club in, and offered me three dollars to get his club. I grabbed a branch, climbed the tree, and knocked the club down with no problem. I jumped down and he said in an angry voice, "Hey, kid, I thought there were snakes in that tree." I replied, "Did I have to get bitten by one for me to prove it to you?" He called me a wise ass, and he would pay me when we got in after eighteen.

But after eighteen, he tried to start an argument with me and only wanted to give me the caddy fee plus 50 cents, a total of two dollars, not the three dollars for getting the club plus the caddy fee. I objected and told him he made a bargain with me to pay three dollars. He said, "Fuck you, boy, I'll kick your ass," and he threw the two dollars on the ground and kicked dirt on it and all over my shoes and pants. His buddies told him to pay the boy. He wouldn't listen to them and started walking to the parking lot.

Luther, the caretaker, was sitting on the porch. I told him what I had done and how this guy welched on paying me the three dollars and showed Luther all the dirt he kicked over me. Luther jumped up and said, "Let's find this jerk." I told him that he was in the parking lot laughing with his buddies. When Luther caught up to him he grabbed him by the back of the shirt, spun him around, and grabbed him right by the throat. The guy was not looking too good at this point. Luther said, "You owe this boy three dollars and an apology for the way you treated him. Did this boy climb a tree and get your club for you when you told him you were going to give him three dollars? And because he was a kid you made up your mind that you weren't going to pay him?" All the time Luther was squeezing the man's throat, his right hand free if he needed to use it. He continued, "Instead, you treated him worse than a dog. Either you pay this boy or you will be barred from this course for life. We don't allow trash like you to rough up our caddies."

Luther let this jerk loose so he could make a decision, then he reached in his pocket and pulled out a five dollar bill. Luther grabbed it and said that the bill just went up to five dollars and handed me the money. When I had it in my hands, I gave this jerk a kick in the balls as hard as I could, and let me assure you I could kick hard. This guy was on his knees crying like a baby, and his buddies were laughing at him. They told him, "That's what you get for messing with a kid who has friends." Luther said he had seen this guy before and didn't like him. I couldn't thank Luther enough and asked him if I could buy him something. He smiled at me and said,

"No thanks, Babe, you don't owe me anything." I was glad Luther got that son of a bitch. I would never caddy for him again.

Ours caddies day golf match between Kautz and Donald Menny and me was quite the match. They were going to whip our asses. The format Menny and I insisted on was that the lowest total score of both team's players won the hole. You had to play out and not give up; you had to finish the hole. It was mental play. The match was even after seventeen; both Kautz and Donald were stymied over at the maintenance shed. They had to chip out while Menny and I each had a shot to the green. Don't ask me how, but both Menny and I hit the green in two, while Kautz got on in three and Donald was on in four. Kautz had a real long putt for par. Things were looking real good for Menny and me. We all ended up two-putting and Menny and I won the match. Those guys did everything to rattle me on the putting green; they said Grumpy was coming out after us. Nothing worked. We won. Kautz and Donald had their money in their hands and were good sports, and most of all we were friends and stayed that way.

Kautz knew a way to get around old Grumpy. Because he didn't caddy that much he was always on the tenth hole, the out-of-bounds corner waiting for those brave souls to try and carry the wall to get closer to the green. He was making more money than we were. It dawned on us that Kautz was no fool. He knew all along what he was doing and got up to the Rock before we did. I think that Grumpy let the first guy up take the corner on ten, so if we try to come down after we caddied, Kautz would grit his teeth and tell us to get out of here. "Don't you guys know that Grumpy will kick all of us down the road?"

So Menny and I decided to walk the golf course perimeter, looking for balls. Would you believe it, we came across one of those dirty bums. He told us to get the hell out of here, this was his hole. I told him to leave us alone or we would take our sticks to him and kick his ass. Could you imagine eleven—and twelve-year-olds having the guts to talk to him like that? He made the right decision and left us alone. Could you imagine us going into the club house and saying that we were attacked by a bum? They would have strung him up. It turned out to be a good day because Menny and I found a dozen balls; many of them were made by Titleist, which were always cut, and when we hit them they would cut easy also.

It was still tough to get a good caddy job at the beginning of the summer because everyone showed up to caddy. When you showed up you gave your name to the caddy master, and jobs were given out in order from the list. One day I counted 16 guys waiting for a job. Some guys would ask the golfers if they wanted a caddy, but you could get sent down the road for that. Every now and than a player would ask for a caddy; then Grumpy would accuse you of asking the golfer. He made sure the golfers wouldn't hear him roughing us up. But it wasn't long before the caddy rush wore off, and the caddies were down to eight, with the late sleepers not showing up till after 11:00 a.m. Some big guys would carry double, but I was too small for that; those leather bags were heavy. There was an art to carrying double; you had to know where to put the bag down, just taking a handful of clubs to the green and tee. This helped you carry the bag less. Some golfers just wouldn't tip, they would pay the fee and that's it. No matter how much you did for them, they wouldn't tip you. The same people wouldn't treat you to lunch and a soda, but you can be sure I wouldn't carry their bags to the car. I would lay it down, wait for my money, and walk away. It was rare to see women play golf. We had a few; one of them was very cute, shaking her ass when she walked. Everyone would look at her; she was something to see; her body and face were beautiful. The older guys would say things that would make your hair stand up. I hope she didn't hear it; she was too nice for that kind of talk. One guy said, loud enough for her to hear him, "I wonder if she got a porch for that swing." I think she liked that. She had her own caddy; I guess we weren't good enough.

One day Luther and I were sitting on the porch, where I wasn't supposed to sit, by the way. We weren't allowed to sit on the furniture either. Anyway, he told me one day he had to go upstairs for some supplies from the closet, and he walked in on this cutie in her bra and panties, on her knees giving this guy a blow job. Luther said he almost swallowed his teeth. He said she never stopped or looked up. Luther said that he didn't stay around to see what he was going to do to her, so now every time I saw her I would have to remember what Luther said about her. Luther could tell a lot of stories; he said he saw it all.

Just after school let out for the summer, Uncle Jerry came over early one morning, luckily catching me before I went out for the day. He said Mommy asked him to fix some clothes poles in the ground, so she could string a line from pole to pole. I helped him, and he liked that. When we finished we sat and had a cup of tea, and I brought up my father again and the bad things he was doing to all of us. What I couldn't understand was why he and Julia wouldn't step in and confront my father about his abuse of his family and Theresa and how he hit our mother in the face and cut her.

Jerry was truly sad to hear those stories. I was trying to make him feel bad, and I must have succeeded because his eyes were watery. He said it wasn't his business, and I said that it was his business that his sister and her children were being terrorized almost every night. He said, "Your father is a nice guy," and I replied, "Not to us." I guess I was trying to draw Jerry into it, and that wasn't going to happen. It wasn't happening to him so he couldn't feel any pain. It probably hurt him to hear this from his Godson and not help him. Eventually my mother heard me and got angry and told me to find something else to talk about. That scared Jerry; he didn't want anyone to be mad at him. He stood up and said he had to go.

That summer Theresa and her girlfriend Betty went everywhere together. They looked so stupid, flirting with all the boys. Theresa and Betty got jobs at the Strand Theater at 24th and Market Street as ushers. The price of a ticket was only 12 cents. When Theresa was on duty we all would act up and keep her running all over the theater. Being aggressive, she would react to every commotion. Betty could have cared less. We all would go in the bathroom for a smoke, and there was so much smoke you couldn't see the ceiling. The manager would come in and tell us to put out our cigarettes. He said that the Fire Marshall would close down the movie theater if he knew all this smoking was going on. We never put them out, though, and he never stayed around to see if we did. He was afraid of us in a group like that.

You would think that this movie job would be good for Theresa, getting out of the house for a while, but it wasn't. I was in some fights with Theresa that were unavoidable, and they were getting worse. Her anger was building up, and she would hit me with anything she could put her hands on, which was dangerous. It didn't prevent her from fighting. She was consumed with anger. I told her one day that she was fighting with Menny and me just like Daddy did, but she couldn't see it. Her friend Betty was the opposite, just sitting around smiling at everything as if she didn't have a worry in the world. Betty was very nice to me and flirted, too. I guess she had to practice on someone. My cousin Luanne came over, too. She would walk up to me and grab my balls and look me right in the eyes and say, "Hi Babe." She had a surreal smile, but she was my cousin so I had to behave myself. Those girls were prime rib for the right guys. I didn't hold out much hope for Theresa because she and men just didn't mix. It was going to take a different environment to change her. She was deeply scarred, with little hope ahead of her.

My father was starting to get his sea legs back after the visit from the two detectives. You can only hold evil down so long before it rises up again. He came in one night and came up the stairs. He heard me moaning in my sleep. He woke me up, put the light on, and asked me what was wrong. I told him I was sick in the stomach and I felt like throwing up. That's when he accused me of drinking, saying that's why I felt sick. If he had known how much I hated beer or the smell of it he would never have put the light on. He was the poster child for drinking and all the failures it causes.

I was sitting up on my elbows when he started thumping me in my chest so hard I fell back on my back. He wanted to know what I was drinking. I kept telling him it was a Coke. By this time Mommy and Theresa were running down the hall way to our room, yelling that he should leave us alone. Menny told him to get out of our room. He stopped with me and ran around the bed and went to Menny, getting in his face yelling, "What did you say, boy?" Mommy burst in the room, and he stood erect. Mommy came up to his face and told him, "Leave these boys alone. They are good boys and will never drink."

Theresa added, "Haven't you done enough around here?" That was the final straw. He ran up to her and grabbed her pajama top, and reared his fist back as if he was going to hit her. Just then my mother hit him in the side of the face. I told him, "Why don't you just leave here?" Holding his ear with a painful look on his face, he told me to watch myself or he would give me something to cry about. Four people were against him now. He had to make a decision; these were bad odds for anyone. He didn't like the lack of respect, and being told to get out now was too much for him. He could see we would take up for each other. He had hurt my mother's arm, which she was holding in pain. Instead of hitting Theresa, he hit the metal bed, making his hand swollen and red. His ear hurt and his hand hurt. He was bent over holding them in pain. He left to soak his hand in the sink, but he ought to have soaked his head in the sink as well.

Mommy stayed and asked me what happened. I explained that he had accused me of drinking beer, and Menny replied that we don't drink. She knew it and that's why she was so angry with him. I was so angry I was going to find a way to teach him a lesson. Those comb teeth and match heads in his cigarettes were nothing to what I could do to him.

The next day after school I went to the medicine cabinet. I took his single edge razor and put a nick in the blade and bent the edge so it wouldn't shave evenly. Too much pressure would cause a nick to his face. I pissed on the blade, let it dry, and put it back in the razor. If it did work he would be cutting his face with a dirty razor. I had read about this in a short story magazine one day. It told how this woman got even with her husband for hitting her. Only now I was going to get even for him hitting us.

A few days later I saw him with a bandage on his cheek. The side of his face was swollen and red like a boil. It kept oozing puss, and he finally had to get it lanced. He was in a lot of pain (just like we were), he couldn't shave, so he looked like a bum, and if he didn't change that blade he was going to have a repeat. He told Mommy that he looked at his razor and it had a nick in it. He couldn't imagine how that could be. He said those blades were new and that blade came out of a new pack. I was able to pull this off like the woman in the story, but she had eventually killed her husband by dipping his blade in poison. My father was definitely becoming scared, hiding his cigarettes and now checking his razor all the time. He was going to be a wreck, but there would be more if he didn't behave. I told Menny what I had done, and he was shocked. He wanted to know how I came up with the idea, and I told him. He wanted to tell Mommy, but I said no, that she would get shook up. Menny said he wished he had thought of it.

Every day I was doing something, but I was home at 5:00 for our usual liver and fried potatoes, which was a cheap way to feed five children. We would fill up on Mommy's apple cake and lemon meringue pies. The apple cake was very popular; we ate it from our hands just like tomato bread. Peach upside-down cake was my favorite. Once I was so full I went out on the porch to sit, and Mrs. Toskas was trying to cut her hedge, which was only about 18 inches off the ground. I went down and told her to tell me what to do and I would do it. She told me that she only wanted it trimmed, neat, nice, and straight. It took a while but I got it right and looking good. She was so happy and thanked me. I would do anything for Mrs. Toskas.

I looked up and saw Joan standing on the porch smiling at me and nodding for me to come up, but her mother was home so I knew nothing was going to happen. I went up on her porch and said, "Did you want me, Joan?" She smiled and said, "In the worst way." She said she wanted to thank me for helping out her mother. She then put one hand on my shoulder and one on the back of my head. She pulled my head to her mouth and practically pulled me inside. That girl could kiss; she certainly seemed thankful. What the hell would she have done if I would cut her grass? She whispered in my ear, "When are you going to wrestle me again, lover?" I was anxious to; it had started to become fun for me. Where else could I hold on to a good looking girl's tit for 15 minutes? When I acted scared and shy I aroused her all the more. I knew the summer was young and so was I.

Up at the yard everyone was playing basketball. Soon a lot of guys were going to try out for the C.O.K. basketball team. We played for hours. I knew I was going to hold back and not go out until next year, so I had plenty of time. Young guys would come from all over Wilmington to play a game with us. Some black guys came too, wanting to see the best our yard had to offer. Continuous basketball games went on till dark.

Some games I would be good in and some games I would just pass the ball off. It was the best experience. If you shot and missed, the older guys would tell you not to shoot anymore—if you can't make it, pass it off. In other words, they wanted to shoot. The experience was most valuable. We even had a disabled boy playing. He was good; he had no problem keeping up with everyone else. I was still smoking and at times I would dry heave or gag. You can't play basketball and smoke. They don't mix.

Often I would stop by the park to see what was going on there. Mrs. Lemon, the activities director, was happy to see me and gave me a big hug. Everyone was calling for me to get in the soft ball game. You weren't allowed to hit the ball over the 10-foot fence. They had to be infield hits. It was a lot of fun, but too many small kids were out there. A hard softball would really hurt them. Dodge ball was fun, and as soon as that game was over someone wanted to play horseshoes, which I loved. The equipment was good, and Mrs. Lemon wouldn't tolerate any misuse.

It was still noticeable that no one would knock on the door to see if we wanted to come out and play; we seemed to be off limits. Even Doris Baylor stayed away. So Menny and I would look for games to play as far away as Prices Run. One day we saw a new baseball bat lying on the diamond near home plate and we both took off on our bikes. We both got there at the same time; we grabbed the bat at the same time, too. We must have fought over it for a half hour and then agreed that we both could share it. It had a crack in it, so we put nails in it and taped it heavily. It worked well for us. With our new bat we would get a game up across from Speakman on 30th Street. Two cops in a patrol car would drive up, open up the trunk, get their gloves out, and join in with us for about a half hour. I am glad they weren't the motorcycle cops that I had thrown tomatoes at. I think they knew this kind of interaction would go a long way, playing with the young men in their patrol area. We really enjoyed it.

Again that summer, Mommy was upset because my father wasn't bringing enough money home to do the bills; she was always behind and was trying to catch up. The two boarders' fees weren't enough. I don't know if my father knew how bad things were at the house. He was letting a lot of people down. Some of the men who used to paint for him were doing good on their own. Mommy said she had to look into other ways to make money. And now we had another little girl to feed.

That past winter, Menny and I had noticed that when Mommy was taking her bath at night, she was looking a little rounder. We never guessed she was pregnant, and she didn't tell us. One day I happened to overhear my father telling someone that his wife was pregnant, and the other person told him he should keep that thing in his pants. That's how I found out she was pregnant: I told Menny and we were both in shock. How could Mommy have a baby with that lunatic? It was a mystery to me and still remains so. When Mommy's time came, she hired a woman to take care of us on a short-notice basis, and on the morning of June 26, 1949, baby Elizabeth was born, whom Mommy immediately called Honey. It wasn't three hours before the babysitter soon packed her bag and walked out, telling Theresa she couldn't take it any more. So our cousin from New York Louise came down to take care of us, we got along very well, and the time for Mommy to bring home Honey flew by quickly.

Honey was an adorable baby, and we even entered her in a contest for the most beautiful baby in Wilmington. Although she didn't win, we all made a fuss over her anyway. She had been born with a knee alignment problem, so at night she had to wear a half-moon brace with a shoe on each end that held her knees in the right alignment. During one of my father's Friday Night Fights, Honey was crying with all of the commotion, which annoyed him. He picked her out of her crib and threw her on the bed, her head twisting and bobbing around from one side to another. The brace hurt her little legs, and we all reacted in a thunderous verbal attack and forced my father out of the room. Mommy spent a while comforting Honey and singing to her. This was a new low for him in our eyes.

At the height of summer, the Blue Rocks baseball team was back in town. We had a nice big ball park. Hundreds of people would be walking toward the main gate. And a lot of times we would break in line and tell the ticket collector, pointing our thumbs behinds us saying, he's got 'em. The next guy would do the same. As soon as we were in, we ran like hell. It wasn't until the fifth or sixth guy that the ticket collector would catch on to our little scam. They would stop everyone and kick the remaining ones out of line without a ticket. It wouldn't work on the same collector twice. You would have to pick a different day and a different line. If you timed it right you could run and jump over the turnstiles. They would never catch us. We had more ways to sneak into the ball game, and never paid to get into a single game. The park had two big green gates that when fully open, were about 12 feet wide. We would bang on the gates and yell "Refreshment truck, open up!" About ten of us stood there, and when the gates were flung open all ten of us would be in and gone, before the guy knew what hit him. We would scatter all over the ball park.

The funniest thing was to see us guys coming over the center field fence; just below the score board during the National Anthem I mean in droves, a continuous stream for at least two minutes. The police would be standing at attention while we all came over the fence like rats off the sinking ship. We would run by the police while they were saluting the flag and tantalize them by giving them the finger. The fans would cheer when they saw us run on to the field and into the bleachers the cheering was almost deafening. The police didn't know what to do about it. I guess we embarrassed them in front of thousands of people. It didn't take long before they had the whole outside score board area boarded up tight as a gnat's ass. The police boarded up the only way we would use to come over the center field fence after a couple of times of trying to get through the barriers we would have to do something else. Sometime the players would let us in through the locker room. Once in we were on our own. We would walk down the hall ways to the grandstand. We had a lot of fun at that ball park. I even became a Blue Pebble. It was a name they gave us kids who practiced on the field with the players. They were rocks, and we were pebbles.

Sometimes I worked at the ball park selling ice cream, sodas, and hot dogs. I liked selling ice cream the most. I would call out, "I scream, you scream, we all scream for ice cream." But most often a bunch of us would stand outside the park, waiting for a foul ball. Kautz was always trying to get them. He didn't want any competition and would always try to scare us off. This is the same guy who didn't want any competition up the golf course on the corner hole. If we were lucky to find a ball outside the ball park we thought we were big shots.

After the game Menny and I walked through the park as a short cut from 30th Street to 29th street. It was real dark outside, and Menny would say that someone was following us. It didn't take much to scare me. I would take off running like a deer. There was a small stone bridge halfway down the hill, and by the time I hit that spot I was uncatchable. Menny was told not to scare me more than once, even more than a dozen times, and he still kept it up. He was using me as a source of entertainment. I could hear him laughing all the way down the hill. I don't know what was so funny.

One summer day I went out in the yard to cut the grass. There was Joan sunbathing. She asked me to put some suntan lotion on her. I jumped the fence. She was lying on her stomach in a black one-piece bathing suit. I poured the lotion in my hand, and she told me to make sure I got it under her suit. I put it on her shoulders and back. She turned over and told me to get her legs. I was starting to get nervous and she was laughing at me. I asked her if she wanted me to do under her suit at the top of her legs. She told me she trusted me to do a good job. I was rubbing her leg so hard that she thought it was a massage. I was finished and reached for a towel to dry my hands off. She reached out and grabbed my hand and said, "Don't forget my top". I asked her if she wanted me to go under her bathing suit, that's when she said, "Travel at your own risk." I started spreading lotion on her chest and lower neck. After I slid my fingers under her top and moved them back and forth I reached for the towel, I was finished. She thanked me again and again. I told her to let me know when I could be of service again. She gave me a big kiss and I vaulted over the fence to safety. I looked back at her with her legs spread apart. She was too much for me to handle.

It was hot one day when Abee London came out of his house with a wagon and a big block of ice. He said he was going to make snow balls and sell them. He had orange, grape, and root beer flavors and an ice scraper. You pulled it along the ice and when it filled up you flipped the lid up and dumped the shavings in a cup, then poured the flavor over the ice. He was going to charge 15 cents. It was so hot; the ice was going to melt quickly. He walked down the center of the street saying "Snow balls!" But he was so quiet, no one heard him. We asked him how he got the ice and flavors and he had no idea. We all hoped he did real well. I saw him coming home, the block half gone and melting. Water was falling from the holes in the bottom of the wagon bed. He went down the driveway where his mother was waiting. She took over, and it looked like he had sold some because the flavor bottles were almost empty.

Mommy asked me to take her back to P.S. DuPont to pick some more berries, as we had done one summer before. So we got our bags and went, including Bonnie and Mickey. We walked about seven or eight blocks. As soon as Mommy saw the bushes she smiled. She smiled the whole time we were there. She couldn't believe that no one had picked the berries. We all had bags, so we all picked till our bags were full. We weren't home five minutes before Mommy was starting to bake pies and make jam. We had to beg for supper, she got so carried away. Our fingers were all purple. No matter. Before you knew it Mommy said "Let's eat."

We heard over the radio that there was going to be a pushmobile derby on Lea Boulevard, but first there had to be practice runs. We all went up to see what it was like. They had snow fences and bales of hay on both sides of the street from one end of the track to the other. At the top of the hill, where all the push mobiles were in a holding area all the drivers were spinning their wheels and trying to look busy doing little things to their cars. They wanted their cars to be the fastest. Some of the cars looked as if they had come off the assembly line at GM. The rule was that the driver had to build the car with some help from a parent. It was easy to see who made them by looking at the cars. Some looked professionally made and you could see the loving care that went into the other ones.

We had fun watching the practice runs. Some kids crashed into the hay, usually because the steering was loose. An inexperienced driver who overcorrected his loose steering ended up in those bales of hay. We found a big tree on the east side of Lea Boulevard, about three-quarters of the way down the hill. We climbed up, and it was perfect for watching the race on that fine Saturday afternoon. I had plenty of cigarettes for the day of the race, and I had a great spot up that tree to see it all. The speakers were so loud. I guess that's because they wanted everyone to hear the call of the race. People lined both sides of the hill, cheering and waving hankies. It was really neat to see it all. It took all day but they did have a winner through single elimination. If you lost one race you were out. That winner would race and race till one was left. If we had to take a leak we went behind our tree, and then ran down to the refreshment stand for a soda and a hot dog.

I was gone all day; I'll bet I didn't get home till 6:00. I was sunburned and Mommy wanted to know where I had been. I told her and said I was hungry, could I please get something to eat. She said she would make me a bowl of soup and a grilled cheese sandwich. I went into the living room and sat in the tufted chair and fell asleep for about 30 minutes. That's all I really needed to get going again. We got our bikes out, raced down the street, put up an obstacle course. We even jumped on a small ramp.

Menny and I had spent all our money at the pushmobile derby, so we got up early to caddy and make some money. Menny and I got a job real fast. We would take turns taking the flag pin out of the hole when it was necessary, washing the balls and watching where the drives went. When we finished that day, we had made two dollars each, which made us very happy. We went into the snack bar and got a hot dog and a soda and went out back and sat on the curb, when two bums came out of nowhere. They went in the snack bar for something to eat. When they came back out their hot dogs looked like subs. I was a brazen SOB, so I told the ugly one, "It looks like you took all the relish and onions, and I bet you didn't leave enough for anyone else for their hot dogs." They never said anything, they just stared. They took off walking down the stony road toward Wilmington, the same way we would walk home. Menny and I waited until they were about 100 feet away when we opened up on them with stones, about the size of baseballs. We threw so many they were running for their life. I'm so glad we didn't hit them. We only wanted to scare them, not hurt them.

After our stone throwing, we decided to sneak down to the corner for some action. A lot of times if the ball hit a tree you didn't see where it went, but if we were persistent enough, we would find some of them. We needed those balls for caddy's day. It was late in the afternoon when Linda, the girl I had seen before, came walking down the middle of the fairway, shaking her nice ass. We just stopped in our tracks and watched her go by. She didn't know that I knew about her blow jobs up in the club house. Her second shot went out of bounds. I ran so fast after it I fell down when I got to the ball. I walked to the wall and held out the ball for her to take it from me. She was reaching in her shorts pocket, and I told her it was OK. She insisted on giving me that quarter. She squeezed my hand and gave me a wink. That made my legs go weak, like jelly. Menny said, "Babe, you should wrestle her," laughing. We watched her walk all the way to the green. We had to watch her bend over and mark her ball. Menny and I were looking as far up those legs as we could. She knew we were watching because she turned and waved as she walked off the green. Wow. What a woman.

If she played fast, it still would be hard to get in by dusk. Menny and I kept looking for balls all over that golf course when we came across her again. She was a picnic area on seventeen; we only walked up seventeen far enough to where the ball goes out of bounds on the second shot. We knew we could find balls there. We found her and her boyfriend, Peter, screwing on the picnic table. You could see her legs flapping and his bare ass, as white as snow. He kept swatting at his butt; I guess the mosquitoes were biting his ass. I am sure they would rather bite her ass if they could get to it.

Menny and I decided to get some rocks and throw them in the woods, close enough but not so they could tell if it was a rock or not. We were hoping they would think it was a bear or something. We threw our rocks in the woods, and it really sounded scary. When they heard the noise in the woods she pulled up on her elbows. He was bent over trying to get his pants up, and when he stepped aside from her you could see clearly between her legs. She reached for her panties. We threw another rock and she let out a scream. Her shorts were lying on the table and she jumped in them and was buttoning them up while both of them were running toward the club house. There was never a dull moment at the Rock. Just a few minutes ago she was winking at me. Now when I would see her again I would see her with her legs spread apart, getting laid on the seventeenth hole picnic table. She was hot, but always getting caught. She'd better work on that a little.

We didn't get home till 9:00 that night. I stopped at Boles's and got a half pint of vanilla ice cream, and as usual Mrs. Napolski asked, "What can I do for you Lucifer? You look like you've been running all day." I thought to myself, "If you only knew." I got my ice cream and Donald stuck his head out around the corner and asked if I was playing golf Monday. I told him we would meet at his store at 7:30. That would give us plenty of time to get off before the 9:00 o'clock deadline.

Our foursome—Kautz, Donald, Menny, and I—got there in plenty of time. What a crew. Donald said he didn't want to bet, so the rest of us played Match Play hole to hole. If two people tied, we all tied. Whoever had the most wins would win the two dollars. We cheated like hell all the way around the golf course. No one wanted to lose. You name it and it happened that day. Donald was laughing out loud all over the course. When we finished we sat under the big oak tree by the putting green and checked over the score card. It turned out that Kautz and I tied, so no money was exchanged because that meant we all tied.

When we walked up by the clubhouse, Grumpy came up and asked if Menny and I if we could clean the caddy shack up a little. Somehow I thought that Grumpy was only asking Menny and me to clean up because I hadn't seen anyone else cleaning up around there. So Menny and I must be his favorite maintenance helpers. It was a lot easier to clean it up than bitch. It only took a few minutes; he only wanted to show us his authority anyway. We dumped everything in the trash can. Kautz and Donald left. Menny and I stayed for a cold soda and to sit back and relax. Grumpy came over saying he had two caddy jobs for us and we would be doing him a favor if we would caddy for them. The two guys on the tee looked queer. I told Menny to watch them to see if they acted up a little. They were acting more like women than women did; this was going to be an experience.

They didn't care who was watching. They were going to have a good time. We told Grumpy that we would take it but we wanted him to give us some relief at the corner ball hawking in the future. My guy hit his ball out of bounds on the second hole. A bum ran over for his ball and told my guy that he had to pay a quarter to get the ball back. I never heard of paying first before. Now my gay friend was pissed off. He handed him the quarter and called him a bitch. Menny and I both broke into hysterics. I was making Menny laugh and his golfer was laughing at me, choking. All four of us laughed all the way to the green.

They didn't care how they hit the ball; they were just out to have fun. I was watching them acting silly, like little girls, on every green. My cheeks were aching with all the laughing. Those gay guys gave us three dollars each and drove Menny and me all the way down 29th Street. That saved us about an hour. They shook our hand and said goodbye. Now that I think back, we took a chance getting into a car with those guys, but they took a chance too because Menny and I would have been like two caged lions with abscessed teeth if they had tried anything with us.

Menny and I were both tired, dragging our beat-up clubs up to the porch. We dropped them on the porch floor and went into the house. We told Mommy we played eighteen holes and took a caddy job for eighteen holes, and we gave her two dollars each. She patted us on our heads; she was so happy to get it but didn't want to show us how desperate she was.

Menny wanted to go down to the ball park because Kautz would be there, but after a great meal of spaghetti and meat sauce I just didn't want to go. I sat on the sofa talking to Mommy about Ireland. She really made it sound like fun and said someday she and I would go over and see for ourselves. Then Menny came downstairs and begged me to go with him to the ball park. He said "Babe, we will come right back." I gave in. When we got there Kautz was right in the thick of things, chasing foul balls. We didn't stay long; we rode our bikes as fast as our legs could peddle and were home in no time.

The next morning Kautz climbed into our bedroom window, by climbing up the back kitchen roof. There was a step ladder that we put against the wall so he could climb up to the roof. He wanted to go into Wilmington to buy a pair of shoes at a store he called Flag Brothers on 8th and Market Street.

We caught the bus downtown, and as we walked toward the store I saw a guy with no legs. He was sitting on a flat board with wheels, selling newspapers. He had on these thick gloves so he could push against the sidewalk and move along. He had a big smile on his face; you had to give him credit for being able to smile. We turned into the store, where Kautz spotted the shoes he wanted. Kautz took off his shoe and told the salesman what he wanted. The salesman measured Ed's foot, making a face, and I asked if he hadn't ever smelled a dirty foot before. He said, "Not this bad." You could tell he was upset because it took about three pairs of shoes before he got it right. I asked the salesman if he was going to sell those shoes that Kautz put his dirty feet in. He looked at us and said, "Will there be anything else, gentlemen?" Kautz paid the man and we left.

Kautz wanted to take his shoes home just to get rid of them, so we took the bus to his house on 35th Street. After that we headed for P.S. DuPont and football practice. We went down on the field, and I saw Herbie and Junie Eisman. Again Junie threw me a couple of passes and I burnt a couple back to him. He walked over and said, "I can see you haven't lost any of that speed; you have a good arm." We had a good time watching them practice. On the way home I came across our paperboy on 31st Street. He was using a wagon to serve papers. We talked all the way to 29th Street. He said that you could make about $12 a week. He showed me how to fold and throw them. We sure could use that money, I thought.

I bet it wasn't a week later that he approached me again to see if I would be interested in taking over his paper route, six days a week for just one hour a day. No delivery on Sundays and we had to collect the money. I told him I had to talk to my mother and brother about it and would get back to him the next day. Mommy thought it was a good idea, and Menny was as excited as I was, so the next day we told our paper boy that we would take it. He said that the News Journal had to approve. They did and we were assigned our route, number 444, which was two city blocks square plus the houses across the street from ours, the west side of 29th St.. At first we would deliver together, and after awhile we agreed to alternate days. One of us had to be home at 4:00 to deliver the papers.

Delivery was easy; collecting was a big pain, but we got through it. Tuesday we had to have the money ready for the route manager. The bill was always attached to the bundles when they were dropped off. We had to carry a lot of change when we collected and then trade it in the stores in the neighborhood for paper money. The majority of the people were very nice. They wanted to know where we lived, our names, and our phone number,

I guess so they could call us up and pester us. We were more careful not to add too many people to our route; we had about 117 houses. That was about the limit; we had to have a life.

With the paper route, caddying, and taking orders down at the A&P store, we were outdoing what my father was giving my mother. He wasn't getting many paint jobs. One Friday Mommy had to go looking for him at his favorite watering hole, and Menny was delivering papers. Mommy asked me to go with her. We were lucky we found him at the first bar; he came out and started threatening her because she was embarrassing him. He looked over at me and could tell I was disgusted with him. That son of a bitch only gave my mother $10.00 and had the nerve to tell her he was going to get some money during the week. He seemed furious at my coldness, and that Mommy did not trust him to bring money home. When we got home, Mommy said to expect Ballsey to come home mad. Theresa was out with Kitty.

Kitty stayed, thank God. Sure enough, when my father came home, he woke us by fighting with my mother in their bedroom. She let out a scream that emptied our bedrooms to see what was wrong. When we got there my father had blood running down his nose. Margaret and Lovey were in the bathroom praying again, but God must have been somewhere else because He never heard them. My father started charging toward me when Kitty stood in front of me and told him to settle down because he wasn't going to hit anyone as long as she was there. So he might as well go to sleep.

He was afraid of Kitty, who also had a father who drank. She was tough. She would say, "How could you beat your wife and your loving children for no reason? I can't believe, Uncle James, that you are doing this." She would tell him she was ashamed of him and what he was doing, and so would her mother be if she knew. "Don't you want people to be proud of you Uncle James?"

It was my birthday that day, but I got nothing, not even a card. No cake, no ice cream, it was just another day. I was disappointed. I got over it quickly, though; that's how you survive.

The next day it dawned on me that I had forgotten to water those plants at the convent. I jumped on my bike and took off to the convent, where I found all the plants dead and dried up. I was shaking in my shoes. I had to think quickly. I grabbed them and threw them down the pit where the new church was going to be, where no one could find them. I had to come up with a good story. I went back before school started and I saw Sister hanging out the wash. I jumped off my bike and ran to her, telling her that the plants were missing and that someone must have taken them about a month ago. She thanked me for being a good boy and gave me a box of salt water taffy she had bought for me. I felt so guilty I almost didn't take them.

Out of the corner of my eye I saw all the pots and dead plants around the corner, hidden by the convent wall. I looked at Sister and gave her back the salt water taffy. I told her I had lied, that I had forgotten to water the plants and so they all died. She said the Sisters were disappointed but realized that an active little man like you are would forget; she said she knew I was enjoying my summer freedom. She was happy I told her the truth because it was the right thing to do. She didn't know that I saw the pots; she made me take the taffy. I was a wreck; I was expecting to be sent back to the fifth grade. Sister told me she would see me in school when it started.

With only a week to go before school started, I was determined to do a lot of things to finish my summer. There was basketball practice to watch at the Yard, and we had our same foursome for caddie's day. I was looking forward for one of us to break 100. Our last Monday before school was a beautiful morning, not a cloud in the sky. Nobody wanted to gamble, so Menny and I made a bet, total score for a dollar. I shot 103 and Menny shot 105. My swing was too fast, but I had won, only three strokes shy of my goal.

This picture is of Timsey JerLiam O'Riordan and his wife Margaret Kelleher on his right.
The three girls are unknown.

The farmhouse where the O'Riordans lived in Bellvue, Co. Cork Ireland

This picture was taken of Jeremiah O'Riordan, Jerem, or Uncle Jerry. March 1936.

This picture was taken of my mother, \ Bina Abbigail O'Riordan Toner in 1936.

The schoolhouse the O'Riordan's attended in Renanerree, Co. Cork Ireland.

The steps the girls fell down that cold, windy evening.

This picture was taken on a sliding board, on Fourth St. From left to right Margaret, me, Menny and Theresa.

My parents wedding picture taken in 1933. Left to right, Tom and Lilly Tobin, Bina and James E. Toner Jr.

This picture was taken of Rodney St.
Top: My father, Menny, Theresa and me.
1940.

This picture was taken of Menny
and me on Fourth St., 1941.

This picture was taken on Fourth St.
Top. Left to right, Menny, Theresa and me 1941.
Bottom. Left to right, Nora and Margaret 1941.

Theresa and Honey. Taken outside my
mother's store, "Toners Luncheonette", 1953.

This picture was taken of me on our store's
front lawn just after a round of golf at the rock, 1953.

This picture was taken of me in England
in 1958 as a Military Policeman.

"The Haunted House". This is the house where Grandmom Kelleher died and the house has
been haunted ever since. Coom, Kilgarvan.
Take notice of the tools and paint cans left by the front door when the workmen ran off the job.

10

Sister Thomas Xavier, my sixth grade teacher, had a nice complexion. I think the nuns sunbathed in the summer. It was easy for them to conceal something like that because they were covered from head to toe. They had no men in their lives, no chance of a man, which did something to them. They were bitter, and mostly at us guys. The girls were good, but we were mischievous, and Sister would use a yardstick on us or her solid oak ruler. They both hurt.

I think Sister was most excited when she was teaching Catechism; she made it very interesting for us. We had to know everything from the commandments to the Holy Days of Obligation. This was the first time I heard that we weren't allowed to go in a Protestant Church or be in a Protestant wedding. Certain books and movies were taboo. I remember seeing lists of books and movies that were banned by the Catholic Church. If you read these books or saw the movies, you committed a sin. I couldn't understand why non-Catholics could see these movies, or read the books and they believed they were going to heaven but we couldn't. It sounded like someone was discriminating against us Catholics. And can you imagine me in Confession adding this to all my sins? I would have been doing penance for days.

While I had a lot going on in school, Theresa didn't seem interested and was not getting up in time. I know she felt inferior to the other girls, but she was doing this to herself; it wasn't her schoolmates doing it to her. This all came from a poor self-image. Someone from her school told me she was too defensive and it made her look bad. She could have walked to P.S. DuPont and gotten a better education because she would have been a better frame of mind, but she had to take a bus to Wilmington High school leaving it hard for her to be on time for her first class at 9: am sharp. We could not reason with her that going to school to be with her girlfriend was the wrong reason and the proof was she couldn't get up on time catch a bus to make it to her first class. This made it hard for Theresa to like school because the teachers had to discipline her for being late so many times. That couldn't all be blamed on my father. She had picked Wilmington High because her friend Betty Dueling was going there, but she only saw Betty for about thirty seconds a day. So she really picked the wrong school to go to.

Nothing was going smoothly for Theresa. She smoked and her school was very strict on smoking. She was 15 and only in the ninth grade. Mommy didn't want her going to dances unless they were school sponsored. Theresa wanted to go to the other dances, like those at the airbase. She had to make a decision whether to honor my mother's decision or not; eventually she went to the airbase dances with Betty. They relied on each other for everything; I didn't know what they did all the time, but it certainly wasn't homework.

I was sitting out on the porch step with Joan one Saturday morning when the conversation got onto Theresa. Don't forget, Joan went to Wilmington High School, too. She told me that Theresa was cutting classes all the time. Joan told me she stayed away from her because she was honestly afraid of Theresa, who was too unpredictable and angry. I told Joan that my sister was having a hard time with my father and his drinking. Joan said she fully understood what a hard time it was for all of us. She thought that Theresa would probably drop out of school soon. Joan also said that every time she saw Theresa she was smoking a cigarette. She never looked happy either, never smiling or laughing. My mother wasn't aware of this and I wasn't going to tell her either. I asked Joan how she was doing in school and she said she had a "C" average and that she would graduate. Some day Joan wanted to be a beautician. I knew she would be good at it.

One day Mommy took me to see Grand Mom and Grand Pop Toner. I was looking forward to seeing Grand Mom. She was always very happy to see us. As young as I was I could see that her clothes were rags. Grand pop had no idea how he should care about someone, only how he cared about himself and only himself. So that was the best that Grand Pop could do for her. Grand Pop wasn't happy to see us; he never as so much moved his head to say hello. He wasn't even intelligent enough to pretend he was interested. Grand Mom said, "James, say hello to Bina and your grandson Jerome." He mumbled something, turned his head, and smiled slightly. No one could tell met that he wasn't aware of other people around him. He just didn't give two damns about anything. I later on would have liked to have known why he ever wanted to get married, just like I wondered the same about his son. He turned back around and went back to removing a fingernail. He had his own medical tool kit; it consisted of a scalpel, scissors, and a nail cutter. It could cut sheet metal if he wanted it to.

Grand Pop had only a couple of teeth left in his mouth. He had worked as a blacksmith when he could and worked on the old trolleys. He wasn't healthy; and he drank too much. Poor Grand Mom looked like a homeless person, which hurt Mommy and me to see her that way. We couldn't help her because we weren't that much better off. I could understand if we didn't have any money because my father was taking care of two families. But this was not the case; he was just pissing it away, just like his father was doing. What was happening to his parents was slowly happening to us, except us children gave Mommy a lot of money every week. Grand Mom's children didn't appear to be giving them anything at this time. Thank God we could help Mommy. We definitely weren't moving.

In October we had a meeting with all the kids who wanted to get corn up at Blue Ball, but I knew this was my last run. I didn't feel like doing it anymore. My fingers were numb from shucking, and I didn't throw corn anymore. I still looked forward to Mischief Night, though, because to me it was like a holiday—the night that we unloaded our hostility. You had better be able to throw, but especially to run because running got you through the night.

It seemed that each year was worse than the previous year. I actually saw a guy throw a brick through a church stained-glass window; I must have run five city blocks in 30 seconds. I wasn't going to stay around and say I didn't do it. I wouldn't do anything to a church—I had my limits. At the same time, Menny and I were gravitating to the more exciting things like unhooking the bus cables from the power lines. The driver would come out of his bus like a raging bull, but he never went far because of the money left on the bus and the people waiting to go home. I ran off like a deer.

All that throwing paid off because I could put the newspapers I delivered anywhere I wanted, over railings, hedges, fences, and right where they should be, by the front door. It always stayed folded when I threw it; I was so proud of myself. Delivering papers was fun for me because I got to throw something at least 117 times. I should have paid them to let me deliver; that's how much I enjoyed it. A lot of times when I finished delivering papers I still wanted to throw something, so we played wire ball. We threw a tennis ball at an overhead wire, and if you hit the wire, and if it was "caught" then you were out. If you missed, it was a hit. If you hit the wire with the bases loaded it was a grand slam. It required a lot of throwing, and that's what I liked the most.

The weather was unusually cold; Theresa said that the guy on the radio predicted a cold winter. Right away I hoped it was going to snow a lot so we could shovel and make some money for Mommy. Theresa said Mommy wouldn't have any extra money for Christmas this year. That put knots in my stomach; I really looked forward to Christmas. We never had a lot of gifts, but we did have a good time.

Right before Christmas we woke up to six inches of snow. The deeper the snow the more money we would charge, so we should be able to make some big money from this storm. After a day of work we had $16.00 between the three of us, but I said it wasn't enough. Theresa had the younger girls with her, which slowed her down. Menny suggested getting the house on the corner of 31ˢᵗ Street with a lot of sidewalk.

We knocked on the door, and the owner agreed to pay us three dollars to shovel the front and back steps and his sidewalks, which went around the corner and took a long time. I went up to the door to collect our money, but he kept yelling for me to go away. I went back to Menny who was leaning on a car and told him that old son of a bitch wasn't going to pay us.

The owner had a black sedan parked just far enough away not to be visible from the house. Bent on revenge, we snuck back around to the street side of the car, opened the back door, and started shoveling snow and slush as fast as we could until the back of the car was full of snow up to the windows. I never shoveled so fast in all my life. We closed the door and ran up 30ᵗʰ Street. His interior was ruined; it was going to be below freezing that night. If he wanted to cheat us kids out of three dollars, he deserved what he got. (A few days later I saw the black car being towed down West Street. With cloth seats and carpeting, it was going to cost that man a lot more than three dollars to clean that mess up. We made sure that we never went to his house to shovel again.) Menny and I went on to the A&P, and in one day he and Theresa and I gave Mommy a total of $26. Mommy was speechless at such an amount. I knew she felt bad about taking it, but we freely gave it to her. We kept only a dollar each.

Around that time a woman kept calling our house asking for Jim Toner. I took one call and told her he was working. I asked where she met him. She replied, "At a party, and what business is it of yours, young man?" I told her I was his son, that I had a brother and four sisters, that Jim was married, and that my mother didn't deserve this kind of treatment from a whore like her. The caller just hung up but kept calling back. Finally Mommy got on the phone and said, "Jim is married but if you want him that bad you can have him. You are welcome to come and get him; I hope you have a good job because you will need it to support him."

That day it was after 6:00 o'clock when my father came home from work. I could tell by the way he acted and smelled that he had been drinking. Mommy told him, "Tell those drunken whores to stop calling here! If you want them that bad, why don't you move in with them?" That's all he wanted to hear; he spit in Mommy's face, slurring his words. He pushed her in a chair and Theresa grabbed his arm, wanting to swing him around, but she wasn't strong enough. He backhanded her in the ear; she screamed and I could tell she was in great pain. Menny and I jumped in, asking why he didn't pick on somebody his own size. "We ain't afraid of you!" He felt challenged and started at us when Mommy grabbed his shirt and ripped it in half. She told him that if he hit Menny or me she was going to have him arrested, and maybe those two detectives would be the ones to do it. She added, "They will love to come see you again, only this time you won't be so lucky." He got right up in our faces and tried everything to start a fight, but Mommy told him not to try it because it would be his last fight.

I know he heard Mommy warn him. He was trying to find a way out of a situation that made him look bad, but nothing was working; Theresa was in a lot of pain. Mommy gave her two aspirin, but Theresa was up all night crying. First thing in the morning Menny and I watched the kids while Mommy took Theresa over to Dr. Rayon's. He told Mommy Theresa had a broken ear drum and asked how it happened. After Mommy explained, he put down his instrument and asked, "How many beatings are you people going to take before one of you is really hurt? She asked what she could do with five children and two boarders; he shook his head and said he would be a witness for her if she needed him. The entire neighborhood could be witnesses; that's how widely my father's abuse was known. More than once his own mother told him to behave himself and to stop drinking, but it was too much part of his life to stop, if he had any respect for his mother he would have quit drinking. He was a sick man who in all honesty couldn't be helped. I think prison would have taught him a lesson that he would have had plenty of time to think about. I couldn't help but wonder what he would have done if Mommy were the one out drinking and having men calling the house for her, how long he would have taken that life. I could only conclude that it wouldn't be that long.

This was Honey's first Christmas, and we were trying to make it nice for her. Bonnie and Mikey's mother had brought their gifts sometime in December, but I wondered how she could not be here with her little girl on Christmas day. You can pay someone to watch your children, but no amount of money could make them feel totally at home. But they were happy, felt our love and gave love in return. Meanwhile Mommy was trying to keep us all from becoming boarders somewhere else.

On Christmas morning, we each got two gifts, a pair of pants for school, and a pair of clip-on roller skates. The girls got fur-lined gloves. Mommy thanked Menny and me for the pair of slippers we gave her; she never took them off that day. After another dinner without my father, everyone wanted to play Monopoly, but I didn't want to play. I felt gloomy and couldn't put my finger on why I felt that way. Just then the door bell rang. It was Catherine Sullivan and her girlfriend, who was allowed to driver her parents' car.

Catherine was a good storyteller, so we begged her to tell us a story. Catherine pointed me out to her girl friend, "this is the boy who's teeth went into my fore head," And pointing out the scar to every one; it happened one night when she was telling a scary story, she said, "ok everyone sit on the floor". Catherine sat in the tufted chair and turned out all the lights but the small one on the phone table. She changed her voice all the time, trying to scare us, making noises, and laughing scarily. Here is her story.

A little boy was lost in the jungle and was cared for by a pride of lions. The boy became as wild as they were; they took him as one of their own. He even went out with them to hunt for food. The females led the hunt for food, and the males lagged behind and only came in after the females made the kill. A big male lion named Wilsey fed first, and the females had to wait their turn. The lost boy ate with the females and had to wait till the very end. He would rip the flesh just like them but there wasn't that much flesh left on the bones and a lot of times they wouldn't wait for him to eat. They would leave him so he would have to carry some bones with meat on them and run to keep up with them. Wilsey would look for a place in the tall grass to bed down for the evening. It was important that the boy know the chain of command so as not to offend the big male lion.

The boy slept right in the middle of the pride, using them as pillows. It was very hard to sleep with all the flies and mosquitoes; the boy kept swatting at them. That would keep the pride from knowing what was going on around them, so Wilsey took the boy down to the river and pushed him down in the mud. The boy caught on fast and started smearing his body with mud. He looked bad but it kept the flies and mosquitoes away.

After exposure to the heat during the day and the cold at night, the boy was slowly becoming very sick. He was feverish and delirious, calling out for his mother. Seeing that the boy was becoming delirious, Wilsey decided to take him to a man who had the reputation of taking care of the sick and hurt animals. He managed to get the boy on his back and took him for miles, the boy holding on tight with his head buried in the lion's mane. When they reached the path that led to the man's house, Wilsey let out a roar that could be heard for miles and jerked his body so the boy would fall to the ground. Wilsey hid in the bushes until the man came out with a lantern and soon found the boy lying on the path, moaning from the high fever that would kill him if not attended to quickly.

The man picked the boy up and carried him in the house. The first thing the old man wanted to do was to put the boy in a tub of water and try to reduce his temperature as fast as he could, but the boy was truly wild and the old man could only get him to drink water. He couldn't eat any cooked food, so the man fed him monkey flesh raw, the bloodier the better. The old man had his hands full doctoring this boy back to health. It was as though he was nursing a two year old lion cub and was having trouble with the boy resisting the changes to his diet.

The boy could hear the wild noises all around them, day or night. This made the boy restless for the return to the wild; he would go out at night to hunt with a knife just like the wild family of lions would do. One night he went out too far and out of nowhere a huge male lion leaped from the heavy growth and pinned the boy down under him. The boy was no match for the big male, which opened his mouth for the kill. Just then the boy called out, "Wilsey it's me—don't you know me? I am your friend." Wilsey stopped and looked at him in the moonlight. The reunion immediately turned into a joyous occasion, and all the female lions came up to the boy and smelled him all over. The female lions formed a circle, roaring. The boy stayed in the middle, and then Wilsey their leader came into the center of the circle and roared. Daybreak was coming fast; Wilsey started pushing the boy out of the circle and back toward the man's house. The boy was resisting with all of his pleas, but none of the other lions paid attention.

Wilsey knew that the boy couldn't grow up in the jungle because it was hard for them to survive as well. Wilsey was ignoring the boy's pleas and again started pushing the boy back towards the old man's house.

With his head down, sobbing, the boy never looked back at the pride of lions that were sobbing also. The boy felt that they didn't love him anymore, when Wilsey knew differently. The old man found him walking the path in the jungle and could clearly see that the boy was exhausted, so he took the boy by the hand and led him back to the house. The boy found his way to the cot and lay down and slept for almost 24 hours. He had been gone for two days and had gone back to his wild ways. The old man gave him a change of clothes and thought he would wash the blood stains out of the boy's tattered shorts. There he found a folded picture of a young beautiful woman tucked in a little pocket near the waist band. On the back was faintly written, Anderson, American Embassy. He put the picture on his bureau, saving it for the right time. He began to teach the boy some manners and hygiene. In about six months he had the boy taking a bath, saying thank you, eating with a fork, and sleeping in bed.

The old man wanted to make an inquiry to the embassy about the boy, but first he tried to piece the puzzle together. How does a little boy grow up with a pride of lions? It finally dawned on him. This was the little American boy who went missing from the American Embassy three years ago. The man sat at his telegraph machine and typed, "I have Anderson, the young American boy who was lost in the jungle." He gave his location, and in less than 24 hours a helicopter was making a lot of noise and trying to land in the grass outside the house. It had all the animals in an uproar. A man jumped from the copter and ran toward the boy, who was clinging tightly to the old man. He introduced himself as Anderson's father and that his son had been lost for years in the jungle. The father tried to hug the boy but he wouldn't have any part of it; his father was a stranger and the lions trained him to be cautious of strangers.

The old man took the father inside and told him that the boy was still a little wild and that he would need a lot of supervision to bring him back to civilization. The father insisted on taking the boy back, but the old man said it would be a mistake because the boy would seem to wild and uncivilized and would get in trouble. "Let me have the boy for a little while longer. You haven't had him for over three years, so what another four to six months?" They agreed that the father would visit every two weeks, and the biweekly visits went very well.

In four months the boy was ready. When the father came to pick him up, the boy wanted to take a short walk out into the jungle. He assured them it was going to be OK. He wanted to say goodbye to his family of lions, but the adults had never heard of such a thing. They had to walk fast to catch up to the boy. After 30 minutes, the boy stood on a mound and made some noises. Soon the lions started to appear from all over. There must have been 50 of them. The big male lion Wilsey came last, walking proudly as only a big male can. He walked up to the boy and he let the boy hug him. The female lions were bobbing their heads. Wilsey let out a roar and they all left as fast as they came.

Twenty years later, Anderson, now a grown-up, good-looking man, came back to the wild for a last visit. He found out that the old man had died a year earlier; and the house was being taken back by the jungle. When Anderson walked into the jungle, he found a mound to stand on and started to make the special noises. He waited for all of his friends to show up so he tried one more time to get their attention. No one showed up; they were all gone. Anderson felt sick inside. It dawned on him why Wilsey didn't want him to stay with them. Walking away, he knew he would never return again, and that the lions had become victims of the law of the jungle.

Just then, Catherine turned on the lights. We were all crying and so was she. It was a great story, a little scary but mostly sad. Catherine could really do those lion roars. We ended up in the kitchen for apple cake and a cup of hot tea. What a great ending to a great Christmas Day.

We sat around a while still feeling the effects of Catherine's story, and Catherine said she had to get home. She was babysitting now. She had quit school and become a full-time nanny. She said she liked it; she would go on vacation with the family and would go where they would go. She was very happy. I couldn't imagine her mother letting her quit school. Theresa told Catherine that she wanted to quit school, and was an usher part time at the Strand Theater at 24th and Market St.

Although Theresa was still having a bad time at school, she couldn't quit like Catherine did because she was only fifteen, and you had to be 16 to quit school. She hadn't made any friends. She had a chip on her shoulder and it wasn't making her very popular. The school that she wanted to go to with her friend ended up being one of the unhappiest places for her she was also getting into some minor fights at school and around the neighborhood. Jeanette Napolski, my friend Donald's sister, was a big girl and Theresa always wanted to fight her. Jeannette was around five foot ten but still no match for Theresa. But Jeanette defended herself, and Menny and I always jumped in and stop it. Fighting for no reason didn't make any sense to us. Theresa was acting like my father. What he was doing to us made her want to fight with everyone else. Theresa was tough, and if our cousin Kitty were with her, they could kick some ass. Kitty went to Wilmington High School, too.

We knew that when Kitty slept over, my father was shut down. I'll never forget a night that Kitty was over and I woke up to hear my mother telling my father to stop those women from phoning him. She told him to get out, that his children were giving her more money than he was. The money he was giving her wasn't enough. She asked him what he thought married life was and asked why he had wanted to get married anyway. He grabbed my mother and ripped her pajama top. She let him have it with the metal vacuum cleaner line right across his eye, cutting him and causing his eye to close up almost right away. We were all standing in the doorway looking at him.

Kitty charged into the room and told my father that this kind of abuse has to stop. "Every time I'm over here, you're fighting with Aunt Bina," she cried, "and these children are a wreck on account of you. They can't sleep at night because they don't know what you're going to do next. Haven't you done enough to this family? Why don't you just leave? I'm sure you can find some women to want their life ruined like what you're doing here." He walked up to her, holding his black and blue swollen eye and got within an inch of her nose and told her to mind her own business. She replied, "It is my business; you made it my business, and you better back off because too many people want to kick your ass. Just in case you don't know it, the line is getting longer every day." She continued, saying that she was invited here and was not leaving. "Why don't you hit me? I'm not afraid of you at all. If I have to permanently move in here, you will stop this terrorism. I dare you to hit me if you're so tough." I said to myself, "Kitty, don't push him into doing something stupid!"

My father had to make a decision. There wasn't any way he could save face. Finally he didn't do anything to her, and she knew he wouldn't. He knew he didn't want her family after him. Stories were out about his antics, but he was in denial. Meanwhile we were all awake. I heard him down stairs with the ice cubes. It was bad enough that he had a black eye to explain, but now a closed eye as well. He was going to try to get the swelling down.

The next day I wasn't any good in school. I didn't understand what Sister was talking about. I would often wonder if she knew about my life out of school. Usually the next morning or so I always expected Joan to ask me what was going on. She wasn't around, and I didn't see her after school either. It was Saturday morning when she got me on the porch, winking at me and making sexy faces at me to get me embarrassed. Menny was telling Joan that I was practicing my wrestling moves. She said her mother wasn't home and grabbed me by the shirt and pulled me over the railing and into the house.

Joan had on a blue sweatshirt, which she pulled over her head. She stood in front of me with a thin white tee shirt on, with no bra. Her nipples were hard. We always started on our knees. She was serious about wrestling with me, and so was I. She threw me down and I grabbed her tits. She threw her head back laughing. I let her throw me all around but never let go of those boobs. She had me on my back. Menny was yelling, "Pin him, Joan." She wasn't strong enough, so she lay on me. She rocked on me until I let her win. I held on for dear life—what a ride. Her nipples were rock hard now.

She rolled off me and lay on the floor on her back, laughing and breathing hard. Menny was telling Joan that she had beat me fair and square. She told me to kiss her and I hesitated, and she pulled me over on top of her. She looked different, like she was shook up or something. She gave me a big kiss and her tongue was everywhere. I got up and left. Menny kept saying that I should have been on top of her and not her on top of me. "I thought we were wrestling," I said, "not having sex." Menny said that she was humping me. "Babe, you must be dumb," he said, but I didn't know if she was humping me or not. A few minutes later Joan came out on the porch. She had on her sweatshirt and combed her hair. She was good looking, and I liked the way she smiled at me. I said, "Joan, why don't you wrestle Menny?" She said she had chosen me to wrestle and no one else. "Be happy, Babe; you seem to be enjoying it," she said. I replied that Menny was having more fun watching than we were.

Menny said that girls got turned on by my shyness. I thought that as nervous as I was around girls, they would leave me alone, evidently not. I was too young for Joan, and she knew it. But she taught me a lot. She didn't have too much to do with anyone else in the neighborhood: no wrestling with anyone else but lucky me. Most guys would have killed to have what I had with Joan.

Wrestling never seemed to affect my blood pressure. Mommy was still taking me out of school regularly to see the doctor. He would check my blood pressure and write the prescription. The liquid was pink and tasted like peppermint. I guess it was working. Mommy said the reason for the high blood pressure was on account of my father. She said that he was the problem with all of us.

The Yard was very popular after school and on weekends. Games were going on all the time: basketball, football, tag, stick ball, and every game was intense. I loved them all. Competition was something I never ran from. This doesn't mean that I won everything or that I was on top. I was just a kid who played his heart out and was lucky sometimes. The most fun was being in the game with the older guys, who tried everything they could get away with not to get beaten by someone younger. Believe me, I was kicked, hit, elbowed, stepped on, punched, knocked down, tripped, cursed at, and threatened by them, and all this happened in a game of fun.

This experience was valuable when I played in games with guys my own age. This is why I always enjoyed playing with referees or umpires, which cut out a lot of brutality in sports. Our toughest basketball games in the Yard were with Ed Tucker, "Mr. Elbows." He was older than we were, and could really hurt us. When he went up for a rebound, look out on the way down. He could throw an elbow in two or three directions. He stood on your feet, too. When I was in a game and he wasn't playing, it was really fun. But I don't want to paint him as a bad guy. He was a very nice person except on the basketball court. He was competitive, as I was, and hated to lose. He made me a better player. I could work my hips really well thanks to him. I could throw a hip and it wouldn't be seen, but it would be felt. But I was still going to wait until the seventh grade to go out for the team.

I was busy with school, being a paperboy, and an altar boy. That would be enough for anyone. Going to school was hard for me, but I rarely ever missed school or got sick. I think it was because I sweat a lot. Really sweat. It would run off me like a river, summer or winter. I felt good in school this year, though. Some kids helped me with my work if they could, which made me feel good. I was learning more and more each year. I knew I was going to catch up and maybe pass other people. My goal was not to be last when they gave out report cards. I felt that someday I would have a thirst for knowledge.

Menny and I were having fun with the paper route, working as a team an hour a day, six days a week. It was easy for us, but we still didn't like collecting. One day I was collecting at a second-floor duplex on West Street. I walked up all twelve steeps and knocked on the door. A girl's voice said, "Who is it, is that you honey?" I just stood there and didn't answer. All of a sudden, the door flew open and a beautiful woman was standing there naked. She had jet black hair, all over. She stood there with her arms open and then shut the door as fast as it opened. She scared me out of my wits. I took those steps down two at a time. When I was four from the bottom I jumped on the landing, hitting it hard, and fell through the open door and tumbled down the front steps to the sidewalk. I was shaking. I don't know how I could ever go there again. I looked up at her window and she was looking down at me, smiling.

I bet it was three weeks before I went back to collect. This time I took Menny. He wanted to see her face when she saw me again. I knocked on the door, which opened fast. It was the same woman, and I said "collecting." She reached for the card tucked behind the wall switch cover. She looked at it and looked at me and said, "I can see you haven't been here for a while. I owe you four weeks." I said, "Yes I know." She was smiling at me and flirting with me as she paid. My face was red and I was fumbling for change. I put the change in her hand. She gave me back some money and said it was a tip that she always wanted to give me. I know I was as red as I could get. As we turned to go down the steps, she said, "Be careful, some people have fallen down these steps and ended up on the sidewalk outside."

We got outside and Menny was giggling. He said, "Babe did you see how she looked at you?" I replied, "Men; she's 23 and married." He said, "With you I don't think it matters. She likes you." I was probably the only guy to ever see her naked besides her husband. I was a very lucky guy. She was not only beautiful; she had beautiful tits, full and firm. They were standing straight out. She was more than any man could dream of. I was always nervous going back there. Menny said she was mine; he was not going to collect from her. She was very nice to me. I could hardly look at her face I was so bashful. Every time I went there, she was always squeezing my hand when I gave her change back.

I loved being an altar boy, even if it was only for Benediction. I felt close to God as an altar boy. Sometimes I showed up sweating, with a dirty face and dirty shoes. I would clean up a little before I went out with the priest on the altar, including combing my hair. The Benedictions were short, only 15 or 20 minutes. I liked the sun shining through the stained glass windows and the incense. It was heavenly to experience. I was behaving myself with the incense; I didn't want a repeat like the time with the fire engines.

When I was on the altar and looked out I would see the same faces. A cute blond about 25 was starting to show up a lot. Her name was Carol Green, and when she walked in, she had to know her walk was illegal. Everyone looked at her, but I bet she wouldn't shake that ass in front of Fr. Lynch. He would kick her butt out of church. I always looked for her and her little smile for me.

One night Menny and I went to Judy Kee's birthday party. I was having a lot of fun with the girls, who were sitting around giggling of course. Then one of the girls wanted to play Post Office. The boys were given even numbers and the girls had odd numbers. Judy put a girl in the closet, my number was called, and I went in and closed the door. The girl asked who I was, I said Babe. I felt her hand around my neck. All I had to do is to remember how Joan kissed and this girl would never forget that night. I could feel her breath on my face as we met.

My lips were open and so were hers; my tongue was touching her tongue. She pulled me close to her, close enough to feel her tits on my chest. She pushed hard against my pelvic area, and we kissed about three minutes. I was too scared to do any thing else. After she left it was my turn to call out a number, and another girl came in. I was feeling around for her, and every time I moved to find her I ended up feeling her up. I said I was sorry for all the touching; just then her lips parted and she ended up being the best kisser that night. She was breathing very heavily and kept humping my leg with her pelvic area, pushing very tight against mine you might say she had woke up a sleeping postal clerk. I straightened myself up before I came out, but I looked down because they were all giggling and my fly was open. Menny was pointing to my fly, so I ran out of the room to fix it.

The game continued and I got called four times. I figured if they called my number, they wanted to kiss me. I don't know why—I wasn't the best looking guy there— but each time I went in, the girl pressed so hard against me I could hardly breathe. Their tits felt good on my chest and their pelvic area against me. What a night! Those girls sure could respond to those open-mouth kisses, but I was still afraid to touch them, these parties were the only experience these girls were getting. They were very vulnerable, but as long as no one found out, they might go along for the ride with caution. It was important that they be invited back to the next party.

I had to bring a date to one party. Who was I going to invite? The numbers were shrinking fast, so I asked a girl named Pattyann. I walked to her home to get her. She was as tall as I was. We had to walk about five blocks to the party; eventually I reached for her hand and she took it. It felt good. I told her how nice she looked. That made a change in her right away. We talked for the whole four blocks and before we knew it we were there. As soon as we went in everyone was looking to see who was with whom. Pattyann and I slow danced a little, if you call standing in one spot and moving your hips dancing. I pulled her tight to me and she didn't resist. She wanted to talk a little. We were having a great time. Eventually the lights were out so we could make out. Wow.

It wasn't pitch black like in the closet or like post office, but it was dark enough. This gave the girls a lot of courage. I was very slow with Pattyann. We kissed a little. She was a good kisser. Not much tongue, but she really held me tight. The party broke up about 10:00, and every place along the way home where it was dark we would stop and kiss. By the time we got to her street we were kissing good and long. Our last kiss was hot and long; she was breathing heavily. The more she tried to cover it up the worse it got. When we got to her door, she put her hand on the door knob, stopped and turned around, and gave me the hottest kiss we shared all night. She thanked me and went inside. I could see her through the window and she turned and blew me another kiss. I flew home in about 10 minutes. What a night. What a party. Now I understand what they mean when they say blue balls; if this kissing had been any longer I would have been sporting my own set of blue balls.

While those kissing games made me feel grown up, I still acted like a boy most of the time. Menny and I often walked through a graveyard a few blocks away that was bordered by Washington Street, Market Street, 31st Street, and 34th Street. Sometimes we were nosy and looked through the mausoleum doors or talked through the air vents. We would just sit and smoke, but we definitely never did any mischief there. To us it was sacred, hands off. At night we played hide and seek and made it scary. Menny had to try and scare me all the time. The gates closed at 9:00 p.m. It was a good climb to get out if you were locked in. Could you imagine getting locked inside a graveyard with an eight-foot fence with points and spikes? That would scare anybody. If that wasn't enough we did some crazy things with our bikes.

It had to be daytime to ride our bikes through the intersections. It's hard to believe we would ride our bikes through a very busy intersection and never get hurt. We didn't do it all the time because we knew if we did it long enough, someone was going to get killed. It's the law of averages. We relied on our brakes and the cars' brakes, but sometimes we went through the intersection at least 15 miles an hour, which was pretty fast. We never felt that we would get hurt. The two worst spots were 29th and Van Buren Street and 29th and Washington Street. The people driving the cars would have killed us if they caught us. Most of the time we rode one behind the other and sometimes four or five in a row, which increased the chances of being hit. We got a high from the speed going through the intersection and the rebel yells. It was an experience like no other. We kept it up until we got older and smarter. Nowadays it would be suicide to try it. The guy on the bike will lose every time, so please don't be dumb.

We used to play touch football on 28th Street alongside the school; the best games were during a snowstorm, which would change the game from touch to tackle in the snow on the cement street. Another good time to get a football game up was at the end of a big, summer rainstorm when the grass was soft and wet and the dirt was muddy. We would go down to Eastlake near the pond. The kick-off was a sight to be seen. Of course we went after the guy with the ball, pushed him hard, and made him slide in the mud for 20 feet or more. We could tackle him and slide with him, too, as the mud flew everywhere. When you came to a halt you were wiping mud from your face and eyes. The best thing was that it was hot out and the water was warm to our skin, but our clothes were wet. It didn't matter what the score was, it only mattered how muddy you were.

But how was Mommy going to clean those clothes? That walk home was tough; we even had water in our shoes. I hoped we had hot water at home to take our bath, other wise I will have to boil the water on the stove and carry it up the back stairs to the bathtub. Mommy saw us and told us to leave our dirty clothes in the back kitchen; it looked like it was going to take a long time to boil enough water to put in the bathtub. We would have to add cool water to cut the time in half. A couple of games like that one and I wouldn't have any clothes to wear.

On the first Saturday in March I didn't have anything to do, so I rode my bike up to the Rock to see what was going on, but the course was closed because it was too wet to play golf. I walked in the clubhouse and saw Luther sitting by the fireplace eating lunch. I was glad to see Luther and hoped he would be in a good mood and not run me off. I think he liked it when I said hello like he was a long lost brother. That day he was smiling; he had his teeth in so he could eat lunch. It was warm in the brown leather sofa by the fire. I felt real comfortable Luther made me a cup of tea, and as I held it in my hands; he started talking about his duties around the clubhouse. He said he found a nice golf bag in the trash can last summer with dog shit in it. Luther said it had taken a while but he got it cleaned up and rid of the smell. I laughed like hell and told him about what I had done to the owner of the bag.

I told Luther that I noticed more women playing golf now. "There are a couple of good lookers playing now Luther, did you see them?" "How could you miss them?" he said, "shaking their lovely asses around, getting everyone shook up, even Grumpy." I told Luther I thought they were good golfers. I described the woman I always saw with this one guy. I thought she had a nice ass. Luther said there was more to that woman than a nice ass.

After Luther told me that everyone, including Grumpy and the bums, would be back that spring, I left him in time to get to my paper route by 4:00. The papers were thin on Saturdays, so I could carry a lot of them on my paper belt. I would give the papers a bump with my hip and pull one out. I would fold it and throw it all in my stride, never losing a step. I would do this for two square city blocks. It would usually take me 45 minutes to an hour. When I got to my beauty at the duplex on West Street, I would throw the paper up to the landing at her front door. Before I could turn, she would come out, bend over to pick up her paper, usually in shorts or a skirt. Either way, I could see what she had for breakfast.

One collection day I went to her apartment. It was a long climb to her door. I knocked on the door gently; I didn't notice that she had a peep hole put in her door. I guess it would probably save her from another embarrassing moment like she had with me. She opened the door; she had on jeans and a sweater that was couple of sizes too small. She didn't have any trouble filling out her clothes. When you looked at her, she was all women. She only owed 50 cents, but she only had a ten. When I reached for my bills they fell on the floor. She immediately bent down and picked them up, backing into her apartment and telling me to come in and sit at the table because it would be easier to count my money. I sat at her table and counted out $9.50. She insisted that I have a cold glass of ice tea. The next thing I knew, it was in front of me. She kept looking at me with a smile on her face. She had beautiful short hair and her teeth were pearly white. I told her that I had to go now because I had more to collect. She walked me to the door with her arm around me and those beautiful tits were firm against my shoulder. When she opened the door she pressed a little harder and gave my ear lobe a little tug. She stayed tight against me till I started out the door. I heard water running and figured it was her husband in the shower. She said she would see me again and not to let her get a week behind again. I don't know how much more of this I could take. She watched me go all the way down the steps. I turned to look up and she waved at me.

I had to sell my change to get paper money to pay my bill, so I took it to Boles's, and Mrs. Napolski wanted to know where I got all that change. I told her that I had a paper route. She told me she always needed change and told me to put her on my list for change. I ordered a sub, with extra oil. It was the first time I ever saw her make a sub. She put everything on it extra and could hardly close it. I couldn't wait to sink my teeth into this sub. I sat at the table and ate it with my half chocolate, half white milk. That milk made it taste even better, a taste that couldn't be beat. I finally finished, but it was a struggle. Mrs. Napolski didn't charge me because she liked me; the name Lucifer was just a fun thing.

One day I went to visit Chubby Morice, who had finally finished his little electric chair and invited me to come down to the basement to have a look at it. The metal cap had a small light that lit when the current was on. Cubby's brother Donald told me to have a seat. I told him there wasn't any way I was going to sit in that electric chair, even though they assured me that the chair was not wired, and therefore it couldn't hurt anyone. Donald sat in it while his brother Chubby strapped him in, and put the metal cap on him. Chubby checked everything out. It took a while, but then I saw the cap light go on and then Chubby flipped a big switch and Donald started screaming and shaking. It was the first time I came close to shitting my pants. Chubby threw off the switch and Donald starting laughing like hell. They had it planned. They knew I wouldn't get in that damn chair, but they did plan to scare someone. I guess it had to be me. I asked Donald if he wanted to go to Harlan School to play basketball with us on Wednesday night. He declined saying that he didn't play basketball.

We had fun at Harlan School, too. It would open its two gyms from 6 to 9 p.m. on Wednesdays, usually in the winter months, October to March. It was warm inside, plenty of basketballs and plenty of games. It doesn't get any better than that. The police would be on patrol all the time. We were good with that much patrolling; we had to be. We all walked in packs, dropping off when your street came up. We figured that they would close down Harlan if we got into any mischief.

On the last day of school, I again was put on probation for at least 90 days the next fall, but this time Sister was very nice and said that if I opened my books at night, I would probably be an A student. "You would be surprised how easy things would get for you," she said. "I know things are hard at home for you, but don't give up on anything. Things will get better for you as you get older. I know you have it in you to do better. Have fun this summer, Master Toner; I can't wait to see your smiling face next year. Read some books this summer on subjects you like. It will open up a new world for you." How great was that?

That summer a lot of my thoughts were on the Rock, caddying and playing golf. We got out of school on a Thursday, and early Friday I was up at the Rock to caddy. The sweepstake guys were there, who met around noon to gamble. They were loud and couldn't play anywhere else but a public course. Most of them were playing with money they couldn't afford to lose. Grumpy asked me to caddy for a man named Peter. He knew me and liked me. It wasn't his fault, but Grumpy put a couple of big mouths with us to make a foursome. I could take Peter but not those loud mouths. On the fourth hole this one guy threw his club up a tree and was cursing out loud. He walked up to me and said, "Hey kid, go get my club." I told him, "I don't climb trees; you threw it you go get it." I told him he was showing signs of poor sportsmanship and was setting a poor example of how a grown-up should act. I didn't like him, so I didn't care what I said to him. I could tell he would like to hit me, but Peter came up to him and told him if he wanted his club to get it himself.

A few holes later, I went down to where the drives land to keep an eye out for Peter's ball. He hit the ball right down the middle of the fairway. Big Mouth hit his right over my head into the woods. I saw it stop by a rock in the high grass. I ran out into the fairway to Peter's ball. Big Mouth came running down the fairway screaming, "Didn't you see my ball, boy? Why don't you get my ball for me?" By the time he got to me foam was coming out of his big mouth. He actually wanted to fight me, and I was only twelve. He got in my face screaming at me to get his ball. Peter caught up to him and told him to back off, to leave the caddy alone, and not to say another word unless he was looking for some serious trouble.

Big Mouth's partner was carrying him the whole round. Big Mouth kept saying he was sorry about his game. His partner Randy said, "I'm not worried about your game, I'm worried about your temper, and the way you're treating Peter's caddy." The last hole was a dog leg to the right around the trees. I heard them say that the match was even. Randy and his partner were in the middle of the fairway, with about 160 yards to the pin. Big Mouth got up and sliced his ball so badly that I wouldn't be surprised if it were in Wilmington. It hit trees, bounced on black top, hit some bushes, and stopped on the edge of some weeds. He looked around for a while and said he couldn't find it. He was going back to the tee and hit another one. You can only do that if your ball is truly lost. It was to Peter's disadvantage for him to do that. He had a chance to be in the fairway only laying three I told Peter I saw his ball and I could find it. It would be to Peter's advantage to make him play his ball where it lay.

Big Mouth would have to get out of those woods Even if he were lucky, he couldn't do it. Peter called him back and told him we could find his ball because I had seen it. Big Mouth didn't believe him, but Peter showed him the ball. It was sitting on some leaves, but there was no way for Big Mouth to get a back swing at it. He had to hit it or take an unplayable lie, a one-stroke penalty. I encouraged him to hit it, knowing that he would be in a mountain of shit trying to get it out of there.

His first attempt was awful. He hit the ball fat. It hit a bush about 20 feet ahead of him. To hit the ball now, he would have to swing left handed. He tried it and missed. He was furious, saying this kid found the ball this time, but no other time, how convenient. He took another swing and dubbed it about another 20 feet. I was standing in the middle of the fairway, watching this man do himself in and losing some money he really couldn't afford to lose.

Peter and his partner were waiting for their turn to hit. It looked like Big Mouth was going to hit again. He had a nice lie and you could see it from the fairway. I could tell by the way he was addressing the ball that he was going to take a big swing. He reared back and hit the ball as good as he did all day, but he just couldn't get out of those woods. His ball hit a tree solidly and came back at him, hitting him just above the ear and sending him to the ground like he was shot. In fact, his partner ran into the clubhouse to get help. They called an ambulance, which took about five minutes to get there. They put him on a stretcher. I could hear him saying that it wasn't fair, that the caddy found that ball like that. "I lost a club on the fourth hole and now I lost the match," he wailed. They took him away, sirens blaring. Big Mouth's partner asked Peter how much they owed. Peter told him $10.00 each and he paid him. The last thing Big Mouth saw as they closed the doors to his ambulance was me smiling at him.

While we were walking back to the clubhouse, Peter told me it was a good thing I found his ball because the match would have been a lot closer.

Peter bought me lunch and a soda and we talked outside the clubhouse. "Aren't you an altar boy?" he asked. "Yes," I said, and Peter replied, "I guess I'll see you in church on Sunday." He said that he was very surprised how I held my ground with that guy. I told him I knew he was never going to hit me no mater how angry he got. That would be a big no-no. He shook my hand and said he was glad to have me on his side: "You knew if he found his ball he would have to play it. You knew he couldn't get out of those woods even if he were on safari." He gave me three dollars and said, "See you in church, Babe."

What a caddy job that was, the first job of the summer. I had made three dollars and Mommy could use it. I knew where there was a seven iron and a new ball and I was going out to get them. I got to the tree and climbed up and picked out the club from between two thin branches. Now I would have a good seven iron to put in my bag. My whole set of clubs were different; not one matched, and I had found my bag in the trash.

Menny and I wanted to caddy Saturday and Sunday so we could play Monday. Grumpy asked Menny and me to caddy in a foursome together. Sometimes I thought that caddy meant slave; that's how a lot of them would treat us. This day our two golfers seemed like two nice guys, but you never knew; one bad shot and they could turn on you, turning from Dr. Jekyll to Mr. Hyde. They must have played there before because they didn't say much; they must have had a heavy bet. It wasn't until after five holes that things started to get real tight, and they started to accuse each other of doing things that were distracting.

We finished nine holes and had not had a single problem. Don't think that I am complaining; it was nice to get a break and have a nice day. They asked Menny and me if we wanted a hot dog and a soda, and of course we never turned anything down, so we said yes. They brought the food out to us as we were watching the bags; there was a backup on the tenth tee again. Menny and I gave them their clubs and walked down to the corner where the low stone wall was and waited. My guy came so close to going out of bounds that the ball came within a foot of the wall. He still had a shot but had to be very careful. He put his shot right on the green and they won that hole; now they were two up with eight holes to go. If they won money we could get a tip. Menny's guy was a mess, asking for yardage all the time, and where were the 150 yard markers. The match was even and we had to help our players out.

We were standing near the landing area on seventeenth hole where the drives would land, but all four of them hit drives into the woods. My guy was barely in the woods and had a shot if he could hit it low. It was a par five; he hit it between two slumps of trees at the curve in the fairway. He could hit the green in three now. Both opponents couldn't find their balls so they took a penalty stroke each, which cost them the hole and now our guys were one hole up with one hole to go.

I told my guy that the wind was at his back so let it rip. He hit it up and the wind took it for a ride. He hit the green in two and everyone else was on in three. I walked up to my guy and handed him his putter and said, loud enough for his opponents to hear, "Be careful. This green is slow." Then I winked at him, but they couldn't see me. The opponents were away, so they had to putt first. They both hit their putts five feet past the pin; one made the return putt and the other one missed. Their total score was eleven. It was almost impossible for my guy to lose; he missed his birdie putt and tapped in for a par. They finished with a total of nine. My guy gave me a five dollar bill and told me to split it with Menny. He thanked me for my help and said he would see us again sometime.

Menny and I got back in time to serve the papers. It was Menny's turn to serve. I sat in a hard wooden chair on the porch and fell asleep. Menny woke me up, telling Joan that I was here. I sat up and could see her sitting on the porch railing. She asked for me to come over; she smelled good and must have just come out of the shower.

Menny told me Mrs. Toskas had just left. Joan asked, "Do you want to wrestle me, Babe, or are you too tired?" I told her I would wrestle her but if she was going to beat me she was going to have to pin me to the count of three. We both got on our knees. Joan had on a loose pair of shorts and a thin white tee shirt with no bra. I could clearly see her nipples standing out. She grabbed my shoulders and I grabbed her tits when ever I could; she kept swaying from side to side. She meant business and soon had me on my back, trying to pin me. Her nipples were very hard and her legs were as smooth as silk.

Sometimes I pushed her shoulders and re-gripped. The more she bent over the bigger her tits got. She was starting to sweat. I turned her to pin her, but she was too smart and had her pelvis on mine and was rocking on me. She must be hurt because she was starting to moan. I started pinching her nipples gently, as she was saying, "Babe, you're bad." It wasn't long before she collapsed on me, breathing heavily and put her lips on me and kissed me for the longest time. She whispered in my ear that she loved it and stood over me and pulled me up to her. Otherwise I didn't think I had the strength to get up on my own. Menny was in a state of shock, shaking his head, walking away.

I followed Menny on to the porch, looking around to see if Joan could hear him. She didn't come out so he sat in the chair. With this puzzled look on his face, he said, "Babe, every time I turn around these older girls are going after you. What the hell are you doing to make this happen?" I told him I didn't know, that I wasn't looking for any of this to happen, and that it would be OK by me if they left me alone. They could see that I was bashful around them, but Menny said he thought that was what turned them on. He said, "Look at the girl on the paper route. She's crazy about you." I might have only seen her naked for a second but the memory was still with me. I replied, "Maybe so, but not in the way you're thinking. I'm too young for that girl. She's working up to sex and I don't know where to start." He said, "It has to start somewhere and sometime. Lucky you."

I suggested that Menny collect from the girl on the paper route, but he said he couldn't handle a girl like that making a fuss over him. He told me to enjoy it while it lasted, and he wanted to know if there were any more stories out there he didn't know about. I said no, because it would be all over the neighborhood and get back to their family. The funny thing was that the girls our age thought Menny was cute and never gave me a second look. I told him that but he said he didn't believe it.

We were back at the Rock by 8:30 Sunday morning, signed in with Grumpy and waiting to be called. I saw someone staggering toward Grumpy; Holy Christ, it was Abee. Menny and I wondered how he could caddy 18 holes. Then I saw Oscar arrive and ask Grumpy for a caddy, and Grumpy called Abee over and introduced him to Oscar. This went over like fart in Sunday School because Oscar wanted one of us. So we hid behind the brick wall. Grumpy put Oscar with a threesome and away they went. It was pitiful to see Abee carrying Oscar's light bag, walking like a zombie. Oscar would never forget this day as long as he lived. I have to give Abee credit for going this far and tackling the hard things.

Finally Grumpy called Menny and me over to caddy for a man and his wife in their forties. She was definitely overweight and you could see that he was a puss. Menny grabbed his bag and left me with Louise, the fat-ass wife. She would always correct her husband, Tom, who could never say anything right. "Now Tom, this is a par five not a par four." "Yes, Louise." It looked like she was nipping from a chrome flask. I told Menny to watch her because she was drinking whiskey and you could smell it on her breath. At each lady's tee when she would make a motion to hit the ball (address the ball) her big ass shook, and once it started to shake it wouldn't stop. We couldn't stand to look at her, so we looked away, and her pussy husband always congratulated her no matter how bad her shot was. It was an easy caddy job; her bag was light and she only used a couple of clubs. This woman could have worked in the prison system.

I watched her nipping on that chrome flask starting on the fifth hole, seeing her moods swing and listening to how she was progressively showing more disrespect to Tom. All he wanted was to have a fun day with his wife at the Rock. If she kept up her drinking she would pay for it on the back nine because the heat was going to build up and work on that liquor inside of her. She had a nice swing and knew how to putt. Unlike most women she was good in the traps. The number two, par five was nothing for her and she was on in three. I must say she wasn't treating me badly but as I said, they can turn on you fast especially if they had been drinking, or drinking while they were playing like she is.

I don't know how we got through nine holes but we did, and I saw Oscar driving up the road, so he definitely quit early. They wanted to go on, but Louise ran over to the parking lot to fill up her flask and take a swig from the bottle. I watched her throw her head back for a big gulp. They offered to buy us lunch, so they brought out two hot dogs and two sodas; we were backed up on ten as usual. I saw her pour some whiskey in her soda. The temperature was in the mid-eighties, and she was definitely going to have a big problem in the afternoon sun. I would hate to have to pick her up somewhere out there if she ever fell down and couldn't get up. I was praying that wouldn't happen. I asked Menny how I always got the bad player, and he always left me with the shit. He told me I was seeing things that weren't there; I let him know that I wasn't seeing anything but I sure was feeling it.

She wasn't like any other woman her age that I had met. She never asked me any questions like what school I went to or what grade I was in or anything like that. She was being controlled by the liquor as if she had a demon in her. At this point she was not in charge of her life, the liquor was. She had Menny and me laughing so hard we were almost pissing our pants. She wasn't doing anything intentionally; it was just happening. She was really starting to be funny, especially when she swung and farted at the same time, or when she bent over to pick up her tee and farted. She never said anything, just as if it never happened, and her husband never said a word. She probably would have kicked the shit out of him. You always laugh worse when you're trying to cover it up, and her husband knew she was two sheets to the wind and it was only going to get worse.

At this point I was practically holding Louise up. She talked and spit all at the same time, and a lot of her words were slurred. Tom came over to me and warned me she had a mean streak in her when she was drinking. He said he didn't like being around her. On the thirteenth green she lined up to putt her ball, and the hole was behind her. Somehow she saw a hole where there wasn't any, even though Tom kept saying, "Louise, what are you doing?" She putted toward the hole that wasn't there. When she got to her ball she screamed at Tom for not helping her. She took six putts to get in the hole; I would have given up my caddy fee just to know how she kept seeing holes that weren't there. Menny kept saying out of the side of his mouth, "Babe, she's drunk as shit. I know you'll be carrying her soon." Yea, thanks to you, Menny.

By the time we got to the seventeenth hole, she was spitting and farting and fighting with poor Tom about anything that didn't make any sense. I guess he was afraid of her; she was a big woman. He was so embarrassed and glad we only had one hole to go. Menny and I watched her walk to her ball on the eighteenth green. It was pathetic, so we were surprised that she could hit her ball on the green in two. She must have wanted to make this putt badly. She kept kneeling down looking over her putt and kept backing up the hill toward the very deep trap behind her. It had to be at least six feet deep. When Tom said, "That's far enough, honey," she stood up and said, "Kiss my ass." Then she fell backwards, sliding head first into the sand trap six feet below. When she stopped sliding the sand was practically covering her head.

I am glad she had pants on, with her legs spread apart. It would have been an ugly mess to look at her with a skirt on. It definitely would have kept the flies off the watermelon. She lay there motionless. Tom cried, "Babe is she dead? She's not moving!" Menny and I jumped in the sand trap. She was saying that some son of a bitch pushed her in the trap, and did we see him. Tom ran for his car; Menny and I couldn't lift her so we dragged her out of the trap over to the edge of the road, which came close to the green. I know Tom wanted to get her out of here before anyone saw her, after this would have been the talk of the club.

There was sand everywhere down the back of her neck and all throughout her hair. Tom came around the corner with his car on two wheels and slid to a stop. He was determined to get her out of here before anyone saw us. I am glad that she didn't feel sick and throw up.

She was so heavy, but we kept dragging her to the car. Tom was practically begging for Louise to help us. We got the back door open; she was on her knees just not going any further, and her big ass was up in the air. I reached under and grabbed her crotch she leaped in the air and jumped in the car all in one move. At the same time he was saying, "Throw her in the back, boys." Menny threw the clubs in the trunk. Tom ran around to us and he gave us three dollars each, he thanked us for our help. We closed the car doors and I asked Tom how he was going to get her out of the car when he got home. He said he didn't give a shit; she could sleep there all night as far as he was concerned. She was drinking more and more all the time now. He looked at me and said, "Screw her," and I thought to myself, no thank you, I'll leave that up to you. I looked through the back window before he drove off, and she was cursing at him for pushing her in the sand trap. What a night he was going to have with her; he was going to have to hose her off before he could let her in the house. We wouldn't forget that day for a long time. We laughed all the way home and couldn't wait to tell Mommy. We were all screaming with laughter in the kitchen for hours. I was trying to imitate her to Mommy which made it even funnier, Mommy didn't know anything about golf, so when I showed her how she was buried in the eighteen green sand trap she ran to the bathroom pissing her pants.

On Tuesday I went up to the park. I never saw so many people playing on swings, or with horseshoes or checkers. Mrs. Lemon had a new assistant; she was standing in the pavilion wearing khaki shorts, and a light tan shirt, she had a whistle on a white rope around her neck. She was in her first year of college and cute as hell. We called her Pat. She was five foot ten, with beautiful hair and nails. More guys were hanging around the pavilion to see her or talk to her. She looked good in shorts and filled out her shirt nicely. Everyone was asking her for help, and she helped everyone who asked. Mrs. Lemon was smiling all the time, she was happy to see this beautiful assistant be so popular with the kids. Pat stayed in the pavilion area most of time. I couldn't take my eyes off her.

The next time we went to the Rock, Menny and I agreed that we didn't like caddying for those sweepstakes guys. They were too loud and didn't treat caddies that well. I would do some ball hawking instead of caddying for them. We found the bums out in full force. One of them had one eye, and Menny said his name was Toner, but I didn't believe it. He had big lips, a big nose, and a distorted face.

One time Menny and I had taken our BB guns to A.I. DuPont field and had come across those bums sleeping on the matted-down grass. I guess they could tell the way we looked at them that we were going to shoot them. They begged us not to shoot them, but we shot them on the legs, arms, and belly. When we walked away they were cursing and saying they were going to get us someday. One Eye said, "I know you. I always see you at the golf course, don't I?" I told him to shut up or I would shoot him again. He fell on his knees begging me not to shoot, while the other two were shaking in worn out shoes. We knew we treated them badly, and they would try getting us back, so when we were ball hawking, we always made sure we were never alone, especially on the holes farthest away from the clubhouse. We were told more than once that they would hurt us severely if given half a chance. We were always on the look out not to get boxed in anywhere so we couldn't get away from them quickly if we had to.

Wednesday was a good day to caddy because a lot of professionals would come out to play like doctors, lawyers, dentists, and salesmen. The doctors were the most obnoxious and were no fun to caddy for; they were too straight laced. They thought they were getting away from the office but they treated us caddies as though we were their patients the salesmen would not join the doctors. They all had their groups. One day I was caddying with a foursome of salesmen. On the first hole my guy told me to take the pin out. I walked over to the farthest spot on the green, holding the flag. Would you believe this jackass putted the ball to me and not the hole where the pin had come from? You should have heard the other three screaming with laughter. This guy was so embarrassed. He wanted to blame me for misleading him. My guy told him to back off. "We all saw the hole, why didn't you?"

We didn't stop for food or drinks but played on. It was hot as hell. My guy's bag was a little heavy. I knew how to carry a heavy bag, putting it down as often as I could, and carry four to five clubs with me that my golfer might need for the next few shots. It was a lot easier this way. The seventeenth hole was a woods hole with a dog leg right, and that jackass guy hit it right in the woods where some bums were standing. So when we got up to the spot where the ball went in, Jackass asked if anyone saw his ball. They all said in unison, "No, we didn't see it." Of course I had to lie. I pointed at old One Eye and said, "I saw this guy pick up your ball." He started jumping up and down, screaming, "I never did that. I never even saw his ball." I said again, "You saw it and you picked it up; now give it back." We had a real good one going on now. Jackass told One Eye, "The caddy saw you, and I want a new ball in my hands now, or I will be putting something in my hands and it will be you."

One Eye threw him the ball and Jackass looked at it and said it wasn't his ball, but my guy told him to shut up and hit it, that they had the whole golf course held up on account of him. I looked at the bum before I walked away and he told me he was going to get me for that. I walked back to him and told him, "Don't let me catch you sleeping in the tall grass again, because I'll get your ass." He was boiling mad because he had to give up the ball, meaning he would loose some wine money.

On the eighteenth tee Jackass told me he was sorry for accusing me of misleading him on the first green. I had been helping them all on the greens, picking up their clubs. After the round he gave me fifty cents. The other two didn't give me anything but a wave and a goodbye, but my guy gave me two dollars. He patted me on the shoulder and said that he would see me again. I went in the snack bar and got a cold drink. I saw Luther and told him about One Eye and he reminded me of how these guys could hurt me and not lose one minute sleep over it. I told him that all the guys knew it and that's why we didn't go out too far ball hawking by ourselves.

Luther asked me if I could help him with a clogged sink in the ladies locker room. He wanted me to crawl into the sink cabinet and take a wrench to the pipe; the trap was full of hair. I handed it to Luther and he said, "Those god dam women have more hair in the sink than they have on their heads," and he cleaned it like new and I put it back together. We were standing at the sink washing our hands when Linda, the one I watched with her boyfriend on the picnic table, came in and saw us at the sink and said hi to us. Luther was embarrassed and I was blushing as she took her cute ass down to her locker. Luther and I left quickly. He would probably pound his winkey thinking about that fox.

I had to get home to serve papers. I was hoping that they wouldn't be real thick. If they were, I would have to split them up and come back for the second half. My favorite customer on 30th Street was sitting on her front steps drinking a nice glass of iced tea. I was sweating as only I could sweat. She had on shorts that let me see all the way up to her crotch. I handed her the paper and she saw me looking and asked me if I saw anything I liked. I was blushing. I didn't say anything, what could I say? She was happy to see me and only too happy to let me have a look where very few eyes have feasted. She told me to bend forward so she could wipe the sweat from my face and neck. She smelled just like a vase of fresh flowers, waiting for hubby to come home. She wanted me to sit on the step with her. I wanted to stay but I was too scared. I hoped I would grow out of this shyness. I told her that I had to finish, or they would call the News Journal on me.

She told me she would see me again. I hated to walk away from that hunk of a woman. I was interested in what she had covered up, and stupid me, I got caught looking. But she put it there for me to see and took it as a complement that I looked. I told Menny about her that night and how she caught me looking up her shorts; he laughed at me for being embarrassed. I couldn't help it. I asked him why he hadn't caddied, and he said Kautz and he were fixing three bikes. To me that was a waste of time. I was making money and he wasn't.

I told Menny that I was going to caddy Friday, Saturday, and Sunday. Friday I went up to the Rock on my own, checked in with Grumpy, and was assigned to three guys. As they got closer, I could see that they were Japanese. He put me with the shortest one, Mr. Akimoto, who said for me to call him Hiro. All three of them had cameras and spoke very poor English. Why me? I was going to have to talk to Grumpy about this.

I had to show them where the tee box was. I was going to be a regular tour director on this job. I had to show them where the hole was, how far away they were from the green, and take a lot of pictures. I had to listen to their babbling all day. I was really caddying for all three of them. I hope they remembered this when we finished. By the last hole, I was drained. It was a tough day, and I never heard English for four hours. I bet I took at least 36 pictures. We walked off eighteen and they were babbling all the way to the pro shop. When I put Hiro's bag on the rack I overheard him asking the pro what the fee was. He told him $1.50. I was figuring on a big tip with all that I did. Hiro came back and gave me two dollars and asked if I had change for a dollar. I had a look on my face of shock and disappointment. I told him I didn't have change. He took one of the dollars out of my hand and went to the coffee shop to get change and gave me fifty cents. Total fee, $1.50.

He told me they were going to get something to eat in the snack bar and kept saying shank you, shank you. I knew where their car was parked because one of them went to it after nine. I had plenty of time. I ran over and let the air out of both back tires till they were completely flat. I went over to Grumpy and told him what I went through for the four hours. He said he was sorry and would make it up to me some day. He had no idea that it was going to be a problem. He did say that the other two men should have given me a tip.

I went back to the snack bar for a cold soda. I needed one. I was sitting there when I heard a big commotion in the pro shop. I could hear Hiro saying they had two flat tires, and that our parking lot was dirty. Mr. Douglas told him to call a tow truck. He was trying to get someone on the phone to understand him. After ten minutes I could hear Hiro shouting, "One hour, that's the best you can do, OK we wait." Hiro came to me and asked me to look after their bags while they sat in the snack bar. I told him I was finished caddying and to look after his own bag. I just stood up, threw my soda bottle in the trash and started walking down the road. Under my breath I was telling Hiro to kiss my ass, you cheap bastard. I found out the next day that when the tow truck came, Hiro had given the driver such a bad time that he left them and refused to tow them anywhere. It took another two hours before another tow truck would come, and that it cost Hiro $50.

When I went up to the rock Saturday it was really busy. On Sunday; I was late going to church and didn't get to the Rock until 11:00. Four caddies were ahead of me. It was after 1:00 when Peter asked me if I would caddy for one of his friends, Linda, about 1:30. I said yes, I'd seen her around the club. She was right on time. Everything stopped when she came out of the locker room. She was laughing like she knew a lot of people were looking at her. Peter was so proud. I thought, "I bet he won't be screwing her on the seventeenth hole picnic table like I saw him before." I was standing with him as she walked up. He introduced her to me and she said that she had seen me around. She said, "Babe is your name." She smiled and winked at me, opening her mouth to emphasize her wink. My legs were weak.

Linda took a lot of practice swings. Peter said he saw a lot of improvement in her swing. I wouldn't know; I was looking at her ass. She was wearing shorts today, so no crotch pictures. She was driving long and right down the middle and was only three over par after five holes. On the sixth hole he asked her how she turned her game around. She flat out told him. Babe was out on the driving range one day and I wanted to hit a few balls and he showed me a few things that I'm not going to forget. I wasn't either, she had let me manhandle her, showing her how to swing properly.

He looked at me, saying, "Babe, I didn't know you could teach too." I told him I was a better teacher than I was a player, she was a good student. I think he was getting a little mad or jealous because she was praising me for everything I did. I was getting nervous. She asked me to help her line up her putts and sometimes stood behind while I lined them up. She would rest those lovely tits on my back. I could hardly stand up at times. She sank that putt and now Peter was really pissed, jealous more like it.

She was only four over par after nine holes. Peter wanted to quit. She walked up to him and told him that she had waited too long time to shoot a round of golf like this one, and if he was going to quit then she was going to quit him. She said, "Come on Babe, the hell with him." Just then he started heading to the tenth tee saying that he was only kidding her. She told him to go and get us both a hot dog and a soda. It's hard to believe how a little patch of hair could have so much control over a man. I told her that Peter's jealous spurts were making me nervous. After all, I was the one vulnerable, the one most likely to get hurt. She told me he would never hurt me as long as she was here. I told her that I wasn't worried about him physically hitting me, but hurting me by making this great day turn into a bad feelings day.

I said, "I hope he snaps out of it and starts rooting for you like someone who cares for you." She said, "Like you, Babe." Just then my face got red. She assured me that everything was going to be OK. She was going to be the best woman player after this round got posted. The hot dog and soda came in handy. I was getting hungry. She asked me what I thought of her chances of breaking 80. I told her she couldn't miss, just stay calm. She kept saying, "Babe, you're so nice, you're so cute."

Peter told Linda he wanted me to help him out too. She told him, "Not today, he's my caddy and he's caddying for me." She could see he didn't want her to beat him. She was still eating her hot dog and taking little bites and smiling at me. I think she was giving me a message, but didn't make any sense to me. She teed off on ten and came close to out of bounds. When we got there, the ball hawker said it was out. He let it lay there for her to see. She was furious and dropped it near the wall. Too many people were waiting to go back and hit it over. She was shaken because she hit her next shot fat and short of the green. A bad chip and two putts gave her a seven. One more hole like that, and this was going to be just another day at the Rock. Peter was trying to console her, it didn't work because she was so mad that she cried a little. I told her she had eight holes to go and she could easily get those strokes back. Relax and have fun. The next two holes she shot par. Now came the 157-yard par three to an elevated green, with steep slopes on all four sides. The wind was at her back. Peter hit first. His ball just got on the green, but he had a long putt.

Linda asked me what to do. I handed her a five iron. I told her to hit it high so the wind would carry it to the green. She hit it good and high and it came down next to the pin for a gimme birdie. She was jumping up and down—what a shot. What a hole to birdie! I said nice shot and she ran over and gave me a big hug. It would have been nice to know what would have happened if she had gotten a hole in one. She tapped in and Peter two-putted. It worked out great. Now we had a long par five along the woods, all the way to the green. Linda had to be careful not to slice one in the woods. She pulled one out there, but it went into the rough. She only hit her second shot about a hundred yards. She was going to have it tough to get on the green in three. She got on in four and two-putted for a bogie six. She was starting to feel each shot. Peter was getting happier as we went on.

With three holes to go she was nine over par, so far, the best round she ever had. She kept saying thanks to me. Peter was tired of hearing it. She knew he really didn't want her to break 80. The sixteenth hole was a 186-yard par three with a lot of crazy mounds around it just like a links course. This was a good hole to make par on. The wind was blowing right to left. She was scared and asked me to help her. I told her to hit a five wood toward the mounds, so the wind would take it to the green. Peter was up. He didn't allow for the wind and ended up on the seventeenth tee. Boy was he pissed. Linda teed off and aimed at the mounds. The wind got a hold of it and it went right on the center of the green. She had a tough putt. The green had a lot of slopes. She asked me to line it up. She stood behind me again and rested those lovelies on my back again. I gave her the line three inches off the right edge. Peter said it was a straight putt. She bent over the putt and stroked it perfectly. It rimmed the cup and almost went in. She tapped in for a par, she looked at Peter and said "Straight, huh." Now he was pissed again.

The seventeenth hole was a long par five, dog leg right. There were woods all the way around and a big clump of trees in the right edge fairway. Linda needed to par this hole. They both had good drives. She was on the left side of the fairway right where she should be. Peter walked over to his ball. She told me if she could par the seventeenth and eighteenth hole she was going to give me a treat some day that every young man should have. After hearing that I was praying that she would par both of those holes; I needed a treat. Well, she did par seventeen and eighteen. Peter and Linda were jumping up and down celebrating the best round she ever had. He was finally happy for her because that was really a great round of golf for the conditions and all. Peter gave me two dollars for helping her. That was nice of him. I was happy. I felt that I accomplished something today. She asked me if I would take her bag to the locker room and put it in her locker and said she would be right behind me. The locker room was empty. Only one light was on, so it was kind of dark.

When we got to her locker, she asked me if Peter paid me. I told her he did; she gave me two dollars and kissed me on the lips. She pulled her shirt out of her shorts and had it unbuttoned and off in no time. She reached back and undid her bra. She looked at me to see if I was leaving I was scared and I couldn't make up my mind what to do, not knowing if she was going to let those beauties out to play. She told me some day soon she was gone to give me a treat, but today she was just going to let me have a look, she walked to me and kissed me on the lips with her bare tits on my chest. Her nipples looked like door knobs. I think she would have taken everything off if I hadn't walked away. I kept listening to hear if she would call me back, but she didn't and I walked out of the locker room without looking back. I would often ask myself about the fondness she had for me and again ask, why me?

One day my father told Mommy that Florida was having a lot of storms and hurricanes, and because paint jobs were scarce up here and painters were scarce down there, he and some guys were going to go to Florida and make some fast money. He would be gone about three months and would send money home every week. He rarely sent money home, and if he did it was only $30, but we were so happy he was gone and no one was getting hit or accused of something they didn't do. At the end of three months he had only sent home $180, an average of $15 a week and he never called to say when he was coming home. He didn't do anything there but drink at night and fool around with the disease-ridden bar whores.

He was only home a few days when Theresa told me that he had come home with syphilis. Can you imagine that; my mother was putting up with a drunken abuser, a non-provider, a diseased womanizer, and a child molester? He couldn't get any lower than that. I wish I didn't have to say all that, but the shame was on him. Mommy was devastated, but she was tough and weathered that storm. It scared me that people were carrying around these diseases. I became even more cautious around women after that, even though I wasn't really doing anything with them.

On my birthday, Mommy made an apple cake and I got some ice cream from Boles's to put on my cake. It doesn't get any better than that. Joan saw me the next day and wished me a very happy birthday. She kissed me thirteen times, one for each year. She moaned the whole time and pushed me into her house. She told me that she had to wrestle me bad and soon we were on our knees, and she tried to go for a fast pin. I grabbed her tits; she threw her head back and was trying to push me on my back. Her nipples were big and hard. She kept saying, "Is that all you got, Babe?" so I pinched her nipples gently and she went crazy, moaning and yelping. As she held my shoulders to the floor, she put her pelvis on my leg and started rocking. The more I pinched the more she rocked back and forth. Those nipples squeezing really got her shook up. She was going to town on my leg, but all of a sudden it was over and she lost all her strength. She collapsed on top of me. Her tit went right in my mouth. She never moved, just breathing heavily. I always wanted to give her a nibble, not to hurt her, but to see her reaction. I gave her a nibble on the nipple. The first time it was ever in my mouth she pulled back on her knees and said I was improving more each match, and she bent back over and put her hand under my neck and kissed me for the longest time, moaning. She told me I was going to make some girl very happy.

With only a few days left before I went into the seventh grade, Menny and I played our last caddies day. We were standing on the first tee when Grumpy had two of the older caddies join us. That made us nervous. Right off the bat they wouldn't walk with us for some reason. We were almost running to keep up with them. On the first hole they were mean as hell and wouldn't hold the pin for us to putt or put it back in the hole. They just let it lay on the green and walked off, not caring how we felt. So on the second hole, redheaded George, who I think is a Jerkoff, birdied the second hole (one under par). He was yelling loudly and wouldn't be quiet for us to putt and then ran off with his friend and left us on the green. When Menny and I finished putting I noticed that George had left his driver on the green. We were next to a big corn field, so I looked to see if they could see. They had their backs to us, so I picked up his driver and gave it an unbelievable throw over the trees into the corn field. It would be a miracle if he found that club.

Menny cried, "Babe, these guys are going to kill us." I told him, "They didn't see me, so fuck 'em. Don't you see how bad they were treating us?" When we got to the third tee, Jerkoff George asked me for his driver. I told him, "I am not your caddy so don't ask me again where your clubs are, or will I get your club, or did I see your club. You won't be getting any help from me, and there wasn't any driver left on the green." He started running back to the second green frantically looking all over for his new driver. Then he took off for his bag that he had left way down the third fairway so we wouldn't have to carry our bag needlessly. He started running back to us screaming that some son of a bitch was going to pay for this, but by the time he got back to us he wouldn't be fit for a good football game, let alone a golf game. You could hear him from 200 yards away; it was clear he wanted to fight with someone. When he got back to us on the tee he looked at Menny and me and was threatening us that we better not have anything to do with this. I told him not to worry, that someone would turn the club in. "They better," he said, "It was brand new. My parents gave me them for a graduation gift." I asked him if nobody turned it in, would his parents be able to replace it for him with no problem. He didn't think so; they had spent all their vacation money on these clubs. So I remarked that he better start taking better care of his equipment.

This jerk's game went from good to bad in just two holes, and he kept telling me to get out of his way. Then he asked where we got our clubs, we said, "From the trash." He asked if I was sure I didn't mean dump. I thought to myself that he would be lucky to find his clubs at all. When we neared the reservoir hole his ball was under a bush. When he hit it, the ball only went a few feet; the grass was thick and six inches high and wet. He threw his club on the ground and pulled out a seven iron. He hit his next shot good and ran off leaving me by myself I waited until he was far enough away and I picked up the club he left and threw it in the reservoir. No one saw me; I was playing my ball and not going to give him back his clubs because he didn't appreciate it. He left his bag in a landing area down the fairway, so while he was walking to the green, Menny and I putted out of turn on purpose and left him on the green to put the pin back in the hole.

At the next tee, George's buddy went first. When Jerkoff George started to tee up, I asked him what he had shot on the last hole. He said "six" and I said, "Menny and I shot fives and we are up before you, boy." This sent him into a rage he could never recover from. He told me I better watch my "boy" talk or he was going to kick Menny's and my ass before the day was over. I told him that it looked to me that he was the one having his ass kicked. "We are playing a lot better than you. If you are so God dam good, do you want to put some money on who can shoot the better round, boy?" I told him that a new rule today just for him was that it was going to be a two stroke penalty for losing a club. That alone will lose him the bet.

His spineless partner was staying as far away from him as he could. He didn't know what to do about me, because I was standing up for my self. He now was driving with a spoon (a three wood). We were on the green, where he left another club. I picked it up and gave it to him so he would think that I had nothing to do with his missing clubs. When he put it in his bag he immediately saw he was missing his two iron and started screaming at me. I told him I had just given him a club and that was the only club that I saw. He told his friend he had lost two clubs now and we were only on the eighth hole. He then turned and looked at me and said, "This better not have anything to do with you, boy, or I am going to kick your ass." I reminded him that I just gave him a club or it would have been three. "Don't worry," I said, "some one will turn it in." He said that if they were anything like us two they would keep them; I bet that's how you got your clubs. I told Menny he was going to pay for that remark, so when we stopped after the ninth hole Menny took all his balls and left him with two. I ran in for a soda and ran back out; we teed off ahead of them.

When they came out of the clubhouse we had already teed off, which of course pissed them off. He was just plain mean and was going to pay a very high price for it today. Then Jerkoff George was making fun of me and Menny, saying that we should give it up. "You can't be having any fun the way you two play," he said, not knowing we were having a ball, in fact all his balls. I asked him what he shot for nine and he said 48. I told him Menny and I shot 46, so if we should give it up, maybe after today you'll give it up too. He didn't know how to take it.

On the eleventh hole he did the worst thing you can do in golf, he shanked it. He was so mad he threw his club over the green. From my vantage point I saw it go deep in a holly bush, almost impossible to see. He kept looking in the sand trap. I told him it was probably under the sand, so he went on his hands and knees rummaging all through the sand trap like some deranged person. Seeing him from a distance would make you think that he should be in a straight jacket. Menny and I were leaving a false trail away from the holly bush. Finally with the sand trap all messed up, he was raking it so Grumpy wouldn't yell at him. His partner told him, "George we have to go now, we're getting backed up." Menny and I winked at each other: three new clubs gone with seven holes to go. I told him not to worry, someone would turn it in, and at this point he wanted to strangle me. His face and neck were redder than his hair. "There you go again with that shit don't worry someone gone to turn it in again," he said, "No one is going to turn anything in. Are you nuts?"

I told Jerkoff George that if he played another round of golf like this one he wouldn't have any clubs left and he would have to get his next set out of the trash like we did. Then he sliced his drive in the woods and couldn't find his ball, so he went into his bag and started screaming again, "All my balls are missing! Some son of a bitch took all my balls. His partner was really starting to get concerned. Jerkoff George said he only had two balls left. I said to Menny, "Did you know he only has two balls left, Big Ones."

He kept saying how he could slice his favorite club. Somehow he was going to mess up with that spoon I had to be careful not to get caught, so on the seventeenth hole he walked to his ball; his bag was up ahead. He was a long way from the green and he knew if he hit his spoon again he had to be careful not to hit the clump of trees in the fairway up ahead. He ran to his bag for a three iron after he stood his favorite spoon up against the tree near the edge of the woods. He ran back to his ball and hit his three iron well, but the ball hit a tree and ricocheted deep into the woods. Oh, was he pissed. He ran up to see if he could find his ball, not caring if we hit our shot or not. His partner was far away and couldn't see either one of us, so I picked up the spoon, the club that he loved so much, and threw it deep in the woods where no human had ever placed a foot before. When I got up to him he asked me if I heard the noise in the woods. I told him that it was probably the two bears that had been seen here for the past year. He said that there weren't any bears around here, so I asked why he didn't go in to find his ball. He looked at me and said I was a wise ass and I better not mess with him. I couldn't wait to see him on the eighteenth tee when he couldn't find his favorite club.

Next Jerkoff George dropped a ball near the woods. He only had a six iron shot but he had to clear some trees on the right. He hit it fine but not high enough. It hit the only tree in his way and went deep in the woods near the picnic area. We walked on the green, putted out, and walked to the eighteenth tee, leaving him trying to catch up. I could hear the clubs he had left rattling in his bag as he was running behind us. When he got to us he had a nerve to ask me to lend him a golf ball for this hole, so I reached in my bag and gave him a Titleist with three cuts in it. I told him it was all I had but he could have one. He looked at it and said it was unfit to use. I told him it was the best I could get out of the trash pile. He threw it in the woods.

He walked over to Menny and asked him to lend George a ball. Menny gave him a Titleist that had a big gash in it that he had filled with soap so you couldn't tell it was ruined. It was just for an occasion like this. Menny told him that if he cuts it he would owe Menny 75 cents. George picked up his bag to get his spoon to drive with, but it wasn't in his bag. He said,

"I know where it is; I stood it against the tree." He took off running across the fairway to the clump of trees, running in front of the foursome coming up the seventeenth hole. They were yelling "fore," but he kept running and they kept screaming at him. He ran to the tree where his club had been, pulling his hair out of his head and jumping up and down as he looked over at us. He ran back to us like a wild man; the other foursome was threatening to turn him in. We had already teed off. He started on me, "Boy you saw me put that club against that tree," and I said, "I saw you carry it to your bag when you went to get your three iron. I saw you put it in your bag. Don't you remember that, George?" "Well where is it? It's not in my bag." I shook my head I don't know. "Don't call me a boy, I am not your lackey."

We were down to where our drives were lying. He dropped his ball where we were and hit his shot to the green. When we got to the green I told him not to worry, someone would turn in his spoon (three wood), if they weren't like Menny and me, and keep it. He wanted to just beat me up. His buddy told him he was away, so he looked down at his ball and said, "Hey, this isn't my ball. My ball didn't have a cut in it." Menny said, "The ball I lent you didn't have a cut in it, either." He said, "Jim gave me a new ball and this one has a cut in it, a big cut." Menny told him that the ball cost 75 cents and we agreed that's what you would owe me if you cut it.

This Jerkoff stood there for the longest time looking down at his ball and said he wasn't going to pay Menny one cent, but we told him we were going to turn him in to the caddy master and he would be barred from the course. We would bring Mr. Douglas in on this because you, George, reneged on a simple promise to pay for a favor. He didn't want to but he paid Menny. He wasn't that dumb. He walked off the green one upset dude, after losing four brand new clubs, at least a half dozen balls, and 75 cents. He shot seventeen strokes worse than Menny and I.

Later Menny and I sat near the putting green drinking a cold soda, just recalling what happened to that Jerkoff. Menny said, "I took a chance throwing those clubs," and I told him I guess stealing his golf ball on the tenth tee wasn't taking a chance. "What you did was riskier than what I did." Menny said, "Babe, if he had caught you he would have beat you up bad." I replied, "I guess you would have not helped me because you didn't want to be involved. I wonder if I could count on you in a pinch."

Just then George's buddy came over and told me he thought I was responsible for George's clubs disappearing. He couldn't prove it but it was the best Houdini trick he ever saw, now you see it and now you don't. I said, "I can't believe that you have the freaking balls to come over to me and declare your opinion when I personally didn't give a shit what you thought." He said I had to be ornery as hell to pull that kind of shit and I was lucky that he didn't like George or I would be in deep shit. I said, "Tell me how do you mean that. I would be in deep shit if you don't have any proof that I had anything to do with it? You are talking out of your asshole, mister. Maybe its because you are one." I told him he was lucky that we liked him or he would be in deep shit. I asked, "Where were you when he was calling us names? You say we are lucky you didn't like him. Did you tell him to shut up? No! If you didn't like him, what are you doing playing with him? Why are you over here trying to convince us that you didn't like him when you came over here on a fishing expedition? You never said a thing to this piece of shit; where were you when he called us bums and that our clubs came from the trash? Did you say anything, friend? Where were you when he made fun of our clothes, how we played, when we beat him by seventeen strokes? You didn't say anything because you're a liar, and you want to see if we will admit to being involved in the disappearance of his clubs, so you can run back to that jerk off and be a hero and tell him we took his clubs. Well it backfired on you; we don't know anything about his graduation clubs. If you learned anything today, it has to be 'Don't treat anyone like you wouldn't want to be treated yourself.'"

His buddy reminded us again that George got his clubs for graduating from high school and it was going to be hard for him to replace them. I told him I didn't care how he got them; if he graduated from high school he proved today that he didn't learn anything. His buddy started walking away, saying that if he hadn't seen it with his own eyes he would have never believed it. He stopped and said, "That golf ball trick was the best, I've never saw a setup like that one. Hell, you probably had soap in the cut ball. Anyway you guys are tough."

I told him I hoped he never had to compete against me someday because he would lose big time. I told him that I blamed him for the shitty day we just went through because he could have prevented Jerkoff George from showing his true colors with the disrespect that he showed us all the way around the golf course. Not one word out of his mouth. "Look at how you two treated us on the first and second hole. You never ever said anything civil to us, let alone walk with us or ever hold the pin for us so we could putt. I hope that I will never have to play golf with anyone like you 'spineless' again." He walked away; having failed in his attempt to scare us into owning up about Jerkoff George's missing golf clubs.

Menny and I laughed for days about Jerkoff George. I got him good, and maybe some day he would start treating people under him a little better. He thought because he had new clubs the rest of us were bums. Menny and I had to keep the story to ourselves because this kind of tale would spread like wildfire. Now we had another secret we couldn't tell anyone.

I asked Menny if Theresa told him about the disease that Daddy brought home from Florida. He said he knew. I didn't understand how Mommy could ever have had a baby with him; it was a mystery to both of us. To the neighbors it looked like Mommy had a lovely new baby, so everything must be OK at the Toner residence. You couldn't blame the neighbors for thinking that. But what must they be thinking? Why would she have another baby? The only answer was that she had six children to bring up, no matter what.

11

It was hard for me starting the seventh grade after such a great summer. There were things happening that no one would have believed. I was as tan as a life guard, now my face didn't look so red when I blushed. Meanwhile back at the Rock we were trying to get in a few more caddy jobs before the bad weather set in Menny and I went up to caddy and grumpy asked Menny and I to caddy for the two men standing by the old oak tree, they looked nice so we said ok. This time I told Menny that I was going to choose the guy I was going to caddy for. I chose the guy in the blue sweater, whose name was Chris. Menny had no choice but to caddy for the other guy.

We walked to the first tee and Chris and Menny's golfer, Ed, were happy to get out and play golf before the leaves started to fall, that made it very hard to find your ball in places. The men told us they had a heavy bet on, so they could use our help with whatever we could contribute to the match.

On the first hole I noticed that Chris didn't count all his strokes, and Ed couldn't tell because he was across the other side of the hole and couldn't see that Chris was cheating. One of Chris's shots hit a Christmas tree and Ed never saw it, so when they finished, Chris told Ed he had five, and Ed said he had five, so they tied the hole, but really Ed had won the hole.

I told Menny that Chris was cheating and tied a hole that he really lost, but Menny said not to tell him any more; he didn't want to hear it. By the fourth hole Chris was ahead in the match and was starting to brag to me how he was going to win $10.00 on the first nine-hole bet.

I was telling Menny how upset I was about Chris's cheating, when Chris's drive stopped at the base of the tree in the rough. He tried to hit it but hit a hidden tree root instead, so he kicked the ball far enough away so as to have a clear shot to the green. He hit a beautiful shot to the green about six feet from the pin. He made his putt and yelled out, "That's for a birdie!" and beat Ed again by cheating. According to my count Chris had cheated on every hole, and was three holes up on Ed with four holes left on the first nine.

On the next hole, a par three, Chris hit his four iron right in the trap. When we got there it was in a footprint while Ed's ball was on the other side of the green hidden in the rough. Chris moved his ball and hit it fat, not getting it out of the trap, and had to try again. This time he finally got it on the green and was laying four but he told Ed that he was laying two, and poor Ed was laying an honest three because that rough was tough. They both two-putted and Chris won the hole. Ed was being beat by Chris's cheating.

Now Chris closed Ed out of their match and won a fast $10.00, and Ed, in shock, wanted to press Chris for the last two holes. (Press means that a new bet takes place for the two remaining holes for the same amount of money.) Ed was a good golfer but couldn't beat Chris's cheating. The eighth hole was a draw, and the ninth hole was a long dogleg right with woods on the right all the way down to the green. Ed's drive was at the edge of the woods and he had to slice his second shot to get it on the green. Chris's was behind a bush, and he had to hit the shot of his life to get it close to the green. He took a big swing and actually missed but made it look like a practice shot. He recovered and took a soft swing and hit it down in front of the green, while Ed's ball also missed the green. They both chipped on the green and were six feet away, both laying three or so. Chris putted first and made it, while Ed missed his, as Chris was yelling "Yes, I won." Again Ed didn't know that Chris cheated him and really tied the hole and didn't lose the press bet at all, or any of the bets. Chris had Ed believing that he had lost $20.00 so far on the front nine holes.

I was really upset because Ed was really a nice guy and didn't deserve this, but what was I going to do? Chris bought me lunch and was really overjoyed with his win so far and asked Ed if he was ready for the back nine. Ed told him that he was going to press Chris for the back nine bet.

That meant they were playing for $20.00. I was hoping that Ed would catch Chris cheating and refuse to pay him.

The tenth hole had a stone wall all around it all the way to the green. Ed hit his drive in the middle of the fairway while Chris's drive was up against the stone wall. He picked up his ball and yelled over to Ed that his ball was in bounds and placed it back so he could have an unobstructed shot. It took balls to do that. They both hit their balls on the green and two-putted for a par, but Chris moved his ball and had cheated to be able to hit his second shot.

The eleventh hole was tied also, and the twelfth hole was the long par three over the creek to an elevated green. Ed hit his shot over the green while Chris hit his drive that bounced off the green in the high thick grass. Chris swung as hard as he could and his ball never moved. He yelled over to Ed and asked if Ed wanted him to shoot first. Ed said yes and Chris hit his improved shot on the green about ten feet from the pin. Ed's shot was nice and about only six feet from the pin with a steep downhill putt, which was going to be tough. Chris two-putted while Ed's ball rimmed the cup, which gave it more momentum to run far past the hole. It took two more putts to get in the hole. He lost that one and didn't know that Chris had whiffed his second shot on the slope of the hill out of his sight.

They tied the next three holes, with Chris pulling every dirty trick on nice guy Ed that he could get away with. I was noticeably upset over this cheating and Chris was starting to see it in my behavior. Ed won the par three sixteenth hole, so the match on the back nine holes was even with two holes to go. The seventeenth hole was the dogleg right past the picnic area, par five. Ed hit first because he won the sixteenth hole, a beautiful shot up the middle of the fairway, not that far but in good shape. Chris sliced his drive toward the woods. I could hear it hit the tree but I couldn't see where it went. I walked with Chris to where the ball hit the tree, and he pointed for me to look for his ball over near the big rocks. When I got there I turned to see Chris put a ball at the edge of the rough and yell out for everyone to hear him that he had found his ball.

Ed had hit his second shot 180 yards from the green, and Chris hit one through the clump of trees and was about the same distance from the green as Ed. Chris hit his ball first and sliced it to the right off the green, almost in the woods. Ed's shot was short of the green and had an uphill chip shot to the pin. Chris was looking for his ball, and before I got to him he had already found it and was sitting up high ready for a great chip shot. I know that he had done something because I'd never seen a lie sitting up so nicely. Nevertheless Chris chipped his ball within three feet of the pin and was cheering uncontrollably. He was laying four but I knew differently. Poor Ed chipped his ball too hard and went twelve feet past the pin to the edge of the green.

They both were laying four. While Ed had the hardest putt, he knew things were looking good for Chris. Poor Ed two-putted for a six and Chris one-putted for a five and won the hole, one up on Ed going into the eighteenth hole. I couldn't take this any longer and was going to wait for an opening to talk to Chris. Walking up the eighteenth fairway, Chris told me that he was going to give me $5.00 for being a good caddy. I told him as much as I needed the money I would only accept it if he told Ed how much he cheated. If I deserved the $5.00 for being a good caddy before I said that, then I should still deserve the $5.00 after it was all said and done.

Chris told me he didn't cheat and wouldn't cheat his friend Ed out of anything. I told him that if he didn't go over and tell his friend that he didn't play fairly, then I would. He turned and got up in my face and told me to butt out; it wasn't any of my business and I was only getting paid to caddy and not anything else. I asked him if this was his final decision and he said yes.

I took his bag with me and called out to Ed to wait for me to catch up to him. He and Menny waited for me. I told Ed that he didn't lose to Chris and that Chris cheated as much as two strokes on every hole and he never saw it. Chris came up behind me and said I was lying and that I didn't like him and didn't want him to win all that money. In defense of myself I asked Ed what I had to gain from saying that Chris cheated him out of $50.00. Hell, he offered me $5.00 coming up the eighteenth fairway because I was a good caddy.

You won't believe what happened next. Ed told me that he was in the war with Chris and he trusted him with his life and that he wouldn't do anything to ever harm him in any way. They were in the landing at Normandy and got through that nightmare and vowed to each other that they would always be there for each other. My reply was, "You trusted him with your life and now you can say you trust him with your money also."

Chris said he could never accept any money from Ed after what I accused him of. Ed said, "Nonsense, you beat me fair and square and it's only fair that I pay you." Chris replied that he wouldn't accept anything. I spoke up, saying, "It looks like I am the bad guy around here but I don't care. I just wanted to make sure that you didn't lose any money and it looks like that is going to be the case. Now if you don't mind, Chris, why don't you pay me the $5.00 you promised me going up the eighteenth fairway?" He said, "I only planned to pay you $2.00 and that's all I am going to pay you, and after what you accused me of you lucky that I will pay you at all." I spoke up and told him that if he didn't pay me he would have a bag full of broken clubs. Menny said that Chris couldn't take both of us on so he should make a decision now. Menny backed me up. As long as we stayed together we would be unbeatable. The big cheat reached into his pocket and gave me $5.00 and I dropped his bag on the ground and walked away.

Menny walked to the parking lot with Ed and met me down by the putting green where I was enjoying a cold drink and a long-awaited hot dog with onions, mustard, and a little relish. When I bit into that dog the juices squirted into my mouth, satisfying me more than I could explain. Menny told me that he also told Ed that he saw Chris cheating all the time and that I was telling the truth. Ed said he would have to think about it for a while because of how much they had been through during the war. Menny looked at me and said, "Babe, was it worth it?" I told him that it was for me because I couldn't see this guy cheating on every hole to win. They were friends and friends don't hurt their friends like that.

Around that time, I finally decided to go out for the basketball team at C.O.K. Mr. Williamson was still coaching; he said that only 12 guys were going to make the team. So before we started back to school we practiced every day for hours, and the day came when the coach would pick the team and gave us our uniforms. I made it I was the twelfth player! I was so proud to be on that team. I tried hard, but believe it or not, the effects of smoking were showing up on me Already, whenever I ran up and down the court, after a while I would dry heave and gag. So I rarely got to play and always had butterflies before the game, but it was good experience for me. Mr. Williamson was a good coach, and we won most of our games. We even beat the Ferris Reform School, a mean bunch, but playing with the older guys in the yard had been tougher.

That year, I finally had to give in that there wasn't any Santa Claus. Mommy really needed our help, and we didn't expect a lot for Christmas. I hustled all the time. I gave her most of my earnings and paper route money, around $10 or $12 a week and whatever Theresa gave her. It added up to a lot of money. The News Journal offered Menny and me calendars to sell to our customers for Christmas. It was going to cost us $12, so we ordered 100. Most of our customers gave us a dollar, but some people only gave us a quarter.

I went to that good-looking girl's house on 30th and West Street to see if she wanted to buy a calendar. When she opened the door, she was so beautiful she took my breath away. She invited me in and bought a calendar for a dollar. She insisted on me having a cup of tea with her and held my left hand the whole time I drank it. She was interested in what I did when I wasn't delivering news papers. I told her that Menny and I were always trying to do things that could help our mother out, and that we worked because my father wasn't able to support us. She told me I was nice and that she was glad that I wasn't scared of her anymore. She said her husband was late coming home from work and asked me to stay awhile. I stood up and told her my brother was waiting for me. Then she hugged me so tight that I felt every part of her against me. She kissed me all over my face and told me she had missed me. There was a lot of water in her eyes. Where was this girl's husband? He should be cashing in on all this affection; if it were me I would have had her on her back for most of my time off from work.

She walked me to the door, taking my hand and wrapping my arm around her hip. When we got to the door, she put my hand on her left ass cheek and slid it across her ass and down her leg. She told me that I was special, and she would never hurt me. Then she winked at me and closed the door. I was a nervous wreck but felt it couldn't get much better than this. I could tell that this girl really felt something for me and was slowly working up to something more. She was horny as hell. If I were older she wouldn't be horny any more. She could get anyone, but she liked me, a nervous, shy paper boy.

Menny and I made $85 profit on the calendars: $75 for Mommy and $5 apiece for us. She was crying with happiness. She said, "If you two young men can make that kind of money, what it is going to be like when you grow up and get married?"

In the spring the call went out for the Christ Our King baseball team. I decided to go out for third base because with my arm, I could throw from anywhere in the park. I found out an eighth grader named Ackerson was going out for third base, too. Right off the bat you could see that he had an attitude. He was an eighth grader and felt he should be first string. I showed up for every practice, ran on and off the field, hustled at everything, and showed a lot of enthusiasm. At our last practice before our first game, the coach called us all together and announced all the first string positions, his starters. He called out, "Third base, Babe Toner." I was shocked. After Ackerson objected that there was no way a seventh grader could beat out an eighth grader for anything, the coach told him, loudly enough for the team to hear, "Babe out-hustled you, he ran everywhere he went, and he picked up bats and gloves for people. He helped everyone, not to mention his arm. He's a hustler and he will start at third base and that's the end of that."

I played baseball as if I were in the street. I was intense and tried to steal every base. I could bunt, took big leads, and talked it up in the field. The coach would say, "I would rather you strike out swinging, than being called out." Still, Ackerson was always waiting for me to fall on my face. I hit in every game, and we won a lot. I loved it. I also knew that I played baseball a lot better than basketball. I didn't have the confidence in basketball that I had in baseball.

The school year flew by, and based on my previous experience, I was nervous on the last day of school. Yes, Sister wanted to see me after school. She told me I did well this year, but I was still to be on probation for 90 days in eighth grade to see if I could adapt to the harder work. It had been the same old message for the past six years. I did get an award for never missing a day of school. What a combination: an award and probation, all at the same time. Sister said I had a good spirit, that what was pulling me through. She told me to keep trying and never give up on anything and I would always come through a winner.

I wanted to do so much, caddy, golf, and do some other adventurous things. A lot of the older guys didn't show up to caddy, but the same rules applied. Check in with Grumpy so he could assign jobs. The caddy fee was now two dollars for 18 holes. I caddied at least three and sometimes four times a week. I loved to ball hawk but we couldn't go by ourselves, especially Menny and I, because of the way we had shot the bums hiding in the grass with our BB guns. If I found five balls, I would be happy and would use them on caddie's day. Menny and I were still committed to improving our golf. I was still trying to hit my long irons and was getting better with my five irons. I was determined to break 100. This could be the summer to do it.

We went up to the Rock one Friday, hoping we would get good caddy jobs before the weekend. We got a job with three teachers, two of whom wanted a caddy. They taught the eighth and ninth grade in Elkton, Maryland, and we got along real well. It was nice to meet some good people. Their girlfriends showed up after the ninth hole and wanted to walk with us the last nine holes. They had been drinking and were very flirtatious, which pissed off those nice school teachers. We didn't want any part of this situation; we just wanted to caddy.

One girlfriend needed to go to the bathroom while we were out on the course. I told her there wasn't any place to go except in the woods, where you had to be careful about the snakes. I told her to back up against a tree squat and pee, and her boyfriend, Billy, took her by the hand and took her in the woods. I saw her pull down her shorts, take one leg out of her shorts and underwear, and do as I said. She told me that was a good idea, and it seemed like the hotter it got the sillier they got.

Then the other girls wanted to take a pee in the woods, too. They heard my idea about how to piss against a tree without holding on, but one of them wanted me to hold her hands so she wouldn't fall over. Her boyfriend got mad and told her to piss in her pants, so she did, and looked a mess. Her shorts were wet and so were her shoes. I told her I could rinse out her shorts and undies in the creek, and that her boyfriend was on the tee, 200 yards away, so he couldn't see. She grabbed me and ran in the woods, stood by a big oak tree, and handed me her clothes. "Nice bush," I thought. I ran to the creek and rinsed them in minutes. I wrung them out and ran back to her. She didn't care; she stepped into her panties right in front of me, looking hot in those undies. She jumped into her shorts and was standing by the edge of the woods before her boyfriend got to her. He didn't notice her clothes. She ran out to him and gave him a big hug. If she could undress in front of me, what must she be doing to him? We walked off the eighteenth green and he ran off with her toward his car. I think he was going to give her a checkup. Our guys quickly gave us two dollars; I think they were embarrassed because they disappeared fast.

The next day we went to caddy, Grumpy said the line was backed up and a lot of bags were on the rack, so we sat in the caddy shack and waited. We were smoking when Abee came in and sat down. He never talked to anyone, just sat there and stared. I asked him if he checked in with Grumpy and he said yes. I thought, poor Abee, Grumpy will probably put him with Oscar. When we saw Abee we realized how lucky we were; he was trying to overcome a very serious problem. It made me sad to see him walk. How was he going to caddy and get home? We would never allow anyone to hurt him, but he probably didn't know we felt that way.

Then Grumpy called Menny and me for a job. A guy named Kenny was standing there, and Menny said he would take him. Grumpy said my guy was in the bathroom, and we still had three foursomes ahead of us, so we weren't going anywhere. My guy came out of the bathroom and introduced himself as Ernie. He must have had a hard time pissing because he had piss all over his fly area. I told Menny we were in for it. Kenny walked like his nuts were dragging on the ground, and he had to weigh over 400 pounds. There wasn't any way he could screw some girl with her on the bottom. If he didn't crush her, he would suffocate her. Menny kept saying, "Babe, wouldn't you pay to see it?"

Ernie was swinging real hard warming up; you could tell he meant business. My first impression was that he wasn't that friendly, but it was still early. I could be wrong but I was a pretty good judge. It wasn't long before Ernie was laying down what he expected from Menny and me, so Menny told him real fast, "Look, pal, I'm not caddying for you, I'm caddying for Kenny and will take orders from Kenny, so back off." Ernie looked over at me; I was laughing and he was fuming, but Kenny told him to shut up and play golf. The other two guys stayed away to themselves like they knew what was coming from Kenny and Mr. Piss My Pants.

When Grumpy told us we were up, the two quiet ones hit first, and then Ernie swung so hard he sliced it. I knew he wouldn't slow down, and if he played his shot far enough left he might be able to keep it in the fairway. We were walking toward the green when he asked me if there were any bathrooms on the course. I told him no, and the look on his face was scary; he never said anything else about it. I looked over at Kenny, still dragging his nuts around. I would give Ernie the line but he just couldn't putt. His second putt was as long as his first putt, and he three-putted that green.

As we walked off the green, Ernie cut a couple of farts. He apologized and said that he didn't go to the bathroom this morning and had some gas. We were walking up the second fairway along the corn field when he just flat out told me, "Babe I really have to shit; what am I going to do?" He said he could never get to the clubhouse in time, so I took him over to the edge of the corn field where there was a big tree and told him, like I had told the girls, to back up against the tree and let it go. I got him a towel from his bag, and he told me he was going to take care of me for this. He was pulling up his pants when I noticed he had shit on his shoes. I told him to hold on and I ran back to the water fountain with his towel. I soaked his towel and ran back and rung it out on his shoes. When we wiped them off they were just like new. He had a few shit stains on his pants; I don't know what he wiped his ass with but I did see a shit-stained hanky on the ground.

Everyone else was on the green waiting for us and wanting to know what was going on. I told them we were looking for Ernie's ball and why don't you guys finish up without us, that we would meet them on the next tee. When we got to the tee Ernie told me, "Babe, you sure are fast with your answers, thank you." He kept telling me how much he appreciated my help and that nobody else would have helped him like I did. Later Menny and I stood off the tee while they were hitting and Menny pointed out the shit on Ernie's pant cuffs. Laughing, I said, "You should have seen him before I cleaned him up; he had shit everywhere. We weren't looking for his ball; he had to take a shit."

Menny said that Kenny's bag was too heavy; Menny looked in and found enough food to open up a store. Menny said that the more Kenny ate the lighter his bag got. I told him he better hope Kenny didn't have to take a shit out here. I told him he would need a big fire hose to clean his big ass off, and we were laughing just thinking about it.

We stopped at the clubhouse because the tenth hole was backed up as usual. Ernie and Kenny got us hot dogs and Cokes. Kenny had two hot dogs and two sodas, and I thought, "Holy Christ, this man was going to shit this place down." Menny went into the bathroom and came out with half a roll of toilet paper and put it in his bag just in case. We ended up having a 30-minute wait before we could tee off on ten. I looked for Abee, but he was gone. I hope he got a good job. Whoever he caddied for would have to be a little understanding because Abee would just be carrying the bag.

We were out a couple of holes on the back nine when Menny called and waved me over. Frantically, I dropped my bag and ran over. Kenny was sitting on the ground in front of a tree with his pants down. I said to Menny, "He's supposed to be bent over, not sitting on the ground." He said Kenny had slipped and fallen backwards and was now sitting on a big pile of shit and that we had to pull him off and get him on his feet. I grabbed Kenny's towel and ran to the water fountain; I drenched it and filled up a bottle with water as well. I ran back looking like I sat right in the middle of a water fountain. We had to pull him up, thank God he helped, and Menny gave him the toilet paper. I had to pour water over his big ass hoping that this would be enough to clean him up. He kept wiping his ass and legs with that half roll of toilet paper and wet towel. It seemed like there was more shit than we thought, so I told him to bend over toward me and told Menny to hand me what's left of the bottle of water. I poured it where I thought his ass was which was not easy. He was so happy that we cleaned him up, he could have kissed us. I looked down; the pile of shit that would have been eight inches high was now twelve inches round with his ass print in it. That was some shit; he must have been saving this up for days.

It all happened so fast that Ernie was up on the green. I told them to finish up; Kenny was happy and like a new man. We made good time, and

201

while we were walking up the eighteenth fairway Ernie went to his left and Kenny went to his right, near the trees. Kenny waved me over. He had his dick in his hand, getting ready to piss, when he wanted to know if it was all right to piss on the pile of sand. I told him there were too many snakes to piss here at the maintaince shed. I reminded him that there were snakes that hung around the sand pile that news scared him causing his little dick to fall back in his pants. Now he is pissing his pants. What a sight. Menny said that I didn't have to scare him, but I said I was just pointing out the dangers of pissing over there. Menny asked Kenny why he had let go of it. Kenny replied, "I didn't; as soon as my Oliver heard 'snake' he jumped back in my pants for me to protect him. So he showed his gratitude by pissing down my pant leg. Babe, you know how unpredictable they are!"

Afterwards Menny and Kenny ran into the parking lot. Menny was helping him into his car. I saw the two quiet golfers smiling at him, getting in their car. Ernie asked me if all my caddy jobs were like this. I told him no, but each one is different. He told me that he appreciated everything I did for him. It could have been very embarrassing for him and I came to the rescue. We walked to the parking lot, and when we got to his car I put his clubs in the trunk. He grabbed my hand and put a five dollar bill in it. I told him he didn't have to and he said, "Nonsense, you earned every penny of it."

I saw Menny up at the putting green. We laughed and laughed about those guys, and Menny said Kenny had given him five dollars and two dollars for me. I told him Ernie had given me five dollars, too. This was a good money day. Menny and I split the two dollars Kenny gave me. We had enough for one day. We got home around 3:00, just the right time to fall asleep before supper. We gave Mommy our five dollars. Thank God we had a little stash; the house payment was tough to make with what my father was giving her. Something about that scared me, so I wanted to build up a stash from my caddying money. Sometimes I had a reoccurring dream that Mommy would die. That used to scare the hell out of me, too. I was too frightened to tell anybody, so I kept it to myself.

The next day Menny said he was going to take a day off from caddying, but I headed to the Rock. It was after 9:00 on Sunday; the place was loaded with golfers, but only a handful of caddies. I just wanted a non-challenging day, but on this job, Grumpy told me to be careful. He thought the golfers were drinking. He was right; they smelt like beer. My guy, whose name was Rob, was loud and pretty drunk I wanted to tell Grumpy I didn't want to caddy for them, but I was afraid he would send me home. So I didn't say anything. If they ruined my day, I'd ruin theirs for sure. I wished I had someone with me.

The heat wasn't going to be good for Rob. He was going to feel it in a couple of hours. He could really hit a long ball, but he couldn't see it. He was yelling at me to make sure I saw his ball, because if I lost one, he was going to deduct it from my caddy fee. He sliced his second shot so badly that it must have gone into two different fairways. He spun around and said, "Kid, I hope you saw that one." I told him I did and that it went straight down the middle. We got to where it should have been. I told Rob that it must have plugged; the ground was wet. He couldn't find it and the others insisted on going back to where he hit it from. They were playing for money so they made him go back and hit it over. He was pissed off, jumping up and down saying, "It's not fair, the ball plugged and you're penalizing me for that."

Rob kept telling me in an angry way that I better keep an eye on his ball. He was the last to tee off on the second hole. The other two were picking up their bags, so they didn't see him hit his ball. It sliced so deep in the corn field that they wouldn't find it until the harvest in October. He turned to me and told me to take him to his ball. I told him it was in the middle of the fairway, a perfect drive. We got up to about 250 yards but couldn't find it. We looked everywhere; I found a big wet spot and said it must have plugged around here. He did everything he could to find his ball. His shoes were very muddy and his club was muddy from dragging it through the soft ground. He said to his two buddies, "This ball can't be found." They told Rob to drop one and just take a stroke penalty. He cried, "One stroke penalty! This is killing me!" He'd lost another hole.

Rob dubbed his next tee shot because he'd started to swing real hard. It only went 50 yards. He hit his second shot up the edge of the fairway, but it hit a tree limb and went up the reservoir embankment. He never saw it, so I told him it was under the tree up ahead by the green. When we got there, there was no ball to be found, just a groundhog hole. I told him it must have gone down that hole, and not to put his hand down there or they would eat his hand off. His buddy told him to drop one under the tree with another one stroke penalty. He said if this kept up, he was going to run out of balls and money.

The other two guys were going to take him broke, and he said he wouldn't have any money to pay me. I told him that he wouldn't be allowed to leave the premises until he did pay me. We argued back and forth about his ability to pay me, and by the ninth hole Rob was so far down on his match that he could never catch up. I went up to Grumpy and told him. He told me to come to me right away if he didn't pay me.

The other golfers were having a good time seeing their buddy lose his shirt. It finally came out that they were playing a ten dollar Nassau. A Nassau is a game in which golfers bet on the first nine holes, the second nine holes, and then on the overall round, which was a good way to cut some of your losses. The best Rob could do was win the back nine, but he hit the ball out of bounds on ten and lost that hole. He hit the railroad tracks on eleven, and I saw the ball bounce back in the rough inbounds, but his buddies said it went out of bounds. When he lost that hole, he wanted to fight. He hit his next ball in the creek where the water ran real fast. The water flow would take it away and he would never find it. By the time we got to the creek it was gone. When his buddies told him to drop one and take a one stroke penalty, he got hot and wanted to blame me. His buddies came over and told him to leave the caddy alone; he knew at this point he was going to lose $30, which was a lot of money. I knew he was only going to give me two dollars, but that was OK, I was glad to just see him lose because he was so nasty.

Next Rob tried to carry the big ditch with the stream going through it. He hit his ball right in the middle, and he was in deep trouble. His buddies were laughing at him. They almost came to blows, and after that hole he was just hitting balls. He tried to be nice to me coming up eighteen, but I didn't pay any attention to him. He reached in his pocket coming off the eighteenth green and gave me two dollars. He told me to take his bag to his car in the parking lot and I told him that I don't work the lot, I was just a caddy. He said he was going to lodge a complaint against me. I asked him if his complaint was going to include that I couldn't find any of his fucked-up shots. He ran up to me and got in my face as if he was going to hit me, but he stopped short. I told him not to play golf if he had been drinking because the two don't mix. I dropped his bag and walked away from him. He was yelling for me to carry his bag; his buddies left him there like the fool he was. This is the trash that finds its way onto public golf courses.

The next caddie's day, I got a group together and we met at 8:30 for some crazy golf. Donald was having all the fun; when he laughed you could hear him a mile away. I tried to run and jump a creek on the twelfth hole, and I ended up getting my feet stuck in the mud. I came right out of my shoes onto my knees on the embankment. I looked around at my shoes slowly filling with water. Donald was laughing his ass off at me. I sat on the rock and held my shoes in the swiftly running water to clean them off. I kind of liked my wet shoes and feet; for some reason it was comfortable for me. I wished I had better clubs. I knew my old clubs were holding me back. I had a good swing, a little fast, but I was willing to practice.

When I got home, Joan spotted me and asked if I wanted to lie out back with her. She got out a lounge chair for me to lie in, I found a pair of wrinkled shorts, and we laid out together. She kept holding my hand, squeezing it for me to know she was still here. She told me she wanted to be a beautician; I told her she would be good at it. She looked at me and said, "Babe, you always say the right thing; that's why you're the only one I let wrestle me. I know how nervous you get, but that's what makes it more fun, you being shy and nervous." She kept adjusting her top so I could see what I was missing. She had the neatest laugh, kind of sexy. I don't know if I could put her fire out; I had the hose, not the nerve.

Mrs. Toskas brought us out some ice tea; she said, "Babe is that all you have to do sit out in the sun all day?" I said I was keeping Joan company. She messed up my hair and went in. Joan told me to lay back and quit looking at her boobs, laughing and slapping my hand saying, "You naughty boy." I told her she made me that way; we both decided it was getting hot. I needed a bath; the shower at my house was too cold with no hot water. I had to carry some hot water up the back stairs; Mommy said no hot water until September.

Where was the summer going? I kept busy every day. While Menny and I were busy, my father was again disrupting our lives. One night, Theresa ran into my mother, crying and saying that my father was trying to pull her onto the floor. I could hear my mother screaming at my father to get out of the house, and of course that pissed him off and he wanted to fight. Menny and I tried to intervene, but Mommy hit him in the face with a wooden coat hanger, cutting his forehead. With four of us against him, he just walked up the hallway to go to bed. Poor Theresa. How could she sleep at night with her pervert father nearby? We could blame his father for these antics, but I also blamed the booze and caving in to the easy way and not caring about the hardships he was putting his family through. He had two young boys keeping his house, giving my mother at least $25 dollars a week. Where was the shame? He had no education and no tact; he didn't know what it was or how to use it.

I was getting some good caddy jobs until the Saturday before we went back to school. When Menny and I got up to the Rock, Grumpy asked if we would pick up the trash, so we went and got a rake and a broom and a small pail to put the dog shit in. Menny and I saw Rob, that wise son of a bitch who wasn't going to pay me a while ago. I recognized his bag; I had carried it for eighteen holes. Everyone was down at the putting green as he walked in the club house with his driver in his hand. I had to be fast because everyone could come back to the rack; I took the pail of dog shit and dumped it down his bag like I had done before, it was very effective. We could hear it slide down the clubs and I ran and put everything away. Menny said Rob wouldn't discover it until his second shot on the first hole because he already had his driver out, warming up with it to use on the first tee.

Rob was carrying his own bag this time, so he didn't have anyone to bitch at. We watched them tee off and head down the fairway, and even though he was 200 yards away, we heard his blood-curdling scream, "There's shit in my bag and all over my grips!" He had no choice but to walk in. He showed Grumpy all the dog shit in his bag. Grumpy told him, "That didn't happen here; you need to trace your steps back and see how this could happen." Menny kept jabbing me, as if to say Babe, you got him back this time. Grumpy added, "It looks like someone would do this to win a big bet," and he looked down the first hole and took off running toward his buddies up ahead. You could see them fighting in the middle of the fairway, wrestling and knocking each other down.

The others finally beat Rob up and tore his shirt. He was a mess by the time he got back to Grumpy. He had a big knot on his forehead, and his left eye was closed. He was insisting on a refund, but Grumpy said he was not entitled to a refund because he quit and it wasn't weather related.

A little while later Grumpy called out another caddy job for "the Toner twins." (Some people thought we were twins, but we were far from it.) We walked by Rob, who was looking dejected. His mouth opened, and I could tell he remembered me as I walked past him; I nodded my head to him and kept on walking. I looked over my shoulder, and he was still looking at me. He picked up his bag by the shoulder strap and started dragging it toward the parking lot. Those paybacks were tough.

Grumpy muttered, "Do you guys know where that dog shit came from?" We never said a word, just smiled. Hoping it was going to be a good day, we sized up our next golfers. They were about 25, and Menny's guy had a girlfriend, Alice, who was going to walk along with us. She was always tugging at her short shorts and halter top. Why did she wear them if she had to keep pulling them down? We didn't see anything wrong with her outfit. She was definitely uncomfortable wearing it in front of some other people other than her boyfriend.

She took to Menny and me right off the bat, preferring to walk with us and saying we were fun and could teach her a lot. From the way she looked she could teach us a few things. She talked all the time; and we could see her nipples getting hard and get soft all day long. She walked up on the green with her hard nipples sticking out and her boyfriend got mad. I heard her telling him we were nice and friendly and not doing anything wrong. Alice was very impressed with our knowledge of the game. She told us on the second hole that all her boyfriend wanted to do is get her in the back seat of his car, and he was a wham-bam-thank you-ma'am kind of a guy. We knew we wouldn't be back there that long either.

I was speechless; I figured anything I could say would be wrong, so I didn't say anything. She kept drinking from every water fountain, saying it was hot out. When she picked up the pin her shorts went right up her ass. Menny and I walked behind Alice if we could. This girl had a good-looking ass, and we kept elbowing each other to look at that. She wanted to hold the pin all the time; she knew how to step back and make sure it was in the hole properly. She spent the first nine holes with us; her boyfriend didn't care as long as she wasn't in his hair.

Alice had a soda and took a big drink from the water fountain, where everyone was looking at her from behind. By the time we got to the thirteenth hole she was starting to get antsy and asked Menny where the toilets were. He said there weren't any, so she asked him to help her find a place in the woods. Because she said she was afraid of snakes, Menny saw a chance to pass her off to me .She grabbed my hand and asked me to find her a place to go to the bathroom in the woods; I said I could hold her as she backed against the tree. I would hold her hands to keep her from falling backwards and she could be done before her boyfriend caught up to us.

She wasn't bashful and pulled her shorts and panties off one leg and grabbed my hands and backed up against the tree. I saw everything, but she didn't care. I could hear her pee, you know that noise the girls make, and she must have peed for three minutes. She took a Kleenex out of her short pocket and wiped herself and put her leg in her undies; I could still see her hair through her white panties. She hurried to get her shorts on before her boyfriend came. As we walked out of the woods she was holding my hand.

Alice asked me if I ever helped other girls in the woods to pee, and I told her she was my first one. She said, "You probably won't forget it," and I said I would try not to. She whispered in my ear, "Not too many people have seen me naked before; I hope you saw enough that you will never forget me." I told her, it's not every day that a young man like me can assist a young girl like you to go to potties in the woods." She thought it was funny the way I put it. Her boyfriend caught up to us and never knew what happened.

He started to get upset when Alice picked up the pin from the green, barking at me, "Aren't you supposed to be picking up the pin? What am I paying you for?" I explained that Menny was his caddy and that I didn't appreciate his hollering at me because he was upset with his girlfriend. Then, as we were standing in the woods on eighteen, another golfer's drive suddenly hit a tree, so Alice grabbed me and pressed tight against me, her nipples hard. She said that she was never going to forget us; I told her it was nothing. I think her motto was "treat me well and I'll treat you well."

As we walked off the eighteenth green she was all over her boyfriend, telling him how good we were. She was rubbing her tits all over him at this point; this man was going to do whatever she told him to do. She told both my guy and her boyfriend to take care of the caddies. He gave us two dollars each and she took two dollars out of his wallet and gave Menny and me a dollar each. We watched Alice walk away. She looked back at us watching and pulled one side of her shorts up, shaking her ass. Menny and I went weak in the knees.

We tried one more time before school started to get another caddy job, the weather was beautiful and Menny and I were hoping for a nice peaceful day at the Rock. We were put in a threesome and were introduced to our players, right off the bat Menny had his man picked out and I was left with the short Italian looking guy. He was mouthy but I was not going to take notice of him. By the second hole he wanted to know what he was paying me for. I told him I thought he knew, and he called out to his buddies that they had a wise ass here and it looked like he was gonna have to teach him a lesson.

Then he came up to me and said again, "What am I paying you for?" I told him to be more specific, so he replied, "Why don't you hold the pin sometime?" I told him it was an agreement that my brother and I had worked out and it doesn't concern him. "If I am doing something wrong, tell me, don't yell at me or try to intimidate me by calling me out to your friends for them to join you in picking on the caddy. To be perfectly honest with you I don't think that you're capable of teaching me anything, especially about golf."

This short turd wanted to fight and I told him I was his caddy, not someone for him to take his frustrations out on. With that he seemed to calm down, because he wasn't getting much golfing in fighting with me. Things were going along well when he hit his ball in the woods on the ninth hole; he asked me what I would do in a situation like this one. I told him to take an unplayable lie and that I would drop a ball back where the ball crossed the woods; he should try to recover from a bad situation. He said no way and he was going to hit his ball here by the tree, but he ignored the fact that he had no hope of getting a clear shot to the green.

He took a four iron from the bag and I placed my self in a position where I could still see his ball and not get hit if he were unlucky enough to hit the tree. He took a good swing and hit the ball solidly into the tree in front of him. It then bounced off another tree and came right back and hit him in his left cheek bone. He grabbed his face and fell on his knees. I ran over and gave him his wet towel and he asked me to take a look at his face and give him a damage report. I told him his cheek was bruised but if he could get some ice on it from the clubhouse he could probably keep the swelling down. His buddies seemed to be more concerned about their next shot than the shot he just took to the face.

He didn't finish the hole and went immediately to the snack bar for some ice, while I waited outside. His buddies were walking to the clubhouse along with Menny when he came out with a small bag of ice. They asked him if he was going to continue and he said yes, he wasn't quitting. Everyone went in for a hot dog and Menny stayed out with me and wanted to know what happened. I told him that the man wouldn't listen to me so he hit his ball into a tree and it almost knocked his eye out. I went in and bought my own soda and stood on the tenth tee for his so-called friends to come out. There wasn't any backup so we could tee off right away. My short turd friend hit one out of bounds and insisted on hitting his next shot from out of bounds even after I told him that it was against the rules that he either had to go back to the tee or drop one where it went out for the sake of time, and take a penalty stroke. He wasn't too happy about it and was grumbling when I told him that was what he was paying me for. He dropped his ball and hit the biggest slice deep into the field, not to be found.

He insisted on my looking for his ball and taking the bag until I found it. I bet I had found six balls when Menny came running to me saying that your friend said that was enough, to come on. When I caught up to them he asked me what took so long and I reminded him what he said about finding his ball. I said he had told me to look for it until I found it, and I found six balls but no Spaulding like the one he was playing. When he said I was ball hawking on his time, I told him that I was following his instructions. He never said another word about it, and I could see that his eye was starting to get black and his cheek bone was swollen.

On the par three in the woods with the elevated green, he hit his ball in the thick grass short of the green. I told him that I could find it for him and he said that he would look for himself that I couldn't find anything unless I was standing on it.

I was standing with Menny, looking at my guy struggle and slip on the wet grass when all of a sudden he was on his ass in the creek, drenched, asking Menny and me what we were looking at. Menny walked away, saying maybe this cool water will cool him off. I stayed away from the wet grass and he came to me for the towel, telling me that it should have been me in the creek and not him. I asked him if he remembered that I told him I would find his ball for him, and how nasty he was to me for that. "This is what I am getting paid to do and you stopped me."

His so-called buddies were laughing at him, with a shiner and soaking wet, still with time to do some more tricks for them. He was livid at their belittling him in front of Menny and me. His clothes had to feel cold against his skin and it would take a while before they warmed up to where he wouldn't feel cold anymore. He was noticeably shivering but I didn't give a rat's ass about him. He was mean and I was not feeling any sympathy for him.

We got all the way to the seventeenth tee without any trouble, when he hit his ball just in the woods where all the big boulders were. He insisted that we could find his ball, but I said it was unsafe and the snakes would scare him, making him lose his footing and fall into the clump of rocks. I caught the eye of his two buddies and waved them over and told them what he wanted to do, along with my warning. They agreed with me and told him that it wasn't worth it, but he said that he could find it and be out in less than a minute.

He was right. In less than a minute he had fallen between two rocks, wedged in and screaming for us to come and get him before the snakes bit him. It took the four of us to get him out and he was crying, scared that he had been bitten by the copperhead snakes that favored those rocks. His elbows were cut and his pant leg was ripped open. It took a while to stop the bleeding from the cuts and burns from falling and sliding down into the rocks. It was obvious he couldn't continue, so he sat on the eighteenth tee bench and waited for his buddies to finish putting out on the seventeenth green. The walk to the parking lot was long; not only did his face and arms hurt him but those wet clothes must have been eating away at his crotch because he was walking like his balls were on fire and no water to put it out. We never spoke the whole time we walked to the parking lot. He handed me two soaking wet dollar bills. I dropped his bag on the ground and walked away from him, thinking he can do the best he can because I couldn't take any more of his shit and wasn't going to help him at all.

I was in the snack bar eating a hot dog when Menny came in. He starts, "Babe, you sure can pick 'em." I told him not to hand me that shit. "You did the picking, if you can remember, or do you have selected memory? I would have loved to see you handle that son of a bitch. I played into his stubborn hand and he did himself in. So Men, do me a favor. Don't tell me I know how to pick 'em because when you do that you never do it in a complimentary way. With you it's always a put down. Do me a favor; don't try to build your self up, by trying to pull me down."

12

I couldn't believe I was in the eight grade already, with Sister Anna Josephine, who I really liked, as our teacher. The girls in my class could have cared less about me. I never had one flirt from them, yet the older girls were all over me. I was still bashful, with a baby face, but it didn't do anything for the girls my age, they never gave me a second look. Although I was looking to see if they were starting to fill out, I didn't care about them either the feeling was mutual. To me it was one less thing for me to worry about,

It was close to Thanksgiving when Sister Francis Letitia, the fourth grade teacher, saw me in the hall and asked if I would come see her after school to do her a favor. When I got to her classroom it was empty of students. I walked in, and she asked me to close the door, and even though she said not to worry, I was still scared and getting more nervous by the second. I sat in the chair next to her desk; she asked me if I had any idea what she was going to talk to me about. I told her no, and she smiled and patted my arm. "I hear you singing sometimes, Babe. You know you have a good voice and that's why you are here. I want you to do me a favor, but it will have to be a big secret." I was practically shaking in the chair. She went on, "Do you remember when you were in the first grade your sister Theresa brought you back to our classroom and you sang 'My Girl's a Corker, She's a New Yorker'? You got a standing ovation! You have a good voice and here's what I want you to do for me. I want you to sing 'O Holy Night' at Mass on Christmas Eve." I stood up and said, "You must have me mixed up with someone else! I could never do that; I could never learn those words. I'm too dumb to learn that song." She said, "I hear you singing it a lot. Don't pretend to me, Master Toner, you are as dumb as a fox."

Sister continued, "You have been on probation now for seven years and you never got left back. You have too much spirit and will do whatever it takes to accomplish your mission. If there is anyone who loves Christ Our King it's you, and you have done everything that was ever asked of you. No one has ever been called on to help the sisters as much as you and the priest. Fr. Lynch likes you, too, and that's saying something. You have an air about you that makes people trust and depend on you. Someday you will be a big success; you would have to be blind not to see that. I know about your treatment at home. You have survived what most people wouldn't, but you have. You, Master Toner, are the only person in our entire school who I would ask to take on a project like this one. You already have a good voice, so all you have to do is learn the words. With your ability, it would be easy for you to do. I will show you how to make your voice stronger, clearer, and sharper. You will be a big hit at a one-time performance that will never be equaled, so please tell me you'll do it." She seemed so happy that it could only have been happiness for me. So I agreed.

Three days later, she gave me the words and I studied them for a week. I knew them frontward and backwards and sang them at least a hundred times. One day I was practicing and Sister asked me to sing it without any accompaniment. She stopped me half way through and said I needed honey. She pulled a bottle of honey out of her bag along with a tablespoon, poured it on the spoon and made me drink it. "Now sing and see how much better it's going to be," she said. I did it and it was great. "See," she said, "I told you I could make your voice stronger." The next time I sang it all the way through. She told me that with a little more practice I was really going to be good.

With only 18 days left until Christmas, we had to talk about how we were going to do this. Sister said that the Midnight Christmas Communion is about 15 minutes, so we would have to have an organist in on this. Sister brought in Lauren Matter, who agreed to keep the secret. The plan was for Lauren to start off with "O Come All Fe Faithful," and then when it was the right time and without any noticeable difference in the music changeover to "O Holy Night." Sister said, "I can see now that it is going to be perfect." I practiced almost every night in the choir. With four days to go I was scared, but Lauren said I was good. She suggested that I sing the piece twice to stretch out the time. The second time through she would add some more organ parts and then I would make a strong finish.

Sister, Lauren, and I met for the last practice, and they said I was ready. Sister put the spoon and the bottle of honey under the organ seat and said to be in the choir by midnight. I was out in the school yard Christmas Eve like everyone else. Menny and I were in a group of about 30 guys. Believe it or not the older guys were drinking. I call it false courage; they couldn't be a part of something big like Midnight Night Mass on Christmas Eve. We started in to church, and Menny and I got separated just like I planned, and I ducked in the choir. I went right to the honey and took a spoonful. I was ready and Lauren was ready, and sister was sitting with all the nuns in the designated pews at the front of the church.

I was standing at the railing and had a full view of the church. Just as they started communion Lauren started her part of "O Come All Ye Faithful" and then I broke in at the right place just like we practiced. My voice was strong; Sister and Lauren had given me a lot of confidence. I saw so many heads turning to see who was singing. I finished my first run; a lot of people were starting to turn around, even some nuns. No one expected to see Babe Toner singing "O Holy Night" in the choir. I started humming at the appropriate spot as Lauren came back with the organ, and I came in with the words "fall on your knees" and took it right through till the end.

When I finished you could hear a pin drop, and then the priest on the altar started clapping saying "Wonderful!" The people in the pews turned and applauded and cheered for the longest time. Sister was waving a white hanky. I reached for Lauren to come to the railing and the people started all over again. I held her arm up high because she made it happen with that organ. I could have never done that without Sister and Lauren.

I couldn't wait to have a cigarette out front before the church let out, but quickly everyone came up to me and patted me on the back. Mommy and the girls all ran to me. The first thing they wanted to know was why I didn't tell them that I was going to sing at Midnight Mass. I told them it was a secret; just then sister made her way over to me, saying it was better than she thought it would be. I introduced her to Mommy, and she was glad to meet everyone. Sister reached under her shawl and brought out a small, beautifully wrapped gift and said Merry Christmas. I thanked her again. She told Mommy, "Only your son could have done that, on this night. He has the spirit in him and I am proud to know him."

It took the longest time to get away, and Mommy was calling out for me to go home. It was almost 1:30 in the morning, and Menny said he couldn't get through the crowd. He told me, "Babe, you sure can keep a secret. Why you didn't tell me? You shocked a lot of people tonight. How did you get your voice so good and strong?" I told him Sister gave me a bottle of honey and told me if I coated my throat with this my good voice will be even better. Mommy said we were all going to have a cup of tea to celebrate Babe's singing debut.

When we went back to school in January, it had all faded away. It was history. Sister Josephine did tell the class, "If you weren't at midnight Mass then you missed Master Toner singing during Communion." Someone in the back of the room said, "If Toner was singing then I didn't miss much." I saw sister Letitia in the school yard and thanked her for her Christmas gift, a small bottle of honey. We both laughed, and she said she was proud of me and that I had lived up to her expectations. I told her it was only because of her faith in me and that I would cherish that bottle of honey forever. Some people wanted to know why I didn't sing at all the Masses on Christmas day, but I never attempted to answer them. They couldn't conceive that it was a special occasion and that it would never be duplicated, with all of its secrecy.

One day I came in the house to find Mommy crying. She told me she had to give up the boarders and it was going to hurt us. Someone was coming to pick up Bonnie and Mikey on Saturday. We were going to miss them; they fitted right in. Mommy said she was going to look for a business to help us out with the house expenses even though Menny and I had done a lot.

I hoped my father hadn't caused this. I saw him that evening in the bathroom using a powder puff to powder his face. I told him the boarders were leaving Saturday and that he was going to have to take care of his family just like all the other fathers around here. I told him his drinking had caused him and us more trouble than he knew how to handle. He asked me if my mother had put me up to this, and I could see he was nervous. He didn't say much after that. I asked him if it were true that he spends at least five nights a week in a bar. "You should be spending that money on us or the house, food or clothing." But I was pushing too far because he hadn't had anything to drink. So that night there was going to be hell to pay because he would stew on this all night.

It was about 12:30 when I heard the door open and close loudly. He was out in the kitchen raising hell. He finally came up the stairs to my bedroom and turned on the light. I looked up at him he grabbed my shirt and pulled me up to him. He said, "Why do you think you can talk to me like that?" Menny said that he didn't hear me say anything and that we had both been asleep. By this time Theresa and Mommy were in our room. He didn't know who to hit first. He went back to me, thumping my chest, telling me to apologize for saying those bad things to him. My mother said that we had been asleep and to leave us alone. She cried, "Why don't you go back to Florida with those drunken whores? Maybe you can pick up some more diseases." He leaped in the air to hit Mommy but slipped on the rug on the side of my bed. He fell on his hands and knees and, humiliated, he stood up and pushed Theresa against the wall. I told him I wasn't going to apologize to him for anything. He spun around to get me and fell down again. This time he hurt his right hand. My mother told him, "That's what you get for hurting your children. You can't even stand up. You're just a drunk, and you had good teacher." There wasn't much my father could do with a hurt hand. I was sure he wouldn't be able to work, but he could drink left handed. I could see he was losing control. With no respect, it must weigh heavy on him. To this day, Menny and I hate beer and the way it taste and smells. To smell it on someone's breathe makes me sick.

One evening Mommy told me she was going to open a luncheonette at Van Buren Street and Baynard Boulevard. She said the owner told her she could take over anytime she wanted to, but it needed a lot of work. Mommy told me that she had told my father that no matter what, he had to work evenings from six to eleven without fail. She and Theresa, who quit school, would do the daytime hours. After a while they hired a woman named Della, who was twenty cents short of a quarter. Very nice, just not gifted, if you know what I mean. Menny and I worked every other night from six to ten.

The name of our store was Toner's Luncheonette. A lot of people came in—jewelers, lawyers, and a lot of rich people. We also had a lot of kids from the Number 30 School and P.S. DuPont High School. Whenever two people wanted to meet, they chose Toner's Luncheonette. We had three phone booths; the phone company paid us good money each month for them. We had two pinball machines and a juke box, all with a 50/50 cut, magazines, candy, ice cream, newspapers, and a ton of food.

We sold a lot of hamburgers and loads of ice cream cones to businessmen. They would sit on a stool and watch me for 15 minutes, and when they had an opening they would teach me how to sell ice cream. When a person asked for a cone I was to ask them, "Will that be one dip or two?" I used the same pitch for everything, and when I pulled it off they would wink and say "good job." To them, selling was their life and a properly trained person could make a lot more money.

I made friends with a lot of influential people and saw them every other night. One night Theresa was working instead of my father, so we all stayed late to help her out. Theresa was in the bathroom and called out that something was smoking. I immediately called the fire department and told them to send someone out. I said no sirens, but it wasn't two minutes before holy hell broke out. You could hear them coming from miles away. Theresa was still in the bathroom, sitting on the toilet, when a firefighter ran in the store. I pointed to the bathroom where the machinery was. You could see the smoke pouring from the door, so the fireman pulled the bathroom door open and there was Theresa still sitting on the toilet. The fireman closed the door and started laughing. Theresa came out laughing too.

Although Theresa was white as a ghost, she could see the humor in it. She and Menny and I couldn't stop laughing. I asked the fireman why the sirens. He said they didn't go anywhere without sirens. He told us the problem was the seltzer pump and shut it off. The next morning we had it fixed. Later we often laughed with Theresa about that night.

One drizzly afternoon, while walking home from school, I saw some girls with umbrellas. I snuck up behind one girl and put my arm around her, not knowing who she was. I normally didn't do anything like that, but I ducked under her umbrella. She turned to look at me and immediately collapsed to the ground. I was so upset that I had made her fall down. As I helped her up, she was rubbing her legs. I apologized and she said it wasn't my fault. I had seen her around but didn't take much notice of her. She looked Italian, but could be Spanish; the more I looked at her, the better looking she got. I kept apologizing, and she kept saying it wasn't my fault. She turned up Jefferson Street, I asked her where she lived, and she said in the house with the big tree in the front. We both said goodbye. Although she wore loose clothes, she had more than met the eye. You could see she was very modest.

After a week went by and I hadn't seen her around, I rode my bike up Jefferson Street found the big tree and the house; I parked my bike, and knocked on the door. This girl opened it in her pajamas and robe. I told her I was just stopping by to see how she was doing I was worried that she might have been hurt. She asked me in and said her parents were in Philadelphia for the day and wouldn't be back until dinnertime. I told her my mother had a store on Baynard Boulevard, and maybe we could go there for lunch.

She asked if I wouldn't mind waiting while she took a shower. I told her to go ahead and dozed off sitting in beautiful tufted chair. I was awoken by her calling me to come upstairs. I walked up the stairs to the landing. She was standing therein her robe with wet hair trying to dry it with a towel. She walked in the bedroom and sat on the foot of the bed, patting the bed for me to sit down next to her. I was my usual scared self. I was concerned that her parents would be upset if they knew I was upstairs with their daughter. She said she was never going to tell them; I laughed and told her I wasn't going to say anything either. She told me that the day I put my arm around her under the umbrella, and turned to see who it was, when I saw you my legs turned to jelly and I collapsed. She said her name was Maria; she was fifteen and in the ninth grade at P.S. DuPont.

Then Maria asked me to put my arm around her like I did that day. I told her sure, not knowing she was going to fall back on the bed, causing her robe to open exposing her tits and the rest of her. She pulled my collar and I fell back too. When I turned to see her pretty face our lips met and we kissed with some soft tongue for a long time.

She took my hand and put it on her tits. Her nipples got hard, so I bent over to kiss them both. She moaned and held my head tight against her chest. My hand slid down her silk smooth stomach to her hairy playground. I played around not knowing what to do and scared as hell to find out. She was squirming all around calling my name. I don't remember anything until I saw her in the bathroom standing in front of the mirror with just her panties on. She reached for her bra. I thought, "This can't be the same girl who's going to put this beautiful body in those baggy clothes." She turned so I could see those beautiful tits one more time before she tucked them away and smiled at me.

I was too scared to ask what had happened. She came to me on the bed, bent over and kissed me as hard as I had ever been kissed before. I put my hands right between her legs, and slid my hand right in her panties ,but she moaned and stopped me and said there would be other times to do this and more. I sat up, wanting a cigarette badly. She walked back in her bathroom still in her bra and panties. I couldn't stop looking at her, and she knew it so she took her time in front of the mirror, turning and smiling at me. Eventually she had to get dressed, which broke my heart.

We walked outside together, and I asked her if she would ever get jelly legs again and she said only when I touched her. Wow! She really made me feel good. We got on our bikes and rode to my mother's store for lunch.

As I walked in with Maria, a few heads turned. Mommy asked who I was with, and I told her this was someone I met a few weeks ago.

I asked Mommy if I could have a couple of cheeseburgers with everything on them, but that I would make the shakes. Maria couldn't believe that I could do that. We sat by ourselves at the window table laughing and giggling. I cleaned up and took everything over to the sink and trash. Maria said goodbye to my mother, and we rode our bikes to P.S. DuPont. We sat near the scoreboard and talked, and I smoked some cigarettes.

She lay back, which I took as an invitation to kiss her. She told me I was a good kisser. I told her that I hardly noticed her before, but she said she saw me all the time and wondered if I had a girlfriend. I said no. She then asked if I would be her boyfriend. I gulped and said yes. I thought it was a good time to ask her why she asked me to stop when I was trying to put my hand under her panties, when she liked me so much. She said that she had no control when her parents would actually come home even though they told her that they might be home around dinner time, and all she wanted was to be alone with me, with no chance of being walked in on. She said that in the right place and the right time she would let me do anything I wanted to her. I said that the safest time would be at night some where there was no chance of anyone catching us. She said that she was looking forward to it; she has thought about it a lot and she wanted me to be her first. Maria said she thought about me a lot and had made up her mind that it would be me. I couldn't believe that this beautiful girl wanted Babe Toner to be her boyfriend. She had a beautiful shape and short black hair. Her lips were so cute, and she had a striking way of moving her mouth to talk. There wasn't a blemish on her face, and she didn't need any make up. When I told her I would be her boyfriend, she was so happy we kissed again, only this time she opened her mouth and put her tongue in mine. What a way to end the day! We rode our bikes back to her house, and I left to get ready to work at the store.

When I hadn't heard from my new girlfriend in two weeks, I rode over to her house and knocked on the door, but no one answered. I looked in the window and the house was empty. I was shocked. I couldn't believe it; what could have happened? As I walked off the porch to my bike, a girl sitting on her steps across the street called out to me, "Hey, they moved." I rode over to see what else she could tell me. She asked if I was Babe, and I said yes. Maria had told her that she met me and was real excited about me. I asked her what happened. She said that Maria's father had gotten into trouble at work and was let go, so they had to move back to somewhere in Philadelphia. I asked her if she had an address, but she didn't and that was a big city to be looking for someone in. I asked that if she ever saw Maria again would she tell her to contact me. She said that she would.

I rode off on my bike, probably in shock from losing a friend like that so unexpectedly. She was always on my mind, but I suffered alone, not telling anybody about her. Mommy never asked me anything but could see I was broken-hearted over something. I didn't have the nerve to tell my mother that Maria my new girlfriend, has left, gone away to Philadelphia somewhere. Every time I went by Jefferson Street, I looked up at the house.

The last day of school, I wasn't nervous at all for a change. I was the only one to win the attendance award, never missing a day of school in two years. Sister gave out the report cards and told everyone good luck in high school. No probation! I walked down to Sister Letitia's room. She waved me in and told her class that I had gone to C.O.K. for eight years and said I was the person who had sung at midnight Mass. She said she wanted to hear good things about me and to come back to see her someday. With that I turned and walked away. Eight years felt like a long time.

It was raining like hell Sunday and there was no chance to caddy or do anything else, so I went to the 10:30 Mass. I always liked to sit in the back, in the last row on the right side. I was sitting in the next to the last row just minding my own business when this wise ass sitting behind me started hitting my head with his missal. I asked him to stop it and he kept it up. I gave him plenty of time to consider what the repercussions were going to be because he knew me and he knew that I wouldn't take this very long. I think he was more interested in entertaining his friends sitting with him than he was in stopping his little childish games. I saw a paperback missal about an inch thick in my pew. I picked it out of the missal holder, made sure I had a good grip on it, and swung around, hitting across his face. It sounded like a shot went off; it was so loud that everyone in the church turned to look where this loud noise came from. This ass was so embarrassed that he left the church. The ushers standing in the back of the church saw everything and never said a word to me, because they even asked him to stop and he wouldn't listen to them either.

The next Saturday, Menny and I went up to the Rock to caddy. We checked in with Grumpy and waited to be called. It wasn't long before Grumpy called our names to caddy in a foursome. We walked over, and they introduced themselves. It looked like I had the fat guy, who told me he couldn't see that well and was going to rely on me a lot. Jesus Christ, how could I be so lucky? It looked like I was going to work my ass off. Menny was laughing, saying, "Babe, you sure know how to pick them." There he went again.

As we finally got near the green on the first hole, my guy asked how far away he was and I told him 35 yards and gave him a wedge. He hit the ball over the green and into the corn field. I told him it was lost and that he should drop one on the green. When he asked me if I wanted him to cheat, I said yes. You could have put a dozen golf balls in his mouth with the look he gave me.

With 17 holes to go I hoped I could hold on. On the second hole along the corn field he put three balls in the corn field. I told him to drop one on the apron (the edge of the green). He said that was cheating, so I told him to drop one in the corn field then. That made him mad. I heard him telling Menny's man that I was a rude son of a bitch. It looked like I was going to take the blame for his game. On the forth hole he hit his ball into the reservoir. As we walked toward the reservoir fence, he asked me what the ruling was on this ball in the water, and if he had to take a penalty shot. I told him not if he played it in there. He said, "You want me to play it in the reservoir?" I told him, "No, You asked me if it was a penalty to play it in there, I told you it wasn't a penalty if you played it in there." He replied that I was a wise ass. I knew if he kept it up I was going to get his ass.

As we got to the par three along Route 202, I told him that the road was out of bounds. He said he knew that and had never hit a ball on Route 202 in his life. But this day he hit three of them on Rt. 202. I looked at him and he said it was my fault for bringing it up. Menny was having convolutions; this guy's score had to be over 50 for five holes. On the next hole he hit his ball on the up slope right against the lip of the sand trap. He had the nerve to ask me how to play that one, so I told him to swing hard. He kept missing until finally it rolled over the lip into the very high grass. Even though he was less than four feet from the green, the way he was swinging it would be impossible to get it on the green. He kept swinging easy, not enough to get on the green. Finally he was on in eight and three-putted for an eleven. I could hear him telling his buddies, "Can you believe that kid? He told me to swing hard."

We finally got to the clubhouse, where my fat friend came out with two hot dogs and two drinks. He ate both dogs and drank both sodas, which of course made me even madder. I walked down to the corner to watch for his ball. His drive went into what looked like a snake hole;

I could see it way in there. I was too scared to go after it, but he said he would and told me to get out of the way. He got on his knees and was reaching in the hole for it when the club I was holding touched his leg. He screamed, "I've been bitten by a snake!" When I asked where, he said, "On my leg, stupid." Oh boy, I thought, he's calling me names now. He couldn't get up on his own, so he motioned for me to help him. He had mud all over his knees. I gave him my hand and let him think I was helping, but he kept pulling on me and not exerting any of his own strength to get up with. I started acting like he was hurting me by his pulling on my hand so hard. He was able to get one knee off the ground and still had one to go. He was straining so hard to get on his feet his face was as red as a fire engine, and he was starting to fart so loud and strain so hard that he finally got on his feet. But he almost burst a vein in his head from straining too hard. His buddies never came over to help us; they stayed away.

As we got near the next green, he asked me for a nine iron. I gave him a seven iron, and he hit it over the green, down the hill to the railroad tracks, and out of bounds. He yelled that he had never hit a nine iron that good in all his life. I quickly put the club back in the bag and pulled out the nine iron and showed it to him. Menny was laughing behind a big bush. Finally we go to the eighteenth tee. On the last four holes he had fallen in the creek twice and had hit some old man with a golf ball on the seventeenth hole and told him it was my fault because I told him to hit it. He hit his drive in the fairway and his second shot in the big pile of sand by the maintenance shed on the right of the eighteenth fairway. He wanted to hit his ball from the sand pile, and I told him he could do it. But he had taken so many swings that he was covered in sand, with little piles of sand on his shoulders. He finally got the ball out of the sand and it was sitting under a tree. He said, "That's not bad, I only lay five." When I corrected him and said seven, he lost it and was angry I was counting his strokes. I told him he wanted to play fair; after all, this could be the hole he could break 200 on. With that he said he was going to turn me into the caddy master. So I grabbed him. I fell on both of my knees and started pleading for him not to turn me in. I had real tears running down my face. "You can't do that mister. I have a sister who needs an operation, and my Mommy needs my money to put food on the table tonight. You are going to cause us to get kicked out in the street and be homeless." I was really balling and grabbed his arm again I was still on my knees saying, "Mister please don't hurt me."

He grabbed me and pulled me up, saying he was sorry. "Please don't cry, I won't turn you in." Now he's balling like a baby, too. When he walked onto the green he had the sniffles; his buddies were watching us the whole time. This guy really looked pitiful. He was wet, with stickers everywhere, and his buddy walked over and asked him what was wrong. He said that he just found out that Babe's sister needed a serious operation; his mother needed the money from caddying so they won't get put in the street, and they don't even have any money for food. They all looked over at me with my sad face. I deliberately put my finger to my eye to give the impression I was wiping a tear away. They all got choked up. Menny was smirking, ready to explode. I asked my fat friend if I could carry his bag to his car. He said that I was kind to ask, that I looked like a nice young man, and that he really felt bad about my family. I put his clubs in the trunk. He said he was going to give me five dollars for my mother and sister and two dollars for caddying. As my face lit up, he said, "I hope your sister comes out OK." I told him he better get home and get out of those wet clothes before he caught a cold. He still had the sniffles. I thanked him again and walked away toward Menny by the putting green where we would always wait for each other.

By the time I got to Menny he was bent over slapping his leg, saying "Babe, I never saw anything like that display that you put on in all my life." I told Menny that the man was going to turn me in to Grumpy about my caddying, but I didn't have anyone to turn him in to. So I gave him a taste of the movies. He went from a wise ass to a mellowed-out human being. Menny said, "Babe you really got him. I don't know how you survived it all. You made him cry to boot!" I asked if Menny had seen the way he looked when he left the golf course—worse than the bums. Menny asked what he had shot and I told him 200, and that I earned every penny of this caddy job. Then Menny wanted to know what he paid me. I showed him the money and told him that the five dollars was for Mommy and the two dollars was for me caddying. I held back two dollars for a new pair of shoes.

When we got home Mommy told Menny and me that we had to take the entrance test for Salesianum School, a Catholic boys' high school, the next Monday. That test was hard; it was all Greek to me. A letter finally came in the mail, telling Menny and me we were going to be in freshman "D." We were to report on September 3, 1951, for orientation. We had to wear a sport jacket and tie, with no long hair or ducks asses (hair style), and no peg pants.

I was collecting for papers one evening when I went to that good-looking girl's apartment on 30th and West Street. The husband answered the door and paid me, but I didn't see her at all. Menny and I were cutting back on the money we gave Mommy because she didn't need our money as much anymore with the store income. We were sharing the paper boy money, about six dollars each, which was not bad for us boys. Things were starting to look up for us.

The next time I collected from that girl from West Street, she was home and told me to come in. We sat at the table. I told her I was here last week and I missed her. She said she wished she had been here. "Do you remember the last time you were here? I let you touch me. I would have let you do more but I didn't know what time my husband was coming home. He doesn't treat me very nice. I wish you were older. I could go head over heels for you." She asked me to stand up and she put my hand in her shorts, under her panties, right on her thick patch. I asked about her husband. She said he wouldn't be home for a few hours.

She asked me if I knew how to make a woman climax. I told her yes. She held on to me as I moved my fingers over her bump. She was wet. She grabbed me tight and shook a lot in my arms and then went limp. She sat down in the chair to get her balance. How could she be having such a hard time with her husband? With me, she would be in bed all the time. She told me that she was going to make it up to me. I asked if her husband could do that. "He used to," she said, "but not anymore." I asked her what she was going to do about her husband. She said things didn't look good. She said to stop by a lot earlier next time I collected, if I got her drift. She said, "It will be my turn to do you. She put my hand back into her shorts and whispered for me to find her bump before I left. We got to the door, I pulled out and she kissed me and put her tongue in my mouth. I had to get out of there. I really had to talk to Menny about this girl. Maybe he could collect and take care of her.

I caught up with Menny and told him what happened. I begged him to collect from her next time and he agreed. The following week he knocked on her door. She looked at him, and he was waiting to be asked inside. She only handed him the card. Menny never saw her close up before. She was a beauty, with a great body. Menny gave her back the card and with a beautiful smile she said, "No offence, but tell you brother to stop around; you're not my type." I waited for him on 31st Street. He had a look on his face that I couldn't read. He came up to me and said that if she was a candy bar, he would have eaten her wrapper and all. He told me,

"Babe, she only wants you. She said I wasn't her type. Looks like she is all yours. Good luck." I told him I didn't want her, that she scared me. She was married and unhappy with her husband and I couldn't get caught in that mess. The next time I collected it was about 8:00 p.m. Boy was she pissed. She asked why I didn't come earlier in the afternoon, so I told her I was working at my mother's store and couldn't get off. She didn't like it but said to keep trying, because she would be there. But I knew she was trying to use me and I couldn't be in a situation like that. I was the one who would get hurt.

I wanted to get some caddy time in so I could play on caddies day. The next time I went to the Rock it had to be around 1:00 o'clock and there wasn't anyone around. Grumpy asked me if I would caddy double for two girls. I turned and saw that one of them was that girl, Linda, who liked to shake her ass when she walked. She was sitting with a beautiful brunette. Did you ever notice that a good-looking girl always has a good-looking girlfriend? Grumpy saw that I was hesitant, but no one else was around on a weekday to caddy. Grumpy said that their bags were light. He told me, "You have to do this for me; I'll owe you one." I told him I would.

Just then the girls stood up and started walking toward Grumpy and me. His tongue must have been hard because he could hardly talk. He actually introduced me, something he never did before. He said, "Linda, Carolyn, this is your caddy today. His name is Babe." Linda said that I had caddied for her and Peter and was instrumental in helping her break 80. She said that one day, down on the corner, I helped her find her ball and didn't take his eyes off me the whole time. She said to me, "You were a naughty boy. I saw you watching me on the green." I could feel my face turn red. Grumpy walked off as fast as he could. This was going to be a day to remember. The girls both had on short skirts just at the top of the knee. This was a new style for women golfers.

My armpits were wet. Linda and Carolyn took a couple of practice swings. I just watched. I never saw an ass move like that. I had seen Linda's ass on the picnic table so that shouldn't be any surprise. If you ever caddied double, you had to go from one to the other for eighteen holes. While walking to the first green, Linda told me that she hadn't forgotten how I had helped her break 80, and I'll never forget you for that. We got to the first green and they were very cheerful and both laying three. They were both looking over their putts and their legs were apart just enough to show a little panty. They both missed their par putts and tapped in for their bogie fives.

Seventeen holes to go. I hoped I could make it. These two girls were very intense about their game. If I gave one a tip, the other one would get upset because I didn't tell her. Carolyn asked me what she was doing wrong on her drives. I told her that her downswing was out of sync with her body. She asked me if I could show her, but I told her that I would have to touch her. She said, "I want you to show me what you mean." Don't worry about touching me; you have done that before. I stood behind her and took her arm and pulled it back to parallel. She fell off balance a little. I had to put my body against her hard, I also had my arm around her waist, holding her tight to me. I thought I was going to pass right through her. I had my right hand over hers and as I took the club back slowly with her, she was rubbing on my privates. I must have felt everything this girl had. She stepped back fanning herself, saying, "What a lesson! I have never had a lesson like that before."

Linda looked a little disturbed about Carolyn fanning herself. It wasn't long before they both were laughing all the time. I couldn't hear why, but they would look at me and start all over again. I couldn't wait to hold the pin again to see what they would show me next. Carolyn had on light canary yellow panties, and Linda had on her usual white. Carolyn was really driving the ball far, so on the eighth tee, Linda wanted me to look at her swing and tell her what she was doing wrong like I did Carolyn. I said I didn't know if I could be of any help. She quickly told me to show her. I got behind her and pushed my pelvic area very hard against her. I covered her hands and took the club back slowly to parallel. I then took her hands and started the downswing hard. My arms were all over her tits. I was talking to her the whole time, reminding her to whip that club coming through. Don't stop; go right through the impact up and over the top, high, all the way around. Boy was she moving that ass. She stepped back, fanning her face, saying, "What a lesson, it feels like a hundred degrees out here today. I can see now that we are going to have to keep you a secret, Babe; you are too good to be shared with anyone."

I think she was trying to wake up my sleeping dog, but I was scared. Linda was fanning herself, too, and Carolyn was bent over laughing, saying, "I told you he was good." They held their legs tightly together like they were going to wet their panties.

We got to the club house after nine holes, and they were fighting over who was going to get my hot dog and drink. Believe it or not they both got me a hot dog and a drink, saying "Here, Babe, you are going to need your strength for the back nine." I never saw girls eating hot dogs like those two.

They moaned as they bit in to their hot dogs, folding their lips over the hot dog and smiling at me. This was going to be the caddy job of a lifetime. They were determined to see me blush. They threw their rolls away and kept the dogs, looking at me and putting it in and out of their mouth like a banana, they kept it up until they devoured their hot dog, they would emphasizing their lips around the dog and biting it gently. I knew Linda was good at it and it looked like Carolyn was just as good.

On the twelfth hole Linda's shoelace broke, so she sat on the bench and asked me to lace her shoe for her. She had her legs wide apart. What a view. She actually had hair coming out from the sides of her underwear. She put her foot on my leg just above my knee. I had the best close-up that I ever had before. I was so nervous it took me twice the time to lace her shoe up. I never saw a girl that close up before; it kind of made me hungry. I had a funny feeling that Carolyn was going to need help on one of these holes coming up, and outdo Linda. I fixed Linda's shoe and she was very grateful, and now that I think about it, so was I.

Carolyn told Linda that her zipper on her skirt was broken and she had to hold it up with her hand. The next thing I knew her skirt was on the ground and she was just standing there in her underwear. Linda quickly put a towel around her. Just then my little dog starting barking. I couldn't believe my eyes. I picked up the skirt and looked at the zipper and managed to wedge it back in the track. Her button was fine, so I don't know how she dropped her skirt. I told her to try it again, so she dropped the towel like she did the skirt. Thank god nobody was around or we would have had a crowd. She just stood there until I handed her back her skirt and stepped into it just like a lady would do. She zipped and buttoned, and she and Linda were looking at each other, fanning and saying it had gotten hot all of a sudden. I was worried that they might see my doggie waking up.

We were walking past the picnic area on seventeen Linda asked me if I had ever heard of bears in the woods. I told her I had heard some rumors about it. Linda and Carolyn were scared and both ran to the eighteenth tee which was elevated enough to let me see up their skirts. When they teed up their ball they both pulled up their skirts up enough to let them bend over and tee the ball up. They were determined to hit good drives. Their asses were swaying—what a sight for a young man like me to see.

By the time we got to the eighteenth green the girls were real quiet like something good was coming to an end. They did give me a last look at their package while they would line up their putts when I was holding the pin. They both broke 90 and said thanks to me. Smiling, we all walked

227

to the clubhouse and Linda asked me to take her clubs to her locker in the ladies locker room. I told them I wasn't allowed in the ladies locker room, but they said it was OK because they would be with me. They had to get their purses and pay me. I put Linda's bag in her locker and when I turned around she handed me five dollars. I told her I didn't have any change but she said she didn't want any. She said that it was for being a good caddy and gave me a good kiss on the lips. Carolyn called me over to her locker in another aisle behind Linda's. As I walked around the corner she said she had something for me. She was sitting on her bench with a towel wrapped around her, already undressed to shower. She gave me a five dollar bill just like Linda. I was speechless she stood up and gave me a gentle kiss on the lips, and her towel fell down; I lost my balance and fell back against the locker. I couldn't help but see that what she had was awesome. She put the towel back around herself very slowly; she wanted me to see the whole package. She said, "I hope I can see you again, Babe," and I said I would like that too. As I went around past Linda's aisle she hadn't put her towel on yet. She was just standing there, knowing that very few women were going to have a body like hers. She turned and said, "See you soon, Babe." She had the hardest nipples I have ever seen.

Linda and Carolyn gave me a day I would never forget, but I couldn't tell Menny because he wouldn't believe me. If I were to tell one person it would spread like wildfire, so I had to overcome the urge to tell someone. I was going to stash the ten dollars. I was getting a good nest egg, over $100, which was not bad for a young lad. When I showed up to play caddies day, Grumpy asked me how it had gone, caddying for those two girls. I told him they both broke 90 and they were very good golfers. He was glad it worked out for me; he was starting to feel sorry that he asked me to caddy for those two. When Menny asked what that was about, I explained and said it was the best three and a half hours I had ever had caddying. He was mad I hadn't told him, but then was happy I had made so much money.

What a summer. It couldn't get any better. One day our park was having a softball game at a park near the Governor Printz Boulevard. The other team had a big guy catching for them named Freddie Mason. He hit a home run every time he was up at bat. I had played against him in a CYO game. In one game against him I got on base and worked my way around to third base. I was trying to intimidate the pitcher; taking large leads and watching Freddie Mason throw back the pitch. All of a sudden I thought I could steal home on him so I ran down toward home plate. Then I stopped and made it look like I was going back to third base. I spun around and took off for home plate. They must have suspected I was going to try this. I heard the ball hit Freddie's glove while I was sliding in. He had the plate blocked, so when I hit him it was like hitting a stone wall. I could hear the umpire call out "You're out!" I also heard every bone in my body crack. I could hardly stand up. I wasn't about to penetrate his defense one inch. I thought I was paralyzed, but Freddie helped me to my feet. My legs were like jelly. He patted me on the shoulder and said, "Nice try, kid." I sat on the bench trying to recover before I took the field. One thing for sure I would never try to steal anything from him again.

Meanwhile at the Rock, they were looking for someone to sell sodas on the reservoir hole on the Fourth of July. I knew I could make more than two dollars doing that. Around 10:00, they took me out in a pickup truck loaded with cases of sodas and ice and a soda box to put the sodas and ice in. Everyone playing golf had to come to that tee today. My ice box was just off the tee between Route 202 and the reservoir hill. It was almost 4:00 when Linda and Peter came to the tee. She asked me if I could help her with some yard work, and I said sure. She wrote down her address on a card and asked me to come on July 6 around 11:00 a.m. and walked away. By 5:00 I had sold most of the sodas. Seven cases, so I made seven dollars. I was happy; that was a lot of money to me. Mommy wasn't relying on our money anymore so I put it with my stash. I didn't get home till 6:00, sunburned and tired.

July 6 came fast. Linda lived near Baynard Stadium. I got there right at 11:00; I would be getting my driver's license soon and couldn't wait. I walked up the alley toward the back of the house, when I saw Linda coming out of her back door, stepping out on to her elevated porch. She had shorts on, and a top on that left no imagination as to her bust size. She greeted me with a hug and showed me her garden and asked me if I could dig it up. I said yes and asked her to show me the garden tools.

She showed me a nice five-pronged digger. The dirt was soft, so by noon I was half done. She sat in a chair watching me. She said it wasn't fair; I made it look easy. She said, "Babe, you sure are strong." I was sweating a lot; she came up to me with a towel and dried my face off. She made sure her bare leg was touching my bare leg. She would come over from time to time to dry my face. By 12:30 she wanted me to take a break for lunch. I was hungry just looking at her, if you get my drift.

She had a nice picnic table and chairs. There was a high hedge, about 10 feet high, going all around her property. It was as good as a wall. It was very private from ground level, but the houses on either side of her could see into her yard from their second story bedroom windows. She brought out a tray of hot dogs, potato salad and sodas. She was awfully pretty and kept smiling at me, which made my legs weak. Thank God I only had a little more to dig. She was so happy with our progress; she reached for my hand to hold and told me how grateful she was that I helped her break 80 at golf. "I told you I was going to make it up to you, and today is going to be the day for you to collect." She said when she posted that score she had the lowest handicap among all the women at the Rock. I told her that was a good day for her, and she said that it would have been even better if she could have celebrated it with me, she would have brought me right back here for the celebration.

When I finished digging I sat on the bench, Linda came over and dried me off again, sitting next to me and rubbing her legs against mine. She was sweating too. She grabbed my hand and took me in the house. I heard her lock the door behind me. She told me to go upstairs and take a shower and get in bed to warm up, and after all that digging I needed a rest. I said I had to serve papers at 4:00 o'clock, she said we had three hours till then. She told me she was going to take a shower after me. I took a fast shower, dried off, and got in bed. It smelled so good, not like my bed at home with that old musty smell. Her bed was so comfortable and big, the room was dimly lit but the bathroom door was open and the light was on. She came into the room, just in her underwear with a towel over her arm; she stopped at the hamper, and took off her wet undies. When she walked into her bathroom you could see she was all women. She closed the door. I heard the water running; that was the last thing I heard until I felt her pull the covers to get in bed. She got in and moved next to me. She said softly, "Babe, are you awake?" I opened my eyes and saw this beautiful woman with her face only inches away from mine.

She kissed me softly saying, "Babe, you mean a lot to me. I have been waiting a long time for this day. I want this to be memorable for both of us. I am going to let you make love to me for as long as you want to." I told her I couldn't believe I was in bed with her, she said, "Babe, I have you here with me now and you're all I want." I was wide awake now and scared to death; I didn't know what to do. It looked like she was going to help me. She pulled my head gently over to her chest; then she pulled the covers down so we were exposed to each other.

She lay there naked. She said, "You can do what ever you want to me." It wasn't long before I was deep in her and she moaned a lot when I exploded in her. While I washed up at the sink she took a fast shower.

She came out of the shower and dried off. I had my hands everywhere. She grabbed me, saying in my ear, "The next time you are going to be even better than you were today if that's possible, seeing as how it was your first time. That's something for you to think about until our next meeting." She was in her underwear and reached for her purse to pay me. I told her I didn't want anything. I told her she gave me something I never had before. She said, "Next time you come over I want to do more to you I know you'll like that." She kissed me goodbye like I was never coming back. I had a hard time serving papers that day. I kept thinking about what we did and what she said about wanting to do more to me. I had a beautiful woman that nice to do whatever I wanted with; those were her words. I lost my cherry to a beautiful girl who cared for me. The next time would be better. Lord, give me the strength to live up to her expectations. School was going to start in ten days, but somehow that wasn't what I was looking forward to.

13

My first day at Salesianum, or "Sallies," was tough. The priests seemed mean and curt and treated us like we were in prison. They called our section freshmen "D" for dummies—and walked us to all our classrooms. They warned us not to be late for class or we would spend the afternoon in "Jug" (detention) from 3:00 to 5:00 p.m.

With my father raising hell at home, Menny and I found it hard to get up on time, and if we missed the 8:00 bus, we were late for school. We lived 21 blocks away, so we were spending a lot of time in Jug. Whenever we walked the hallways and came to a right or left turn, we sometimes ran into a priest coming from the opposite way. When we made the turn they would hold out a straight arm with a fist folded and push it right into our faces, stopping us right in your tracks. They would have the nerve to ask, "What's your hurry? Where are you going?" They loved to pull your hair at the temples, which was so painful it made you stand on your toes. I found out there were three real bad priests. The worst one was Fr. Dougherty, who was short with red hair, a very mentally disturbed man and was allowed to rain havoc on the student body. He would have been unsuccessful in any career. My big question was why he was allowed to terrorize students for so many years. The other priests could see him in his day-to-day abuse and yet not rock the boat.

Then there was Mr. Campbell, another mentally disturbed person assigned to Sallies before he was ordained a priest, who roughed up more of us kids than anyone and did it in the name of all that was holy. Mr.

Campbell was so bad that if he should ever be ordained a priest it would be a mockery to religion and for what Salesianum stood for. Finally there was Fr. Kelly, a balding frustrated man, who tried to cover up the fact that he was in the wrong career field. The only position that he could have successfully worked in would be in the prison system, because he was doing a bad job for God. They were the three "SS troopers" of Sallies, SS meaning "Sallies' Saddest."

Menny and I were having the shit knocked out of us at home, and the same thing was happening when we went to our Catholic school. I thought that God was everywhere, even at school, but He wasn't anywhere to be found in this hell hole, and I was looking everywhere for Him. There were some good priests at Sallies, but the bad ones did more damage than the good ones did good deeds. The bad ones had chips on their shoulders and didn't like us freshman "D's." We didn't have much of a chance. Not only did the priests not like us but the "A-B's" and some "C's" never spoke to us. I am sure the "A-B-C's" didn't experience the "D" treatment and probably will defend how great the school was for them. I can truly understand if someone would say that. If they didn't experience the treatment that we experienced than it must have been a great school for them, but not for us. The only reason we went to Sallies was that we heard it was a good Catholic school. Mommy wanted the best for her two boys, and felt safe that we were going to get a good Catholic education. To tell you the truth Menny and I did too.

When I got home from school one day Joan was sitting on the porch. She grabbed me and gave me a big kiss and said that she only just found out that I sang at Midnight Mass nine months earlier. She said she didn't know I could do that, and I told her all she thought I could do was wrestle. She went on, "Is that what you call it, wrestling, Babe? I call it hanging on to my boobs. But I am not complaining. I loved it, and we had fun doing it for years, but lately you haven't been around. Have you found someone to take my place?" I asked her what self-respecting girl would look at me twice. She said, "Take it from me; you have an appeal to older girls in their teens and early twenties. Those girls see better than these young kids you go to school with. I hear a lot of talk about you and you are very well liked."

Joan continued, "Look at me. Aren't you wondering why I am so attracted to you? It's because you are a decent, strong, honest young man that is going somewhere. I know about the ornery shit you do. I let you hold on to my boobs when we wrestle because you don't know what you were doing and it's funny as hell. I can see that you are getting more inventive. You are even getting me aroused, but I trust that you would never hurt me. I know you like me in my t-shirt with no bra on. I chose to let you to play; otherwise you would only look instead of feel." I thanked her for being so honest with me and said I would try to never let her down. But she warned me, "Babe, not everyone is going to like you. Now give me a big kiss. I have to go in and take a shower, and again congratulations on your singing debut."

One of our classes at Sallies was Bible History, which was a waste of time. You couldn't use Bible History in the outside world, even if you lived in a convent. Menny and I were in Jug so often we probably had a bad name from that. I never did anything wrong. I tried my hardest to appease them, but it just made it worse. None of the priests ever asked us why we were late so much; they didn't care. They were running a prison and we were the inmates. Menny and I told my mother about it all the time, but she wasn't about to complain because she wasn't paying any tuition. Mommy said that we didn't have the money to pay the tuition so she never paid them.

One shell-shocked priest, Fr. Neidameyer, was a veteran of the Second World War. The seniors in study hall would make noises like sirens and bombs going off. He would run out of the study halls screaming. The poor guy was scared out of his mind. I felt sorry for him. I met him some years later at a graveside ceremony and wondered if this was where they put their handicapped priests, in a low-key position that didn't require any attention from anyone. We talked for a few minutes, and I told him that I had gone to Sallies, I remembered him there, and thought he was one of the nicer priests. He thanked me for that and we shook hands goodbye. I never took part in the siren and bomb noises that the seniors made to scare him. As far as I was concerned this priest was a hero being in the war and suffering from combat and what it does to some people. I am convinced that when some other priests would lay prone on the cold marble floor with their arms stretched out in front of the Bishop, taking their vows, that they never had any intention of keeping them. They were just waiting to take advantage of some unsuspecting person in the parish. You could see how they were on the outside, but you couldn't see how they were on the inside. As a result, it didn't take long for us to see that Sallies was over rated.

I wasn't an altar boy any longer, either. When you graduated from Christ Our King, your altar career was over. It was just newspapers, golf, sports, working at the store, and Linda. I was pretty busy, but I hadn't heard from her in a while. And the husband of that cutie on West Street called and canceled the paper. What a relief that was I wasn't going to be sucked into her personal problems.

Meanwhile my mother never knew what my father was doing at night and couldn't count on him. We were supporting him and not the other way around. He promised my mother he would help out at the store at night. When he didn't show up for work we could conclude that we might be in for a rough night. He would come home angry and wanting to fight with us. One night he came in to our bedroom and accused Menny and me of having a hole to look through at people in the bathroom because the bathroom backed up to our closet. This was probably something he would do and wanted to find out if we were a couple of perverts like he was. He came in to our bedroom and immediately opened the closet door; we didn't have a light in there, so he held his cigarette lighter over his head. As he lit it, the closet burst into flames; he looked up to see what was on fire. It was the black witches' wig that must have been very flammable because the whole closet was lit up and the old witch's mask was aglow and our two-foot owl was right in his face. This knocked him back against the closet door. He fell out of the closet onto our bedroom floor, gasping for air and white as a ghost. He could barely stand up and walk away with his tail between his legs. Menny quickly put the fire out. We were afraid that there might be a fire in the attic or somewhere else, so we inspected the closet very carefully. He never went in there again; still it wasn't necessary for that to have happened.

By December Menny and I were spending a lot of time in Jug, and the punishments were ridiculous. They would make us write something stupid 500 times. If they caught you talking or laughing they would take you to the front of the room and make you kneel on two pencils with your arms out holding a four-inch-thick book in each hand. If it was concluded that you didn't hold them long enough, you had to start over. Just plain torture, I heard someone say Inhumane was another description, all because of some childish thing an immature boy might do. The best treatment would have been not to draw attention to this childish thing or to call the person up to where the priest was sitting and tell him to knock it off. No, they wanted to entertain the detention class.

Most of the people in Jug were from the "D" class and some "C's." Some priests would walk around with their prayer books in their hands; often I would see them reading from these black books. I thought they were praying for forgiveness because I couldn't figure out what else they would be praying for. One priest could drink a case of beer in one or two nights. I knew that because I was one of the chosen few who were to take the empties out and pick up the new case on the porch. His room was dirty, but nobody sent him to Jug for drinking too much. Where was the priests' detention room? Sallies didn't have one for priests, just for us dummies.

I was friends with some of the crowd from the Forty Acres neighborhood that were also known as the crowd from Saint Ann's parish. One of them was my cousin; Joe Elwood (now deceased). We were all in D, and the priest made sure we were all treated the same—very badly. We wondered why none of the good priests tried to stop the bad treatment, turn the bad ones in to the Bishop, or try to win them over to their more tolerant ways. As the year grew longer, Mr. Campbell was becoming a very violent man. One day Bill Gas wanted out of Jug and asked Mr. Campbell if he could be excused. Mr. Campbell asked if he would take a hit to get out of Jug. Bill told him to plant one on him and pointed to the side of his cheek. Mr. Campbell hauled off and slapped him on the side of his face so hard that it spun him around 90 degrees and left an awful hand print on the side of his face. Bill's parents had to see it; what must they have thought? I am sure Bill played it down, but from where I was standing that was violence.

Every day Mr. Campbell tried out some nasty things on us. These ideas didn't come to him on the spot; he would have had to call on his evil thoughts and think about them first or these evil people had a hand book that they could turn to for help. He would stand on your toes and twist his heels on your toes through your shoes. That was so painful it brought tears to your eyes, It only took one of these sessions to ruin your shoes, and he destroyed my new shoes I had bought with my hard-earned caddy money. He hurt my toes so bad that they bled and I limped for days. I wish I could tell you that I did something very bad to be so honored with this inhumane treatment, but I didn't. All of us in Section D despised him.

The bad priests would tell us stories of individuals who got in a confrontation with a priest and went to hit him. God paralyzed their arms to protect the priest, and those boys never hit anyone else again. I think the priests were just trying to scare us because we might have some retaliation building up in us, and these stories would make us think twice. We must have been awfully gullible to believe these stories because no one ever lifted an arm to hit back. I found out fast that the devil doesn't always wear red. I've seen him wear black.

One day in my travels, I met a gentleman who told me that at one time he had been a priest at Sallies. He was the most foul-mouthed, nasty man, who didn't like anyone or anything. Who recruited this man to be a priest, and what kind of a test was he given to be acceptable into the priesthood? How desperate was his recruiter? How blind and desperate must these recruiters be? This really upset me.

I hadn't seen Linda for a long time and I was expecting to hear from her but she never called me. I had gone over to her house a couple of times but she wasn't home, so I kept trying until I could catch her home. It had been almost seven months since I had seen her and I'll be honest with you, I missed her. By spring, there was still no word from Linda.

One day I saw kids in the yard practicing track and field events. Bill Maloney and I decided to help out. We decided to coach them and get a team together to enter the state Catholic schools track and field competition at Baynard Stadium. I had them practice passing the baton like in the relay races. We also did high jump and all those other events. We practiced every day. Come the day of the event we all met at Baynard Stadium around 10:00 a.m. Every Catholic school in Delaware showed up with a team; it was almost chaotic. When all the dust settled, C.O.K. won. What a triumph this was—helping coach a track team that won the state championship. We were all ecstatic, just wild with celebration. Then somehow I missed the bus. I was walking up Broom Street when they went by, cheering and waving at me. I wasn't on the bus with them, so maybe I missed some escapades, but it didn't matter. I knew what I had done and that was good enough for me.

Linda lived just off Broom Street so I decided to walk over a few blocks and take a look see; maybe I'd be lucky and catch her home. This time I went around to the back of her house, and the yard was a mess. I looked up at the back door and saw an envelope attached to the screen door with big letters that said BABE. I ran up to the door and quickly opened it up; it was a note from Carolyn (the girl with the broken zipper). I sat on the little bench by the railing and started to read Carolyn's note. She wanted me to stop by her house some evening after 6:00 p.m. so she could talk to me. She said that she had some news about Linda, and had written down her address in the Forty Acres, not that far away. I knew where it was and when I got a chance I would have to go and see what this was all about. Missing the bus from the track meet had been a blessing.

Meanwhile Menny and I were talking about giving up the paper route. But we agreed to wait a little longer; the News Journal put the word out that it was going to take all of its paperboys to the Carnival. We all met at Maryland Avenue, where the Carnival was to be held. We were so proud of the new boots we were wearing, which Mommy bought us. They went all the way to our knees, made of black leather, and laced all the way up. We went on all the rides and ate all the food, and the last thing we went to see was the chimpanzee show. We all stood behind a rope barrier. We were cheering when a dirty-looking gypsy woman came out and started walking down her trailer steps. She had a big monkey or chimpanzee, walking with her on a leash past us kids. This undernourished animal looked like he was in one Tarzan movie too many. It grabbed Menny's leg and started to bite him on his legs but wasn't able to penetrate his leather high-top boots. We were all screaming. He was working his way up the leg until he got to Menny's knee, and when Menny put his hand down to stop it, he bit his hand too. Menny was kicking and screaming, in fear of being killed. The dirty gypsy woman finally pulled her chimpanzee off Menny and put him in a cage where he belonged. She asked Menny and me to come into her trailer so she could see Menny's bites. Thank God for those leather boots or he would have been seriously bitten. He had a puncture wound in his hand near his baby finger, and a big mouth imprint over his knee.

The woman wanted to know what Menny had done to provoke this chimpanzee to attack him, but we said "nothing." She said, "You must have done something to him; he has never done anything like this before." I told her maybe he was tired of being mistreated by you and kept in a cage with nothing to eat. She never looked up at me after hearing that; she was looking at Menny's wounds saying they were not bad that they were just a scratch. She said that once the monkey tasted his blood, it went crazy. She said, "Your blood is sweet." She reached down on the floor, picked up a dirty rag, and wrapped it around Menny's hand and said the bleeding will stop soon, this rag will help; she didn't want us to tell anyone about this.

We got a ride home and I told Menny that I wanted to tell Mommy. He got very angry and said no. We went to bed, but I got up a few minutes later and went into Mommy's room and told her that Menny had been bitten by a monkey. She let out a scream and jumped out of the bed and took off down the hallway to our bedroom. She took a long look at him and said to get dressed. Mommy went back to her room and I could hear her calling a cab to come at once, she had an emergency. That cab was at our house in two minutes. They went to the hospital and were home in one hour. Mommy woke me up to tell me what the doctor had told her, that Menny would have died in his sleep if I hadn't told her about this attack. She said, "Babe, you saved your brother's life." I looked over at Menny and we both started to smile. Menny said, "Babe, you did save my life." That was something, because he didn't want me to tell Mommy. Thank God for those high-top leather boots and brother Babe.

I didn't have to work in the store that night so I decided to take a ride over to Carolyn's house to say hello. When I got there the lights were on and I knocked on her door. I could tell she recognized me before she opened the door, and she was all smiles. She opened the door and said, "Hi, Babe. I didn't think I would ever see you again, it's been so long since I left that note." She gave me a big hug, boy was she pretty. It felt so good to be hugged that I didn't want her to let go.

She said that she was baking a cake and wanted me to come out in the kitchen and talk to her while she was baking. She still had on her work clothes including her high heels which gave her beautiful legs an even better look; she stood in front of her stove with her legs apart. How much more sexier could she get standing like that.

We talked about golf and how she would like to play more. She said that she will never forget the lesson I gave her that day when I caddied for her and Linda. I told her that I would never forget that day either, she smiled and said that no one has ever manhandled her that way before, and it made her a better golfer. She said that it was obvious that I got her note how else could I have found her. She turned away from the stove and walked towards me and said that Linda had to leave suddenly. "Linda asked me to tell you how much she misses you, Babe. If she could see you now she would really miss you. You're becoming a hunk of a young man." I could feel a blush coming on.

She went on to say that Linda's sister passed away and Linda had to take a job transfer to Ohio to be near her family. "I know she will write me, and I will pass along any messages that she gives me for you." Carolyn then said hasn't it been a while since you have seen her, and I said it been almost nine months. She has this look come over her face like I said something that startled her.

She reached for my hand and took me to her back door and put the outside light on for me to see better through the window she had put her arm around me as I started to look out the window at the well-lit yard. I straighten up and turned and she was right there in front of me. She told me that Linda told her everything we did that day when I was at her house working in the yard. I said, "Everything?" and she said "Yes, everything. I would like you to help me in my yard Babe. Will you do it?" I never hesitated and said yes.

She was so happy to hear that she gave me a hug and a kiss on the cheek, she wanted to know how was I able to do all that yard work. I told her working in my yard which was enormous compared to your yard. My brother and I would spend days just digging. She asked me for my phone number so she can contact me to get something set up.

We sat at the kitchen table and she held my hand, I asked her if she dresses like this everyday for work. She said that it was expected of her to look nice every day; I told her that it wasn't hard for her to do that. She smiled and said, "Flattery will get you everywhere with me, Babe. I don't have a boyfriend because I am too fussy and besides I am only 23 and I am doing fine on my own." She was so good looking, she could have ten boyfriends she definitely didn't need me. She squeezed my hand and said she felt safe around me and she could trust me and that is important to a girl.

As the school year was coming to an end, I did everything not to go to summer school and really worked hard. I saw my report card, which had all D's and one F. I failed Spanish. I really struggled with that course; as a result I went to summer school at Sallies one hour a day, four days a week, for four weeks. I passed and prayed that God would help me in my sophomore year. It couldn't get worse. The thought of it would be like the feeling one would get being put back in a concentration camp and would make me nauseous to think about it.

I had a message during the week from Carolyn asking for me to help her with some yard work on Saturday, so I went to her house at 10:30 a.m. as she wanted me to. I took an extra pair of pants and a clean shirt, just in case I got dirty and sweaty. She must have seen me because she came out of her house and stood on her little porch looking down at me and said, "Hi Babe, it's nice to see you." From where I was standing it was nice to see her too. I thought to myself what a hunk she is, and what did she have in store for me this day. Her smile could turn most men into a slave to her. The best part is that she didn't know she had that power over men, she just thought of herself as average girl, who thought I was something, and wasn't afraid to show her appreciation for giving her a hand.

She took my hand and walked me over to a sandy patch that ran to her back property line; she asked me if I could lay brick in the sand so they would be nice and flat. I told her that I could, she said if I could it would look beautiful. We raked the sand evenly so it would still remain hard and level. I patted the sand down with a shovel, and then we would pull a piece of wood (like a two by four) over the sand and pat it so it would be perfect to lay brick on. That took a while but once I started and Carolyn handing me the bricks we made good time, it was really going to look good if I had to say so myself. Carolyn couldn't get over how handy I was and how this project was turning out. She had no idea what we could do with some bricks.

She kept stacking the bricks in front of me; she was really fast and could work hard too. She said she always wanted a yard with a brick walkway splitting it in half. Just like Linda, Carolyn said let's stop for a lunch break. I wasn't that hungry; I never am while I am working. I seem to lose my appetite. She offered me a cold ice tea. I saw there wasn't too much more to do so I got right back into it and in no time we were finished. I was sweaty and she looked wetter than I did.

The whole job was easy for two people. I guess from a girl's point of view I looked dirty, with wet pants and a sweaty shirt from my view, I was OK. She asked me if I brought a change of clothes. I showed her my clean things rolled up on the chair. Then she took my hand and said, "You might as well take a shower. I am sure you'll feel a lot better after that. You go ahead and I'll put some things away and come up and join you when I am finished." I thought to myself that Linda must have given Carolyn our game book because this is turning out to be what Linda and I did.

Carolyn's bedroom was in the front of the house and she had a small table lamp lit that gave me a nice comfortable cozy feeling that immediately relaxed me for what I could imagine was going to happen between us. I flicked on the bathroom light, ran the shower water for a few minutes and jumped in. The hot water coming out of the shower was a treat for me; we could never take a hot shower at home. Mommy said that we couldn't afford the hot water bill.

I had stayed in too long and had to get out. There were plenty of towels to dry off with, and I opened the bathroom door to let the steam out when she came around the corner with just a towel around her. She asked me if I was chilly and I said yes so she told me to jump into bed and warm it up for her. Being the dummy I was I asked, "Are you sure?" and she said, "Yes, silly, I am sure. I am going to take my shower now and I'll wake you when I get in bed with you." I thought to myself that Linda didn't leave anything out; she wants it bad.

Her bed was so comfortable; when I lay there I saw her close the bathroom door minus the towel. My little Oliver was starting to act up and was standing straight out at attention. Believe it or not I fell asleep and I woke up as she was getting into bed. She smelled like a field of flowers, if she was a sub I would have ate her up. She told me that Linda had me first, so she had to wait her turn and I want to make this something special between us that we can always share forever. She could sense that I was nervous that's when she told me that it was OK to touch her where ever I wanted to; she pulled my head gently onto her chest seeing her nipples standing out just like my Oliver. She said that it has been a long time since she let a man touch her I can't control how I feel about you so I have to give in to my desire to have you.

I guess I am becoming overly excited when she threw back the covers and opened her legs, I gently touched her and she started squirming and moaning loudly. She kept saying don't stop, please don't stop. I'd better be able to satisfy her or she is going to be very let down. She guided my hand all over her body. She reached for a little cellophane wrapper from her night table while she unwrapped it and asked me if I ever had one of these on before, holding up a rubber for me to see. I told her no, I couldn't believe how much she helped me with it she made sure that it was as comfortable as it could be for me. But I still couldn't understand why she wanted me to wear such a contraption.

When I returned, she asked me to do it from the back on her knees. She called it doggie style, and it seemed like it went deeper because when I exploded again she shook all over and fell forward face first into her pillow passed out. At first I was scared, but when I looked at her face she had a smile on it and I could look at her from behind and see that she was breathing. I didn't try to wake her. She looked to comfortable, so I wrote her a note telling her how lucky I was to know a nice girl like her, and that I will be thinking of her until the next time we can be together, sweet dreams. I took the note and laid it next to the rubber wrapper.

I left quietly, and turned on some lights so it would look like someone was still up, I checked all her doors and made sure the dead bolt was on the front door and left by the back door where my bike was. When I left I felt safe for her and thought she would probably sleep through the night and wake up refreshed looking for me to be next to her. How disappointed she would be when she would finally realize that I was gone. What little strength I had left I had to go to the store and get something to eat. Everyone wanted to know where I was all day so I told them that I was helping some woman with her brick pathway in her back yard. I didn't finish so I'd have to go back.

Summer school was definitely a pain, but I made sure that one hour a day wasn't going to ruin my summer. I enjoyed playing golf, more now than ever. I was hitting the ball good and would go to the driving range a lot, but practicing by yourself is not fun. I also practiced putting for hours. I also caddied all I could. I knew I was going to make at least two dollars each time, which isn't bad if the golfer is nice. Most jobs were good, some were OK, and I've told you about some of the bad ones.

Menny and I went up early Saturday and checked in with Grumpy. He said for some reason it was slow, but he would get us a job. He called us quickly and introduced us to a man who said that the two other fellows in the blue shirts were Oblate Brothers, not priests, and that they assisted the priests in all their needs, except to have sex with the nuns. Menny and I burst out laughing. This guy said, "Let's have fun today, and keep it clean." They were from Philly and he was paying the bill. I asked him if that meant he was going to be too broke to tip the caddies. He laughed and said that he could see this was going to be a fun day.

He took us over to introduce us to Brother John and Brother Joe. We shook hands and walked to the first tee. My guy was Brother John. He was a little stiff, so I told him that God wouldn't mind it that he had a good time today, that's why He gave us golf and why He provided me today. Brother John laughed and hit a good one over the road. "See what I mean," I said, "great shot." The guys paying the bill told me these guys were not allowed to have or inherit any money. Anything they inherited would go to the church. I told him that was going too far, that the Church was going to keep him away from women and money, too. I told him, "You must have them tearing the doors off the place to get in."

He replied that he had never heard it put that way before. I told him it was the painful truth. These two guys were so humble it almost made you sick. Don't get me wrong, it was good for them; they saw things differently from the way we saw things. I asked Brother John if he had ever heard of Salesianum. He said he had and asked me if it was a good school. I told him it was. I left it at that because he would have not understood anything else. The brothers saw the bums near the course and took a big interest in them. I told Brother John that the bums would have his clothes on their backs if he weren't careful. He felt sorry for them because they were so deprived. I told Brother John they were bums by choice that they took the easy road, and unfortunately, it didn't include God. "Don't even go near them, Brother, unless I am with you. Stay with me." We walked by one bum who was really dirty looking. Brother John asked me about my name, Jerome, and said that St. Jerome helped to translate and write the Bible. I asked him was that the same Bible that we as Catholics were forbidden to read? He wasn't sure of that, and I told him there was another Jerome, an American Indian named Geronimo, who wrote history too.

I went on, telling Brother John not to be mad at me, that I was taking the other side to show him both views. I told him I'd shut up if he preferred, but he said, "Please don't, I am enjoying it very much." The guy paying the bill had Menny help him carry out the food after nine, and we each had a hot dog and a soda. Brother John stayed next to me the whole time. He told me that he served blindly, which was probably not too good, but it was easy and he trusted the priest. I told him to stay in Philadelphia because I could show him priests who were working for the Devil and that they could be considered a disgrace to the Catholic Church.

He said, "Jerome, you sure have a way with words; I never looked at it from both sides before. You sure are a pleasure to be around." I told him I thought he was stuck with me and was making the best of it. He said he was walking in the valley of the blind—see no evil, hear no evil, speak no evil, which was easier. I told him that my life was different from his: I see the evil, I hear the evil, and at times I speak the evil. I was surviving on a daily basis and to see my life would make him sick to his stomach. But, I went on, "I will survive and I will make my mark. I have in me what it takes to be someone, and some people can see that in me and some can't."

Brother John was touched. He said, "You're a bright light. From now on I am going to look for guidance and get involved with families in our parish, and maybe get into coaching, even if it's just helping out." I told him that was a good idea and God would guide him all the way. He said he couldn't hear it any better. He said that if someone told him that some young 15-year old-young man would be an inspiration for him he wouldn't have believed it. I told him if he felt that, he would have all the fuel to finish the job.

Brother John and I had hit it off real well. As we walked off eighteen I put his bag on the pro shop rack. The sponsor came up to Menny and me and split the five dollars for caddying, and we thanked him. Brother John came up to me and gave me a big hug good bye. I don't know why but as they walked away, I felt sorry for him. I think the sponsor did too or they would have never been there that day. When they got out of sight Menny wanted to know what that was all about and why did that Brother give me a hug. I told him that I got to his heart and he thanked me for that. He was going to go back and help kids like us. I told Menny, "Let's break that five and get the hell out of here."

We went down to my mother's store, where she was always glad to see us. Menny had to serve papers and it was my turn to work at the store. Saturday night at Toner's Luncheonette was something. It ran the whole gamut; all three phone booths were in use, as well as the two pinball machines. Let's not forget the juke box, playing all the latest songs. My mother was doing well because Toner's Luncheonette was doing well. She was having enough money left over from the store bills, salaries, and our house bills to still put money in the bank. Boy was that good news. I dipped a lot of ice cream at night there, which gave me very strong wrists. If a nice-looking girl came in and said hi or just winked at me, I would blush. I would try hard not to, but I just got redder.

Although Menny was getting ready to get his drivers' license, he had been caught driving without a license. I think they might have made him wait as punishment. We both bought Cushman motor scooters. Mine was slow, and Menny's was faster. He spent a lot of time on his. I was too interested in other things with two legs and not two wheels.

It wasn't long before Carolyn had left a message to do some more yard work on Saturday at 10:00; I got all excited just thinking about it. I thought that was the second time I had done anything like that to a girl and it looked like it wasn't going to be my last. It was Menny's turn to work at the store and his turn to serve the papers. That was a relief for me; I could take my time with Carolyn and not have to rush home. The closer Saturday got the more nervous I was to see Carolyn again. She definitely gave me something to look forward to being with her, she had a way of making me feel relaxed around her and that I was important to her. How lucky can a guy be? And no one knew about it either.

I got there at 10:00 sharp. Someone said that the temperature was going to be in the eighties. I pulled into the back yard where Carolyn was sitting on the back steps waiting for me. She looked so pretty sitting there in her navy blue shorts and short sleeve blouse. As soon as I put my bike up she was all over me like a warm blanket. Hugging me real tight, she couldn't thank me enough for the way I left her that Saturday night. I concluded that I was very big in this girl's life and we were definitely getting hooked on each other. She said that she loved my note and would cherish it forever and how thoughtful it was of me to leave some lights on in different rooms like I did. Then she said she was sorry but she must have passed out because she didn't wake up until 4:00 in the morning. "I was naked under those covers but the way you had me tucked in I was real warm. The last thing that I remembered was you exploding inside me."

She said that she got up and put a robe on and took my note downstairs and read it over and over sipping on a cup of tea and heaving some cookies to go with it. She said, "Babe, I was starving. And hungry for you, It was awfully thoughtful for you to put the dead bolt on for me."

"I sat there for at least an hour having a second cup of tea and some more cookies just thinking about you and what you might be doing Sunday. I wanted to call you all day and invite you over for Sunday dinner, just you and me. Babe, wouldn't that have been fun?" I told her I was up the Rock caddying all day. She said when she went back to bed and it was very hard to get me off her mind and shake the sexual desire that she was feeling for me and trying to go to sleep. "I put my hand between my legs and soon fell asleep but it wasn't like you, Babe."

She looked in my eyes and said, "I'll be honest with you, Babe, I feel like taking you up stairs right now and spend the rest of the day locked in your arms, but I'll wait." She asked me if I felt like some yard work, I said sure. She wanted to pay me for the work that I did the last time I was here, but I refused. I told her what she gave me was priceless and I would never accept a penny from her. "I know you mean that, Babe," she said. "That is why I am so attracted to you. You like to show more kindness than you receive."

She was worried if I would be offended if we pulled weeds, but I told her that's all we do at home is pull weeds. We finished that job and she asked me if I could fix some cracks and missing pieces in her cement. I said that I would need a trowel or something like that to do a neat job. She went in her little shed and came out with an old trowel that was perfect for what we were going to do. We mixed a bag of cement and started to patch every crack and hole in her back yard. It really started to look good. We mixed another bag and I started to repair the cracks in the cement steps and fill in the space that was there from coming away from the brick wall of the house. When I finished they looked like new. I had cement on my pants and hands, my pants were all wet but they would dry fast in this heat. Carolyn took a wet rag and started to wipe my pants and when she got to my fly, she looked up at me and smiled.

Even though it was lunch time I wasn't hungry, so we just took a break and had a cold glass of ice tea. She came over to me and sat on my lap and told me to touch her and see if I could arouse her. I slid my hand up her shorts and touched her in her most sensitive area between her legs and she said that's enough, that we had to wait a little while longer for me to really take care of her. She told me again how good I was to her when we made love. With the sweat running down both of our faces, she asked me if I wanted to do any more in this heat. I asked her if she was satisfied with what we had accomplished today, and she said she was. I told her if she could hook up the garden hose I could clean out the wheelbarrow before the cement got hard. She said, "Go for it. While you're at it let's clean the side walk off too."

When we were finished she told me to let her have my pants so she could put them in the wash with hers. There would be plenty of time for them to dry. I told her that I was going to give up the paper route and I didn't have to be anywhere tonight either. She was so happy that I could stay for a while that she was almost in tears. I went in the house and took every thing off and put them on the top step. In the bathroom she had laid out some towels for me to use. I could step out of the shower on to a nice fluffy carpet. The water was hot again and I regulated it to my liking and finished fast. It was hard for me to shower when Oliver wouldn't settle down. I put the towel around me and Oliver was trying to sneak a peak out the fold.

I opened the bathroom door and there she was standing in front of me naked, walking to me. She pressed up against me with her chest, and Oliver was not playing anymore; he was wide awake and needed a rub down. She kissed me like Joan did and put her tongue in my mouth. I touched her and she nearly collapsed. She told me to get in bed and warm up the sheets, she wasn't going to be that long. I didn't fall asleep this time; Oliver wouldn't let me .She ran to me and jumped into bed right up against me, and wherever she turned Oliver was right there. She grabbed him and said that she went to the doctor and I didn't have to wear a rubber anymore, wasn't that great. She wanted to know what it was like to wear a rubber, and I told her that it took away a lot of the feeling. She said that I would be able to feel her better inside now and she would be able to feel me better as well.

I could tell that she wanted to get laid in the worst way; she threw back the covers and told me to come get her. I was right. It was better without that contraption. She ran to the bathroom and came back, now it was my turn to go.

She sat up and said Linda was asking for you, and had sent her some pictures that were taken a little while back after she had gained some weight. She showed me a picture of Linda and I remarked look how heavy she got. Why would she do a thing like that? She was too pretty to let her self go like that. Carolyn assured me that she would lose it; she had too much going for her to gain and keep all that weight. "I can assure you she will lose it all if she hasn't already."

Carolyn was happy that I didn't have to run off and that I could stay with her for a while. She said that she was lonely for my company. "I know that I am older than you, but I love you very much." I didn't want to make any sense of it because it felt too good. No self-respecting woman would ever let a man have the freedom to explore her body like I did if she didn't love him. She put her hand over my mouth and said not to say a word.

She told me that she had been putting off telling me all day, but she had to go away for a few weeks on a business trip and would call me when she returned. Tears were running down her cheeks. I never saw her cry like that before and said I was sorry if I caused this. She pulled her warm body close to me and said she would miss me more than I would know. She said I wasn't to worry about her; she would contact me and not to think anything was wrong just because I don't hear from her. I told her I should be getting my drivers license soon and couldn't wait. She kissed me long on the lips and I got dressed and left quietly.

In August we were getting ready to go back to school. I was at my paper drop-off spot right at 4:00 when the wise-ass manager of the paper boys drove up with his buddy. Through the windshield I could see him tapping his buddy's leg, as if to say, "Just watch what I do to this kid." I got to his door and his window was down. He asked if I knew who he was, and I said yes. Then I asked him if he knew who I was. He said, "Yes, you're that wise ass who works for me. You're supposed to be here at 4:00 sharp." When I said I was there before 4:00, he replied, "Starting tomorrow and every day after that, you better be here by 4:00 or I am going to kick your ass."

I get enough of this shit at home, and I didn't need this from anyone else especially this short rump. So I asked him if he was talking to me and he said, "Is there anyone else here, son?"

"Don't call me son. You call me Babe like everyone else."

"How about if I call you Baby, like how you act?"

I replied, "I wouldn't deliver papers for you for double the pay, and you have a lot of nerve trying to show off to your friend. I will tell you now you can deliver those papers today, because I am not, I quit."

He opened the car door and came out onto the side walk. He started begging me to reconsider, that he was just having fun with me. I told him he chose the wrong words and the wrong time to try to flex his small muscles at me. He asked if I would deliver this week so he could find a replacement. I told him no, and as far as I was concerned, my customers are paid up. He could stick this pile of papers up his ass.

I walked away and he ran after me. "How do I know who gets a paper? What are their addresses?" I told him he should have thought about that before he started roughing me up. He was begging me, but I still insisted, I quit. I then went in the house. I found Menny and told him what happened and he agreed with me to let him serve the papers. I saw him at 9:00 p.m. still serving those papers. The next day the manager looked me up and told me he needed my help, but I told him if I told my mother what happened yesterday and how he spoke to me he would lose his job.

14

When school started in the fall, I would be in tenth grade, or better put, back in prison. The priests were eager to hurt someone. They had the summer off with no one to terrorize and were walking around just like prison guards.

My English class was in the library on the ground floor a converted bed room in a converted house. They called it a library, but it looked like a collection of books bought from a garage sale. On the top row of the book cases were silver trophy cup that were won by the students over the years. Because I always liked to throw things, I threw spitballs into the cups before class started. I bet I threw at least a couple hundred of them, making some shots and missing others. One day Father Kelly saw me throwing the spitballs. He ran up to me and told me to get out. I asked what he meant by get out. He said get out. I asked him again what do you mean get out, "Out of the room or out of the school?" What? He answered again, "Get out," screaming at me like I did something bad. So I walked all the way to my mother's store on Baynard Boulevard and Van Buren Street. As I walked in, my mother was having a cup of tea with Rev. Dunn, a Protestant minister, one of those people we Catholics were told to stay away from. He was dressed in his blue gray clothes with a little white square in the front of his collar like the priests wore. My mother wanted to know why I was home early, so I explained that I threw some spitballs into some trophies that were sitting on top of the library book cases when Ft. Kelly came in and saw me and told me to get out. I told Rev. Dunn that all this happened before class started, so I wasn't disrupting anything. This priest kept screaming at me to get out.

I could see that Rev. Dunn was in shock, with his jaw hanging open. He said not only did the punishment not suit the crime, but they didn't take the confusion out of "get out." He said he couldn't allow this to happen to me. "Your mother and I have been talking about your father and all that. I am not going to allow you to be treated at school the way you are treated at home by your father." He stood up and said, "Come on, Babe, I want to take you back to that school. I am going to get to the bottom of this."

He put his arm around me as we walked out to his car, and we drove to Salesianum. He had a hard time parking because his big Lincoln was too big for city parking. I was out in the street giving him direction as to the distances between cars. We finally parked and walked into the Eighth Street entrance. We went up the steps to Father Lawless's office, where Fr. Dougherty was sitting behind Fr. Lawless's desk. Rev. Dunn immediately introduced himself and said he was a friend of the Toner family and was here with Jerome Toner to discuss the discipline of this young man. The look on his face plainly said he didn't want to shake Fr. Dougherty's hand nor did Fr. Dougherty want to shake his.

Rev. Dunn was treating Fr. Dougherty as if he was in charge of this school. Actually Fr. Dougherty and Fr. Kelly kept a lot of things from Fr. Lawless, the Principal. Father Lawless was a very kind and sympathetic man. Anyone who ever went to Sallies will tell you that, but it would be very difficult to find anyone to speak well of Fr. Kelly or Fr. Dougherty or Mr. Campbell. Rev. Dunn started right in on Fr. Dougherty, saying that Father Kelly just told this young man to get out but wouldn't tell him what he meant by get out. The boy asked him what he meant but got no answer, so he left the school and walked to his mother's store, some 18 blocks away. "He thought he was being kicked out of school for throwing spitballs before class. Mr. Toner didn't disrupt his class at all, only Father Kelly did."

Fr. Dougherty's face was red. Rev. Dunn said, "Let me ask you a question. Do you know anything about this young man?" Fr. Dougherty replied that they kept folders on all our students, so Rev. Dunn asked if he would get the file on Jerome Toner. Fr. Dougherty went to the file cabinet. Going through the alphabet, he said nervously, "T, Toner, and Jerome." He brought the file back to his desk and when he opened it up for review for us to see, he was shocked to find only a single sheet of paper.

Rev. Dunn asked Fr. Dougherty what the file said about Mr. Toner. Fr. Dougherty kept looking at the sheet for the longest time. He then said, with his face down, "It says here that from September 1951, to the present time, he has been late for school 43 times." Rev. Dunn asked, "What kind of a person is late for school 43 times?" Fr. Dougherty smirked and said he didn't know. Rev. Dunn asked him, "Why didn't someone in this school sit down with him and ask why he was late so much? I can only conclude that you weren't interested. You were only interested in punishing him after school in Jug. If you would have taken the time to ask he would have told you." Rev. Dunn looked at me and asked if anyone in this school asked me why I was late. I answered no.

He asked Fr. Dougherty if he was at all interested in why Jerome was late 43 times, and the priest said yes. Rev. Dunn told him, "Jerome's father often comes home after midnight, drunk and in a rage, hitting his mother, sister, brother and Jerome. The police are called most of the time. It would be hard to go back to sleep, and by the time they did get back to sleep they couldn't get up in the morning because of the interruption. If they miss the 8:00 o'clock bus or if the bus is running late, then they are going to be late for school. They get beat up at night, and then come to school and get beat up at school, and no one cares here either. You punished him for being late by placing him in your detention center you call Jug for two hours after school, so now if he's lucky, he might be home by 6:00 p.m., and the cycle starts all over again."

Fr. Dougherty was devastated hearing this news from Rev. Dunn, who continued, "I defy you to show me where Jerome Toner got into trouble in this school since day one." Fr. Dougherty looked into the folder, looked up, and said "none." Rev. Dunn said, "That's right, none. These are good young men. This boy has had the hell knocked out of him night after night as well as the rest of the family and yet he has never got in any trouble; now that is remarkable. It's a miracle that they would ever want to go to school, so when they go to a Catholic school like yours, you let them down and just put them in Jug for being late. Jerome looked up to you; you represent the Catholic Church and all that is holy and fair. From what he tells me, you and Father Kelly treat him and his brother and the 'D's' very badly. If this is a Catholic school, then why do you treat him with such disrespect?" Father Dougherty told me to go back to class, but just then, the dismissal bell rang so I stayed, sitting in the high-backed chair. Rev. Dunn told Fr. Dougherty, "Someone needs to make atonement and change some of your in humane policies in this school. If things don't change here, I personally will go to your bishop about this school and the treatment of some students here. This is not Christian behavior. I promise you I will do it and bring plenty of witnesses. Don't make this happen. Clean up this place or I will go to the press as well."

Fr. Dougherty was speechless. Rev. Dunn took a card out of his pocket and placed it on the desk. He turned to me and said, "Come on, Babe, let's go." I stood up and he put his arm around my shoulder and we walked out. Rev. Dunn stopped at the door and turned and told Father Dougherty that I would be in school in the morning, on time or late, depending on how it goes tonight. He dropped me off at the store. Mommy wanted to know what happened. I explained, and I was curious to see if the priests would change their evil ways.

I went back to school on Monday. They were cautious around me for a while, but it soon wore off. They just didn't have any time for us, not even a cordial hello or anything like that. To be honest with you, we were at our best when they weren't around. At Mass in the gym they asked us to pray for this and pray for that, but no one was praying for us, the dummies in "D." We were the trash in the school. I hope Saint Peter, who is working the turnstiles in heaven, will not allow any of these bad priests in.

Menny and I found that a good way to relax was on football game nights. We went to the game with some other guys and headed for the center field fence; even though they tried to board it up we still found a way to get through the repairs. We would hide there until they started playing the national anthem, when we would pop up and go over the fence like rats. There were tons of us because we weren't the only ones to think of it. There were so many of us that came over the fence that the people in the seats started cheering loudly for us while they were playing our national anthem. We ran past the police standing at attention saluting the flag, giving them the finger. Those cops wanted to kill us. We would hide in the bathroom or sit in a vacant seat. They never got me. I never paid to get in any sporting event ever.

One guy worked the Sallies side of the football field in the box seat area. I think he was a Sallie's alumnus who didn't like kids. We must have looked bad to him because he would say, "Hey Toner, what kind of trouble are you getting into tonight?" I would never answer him; I didn't like him either. He came in our store one evening and recognized me and said, "I didn't know you worked here." I told him I didn't but that it was my mother's store. Mommy was sitting down at the end of the counter on the last stool, near the glass covered cake and pie display stand. He then asked me how I liked Sallies. In a very strong, loud voice I said it was the worst fucking school I had ever heard of. I looked down at my mother, who had spit out a mouthful of tea all over the glass display. He picked up his paper and walked out. Good riddance to him.

In the spring of 1953 Menny and I told some of our friends about Joan undressing in front of her bedroom window, so about twelve of us decided to meet in my back yard at dusk. We would need to get as high up the tree as we could to get a full view of Joan and her lovelies. We all smoked and I know with all of us smoking at the same time, it had to look like a Christmas tree with blinking lights. We were anxiously waiting for Joan to appear.

Out of nowhere her bedroom light went on and Joan appeared. She pulled open her blouse and was standing there in her white bra. We were all sitting on different limbs. We all stood up and leaned forward to get a better look. The cherry tree started to move, and I was getting closer to the ground. Suddenly we were all lying on the ground and Donald was laughing as only he could. The tree's roots must have been shallow because the tree fell over, with the roots sticking out of the ground. We were hysterical, but no one was hurt because it fell over slowly. We were all on our backs still smoking and laughing. We had to get out of here, so we all jumped the back fence and ran up 30th Street.

The next day, I went out in the back yard and was looking back toward my house. Our yards were long, so I couldn't have been any farther away from the downed cherry tree. Mrs. Toskas came out and walked toward the tree, turned around, and came back to me. She asked me if I had anything to do with her tree being down on the ground. I told her no, but I don't think she believed me. I couldn't tell her the truth, but I felt bad about lying to her. I liked her that much.

I really felt bad because Mrs. Toskas looked after us kids like a mother. Many times she gave me dinner, usually Italian-style cooking. She knew there wasn't anyone home looking after us, and she was the only person to hold out her hand to help us. God will bring her to heaven to be with Him. I was lucky to have two mothers.

The #30 school had a long stone wall where Menny and I would often sit and talk for hours. One day Menny, George Booth and I were sitting there when George's gym teacher from P.S. DuPont was approaching in his blue Dodge convertible. He had his arm around a woman sitting next to him and was very proud of this moment. As soon as he passed by, I cupped my hands and yelled through them, "Fat Nat, the Jewish Rat!" It was too late; I knew this was going to be a big mistake. We all hid in case he came back around. George was scared that he would recognize any of us. "You guys don't go to P.S.," he cried, "I do." When nothing happened, we quickly forgot about the incident.

The school year was coming to an end fast. One night Menny and I sat with Mommy and told her we didn't want to go to Sallies anymore. She started crying, saying she wanted us to finish school. We assured her we did, too, but not at Sallies. We wanted to go to P.S. DuPont. I told Mommy that Sallies wasn't a school; it was a detention center for misguided priests. We assured her that we would graduate from P.S. DuPont High School, and she could count on it. She felt better and she said to be sure to sign up in time.

I was never so happy to leave a place in all my life. I made sure I wasn't going to take anything from that school with me. I threw my books down the hallways. I threw them in the gym, and I didn't care who saw me. No one asked me what I was doing. My name was all over these books, but I didn't give a damn. I wasn't going back. I walked out of that school and never looked back. I felt sorry for some of the guys whose fathers had graduated from Sallies so they had to go there. I wasn't going to be any part of the graduating class of 1955.

Meanwhile, I kept going over to Carolyn's house, but no one was ever home. One day I stopped by and her neighbor came out onto the porch and asked if I was that young man who worked in Carolyn's yard with her. I told her I was, and every time I came over here, Carolyn was never home. All of a sudden this woman had a terrifying look on her face. She said, "I guess you don't know! Carolyn was killed in an automobile accident while out in Ohio. I'm sorry to be the one to tell you." The news buckled my legs and I fell against the porch railing. I had to sit down so as not to fall. The neighbor said it happened when she was visiting her girlfriend, an old friend. I asked her if she knew the girls name. She said, "I think it was Linda, and that all three of them died in an accident with a truck."

I asked her if she knew who the third person was. She said as far as she knew it was Linda's little girl. Carolyn had showed her a picture of her daughter and she was beautiful like Linda. I then said I didn't know Linda had gotten married. She said she didn't; she was single. Carolyn had told me that she couldn't come back to Delaware because the father didn't know about the baby and she didn't want to have that burden put on him because he was a young man. I had told Carolyn that was awfully thoughtful of Linda to think that far ahead. I must have looked pretty bad. This woman wiped my face with a towel she had in her apron pocket. She held on to my shoulder while she wiped all the sweat from my face and neck. She said she was sorry and that I must have been a good friend to react like this.

I asked, "You said you saw a picture of Linda's little girl. Did Carolyn ever tell you her name?" She replied, "Yes, she called her Gerri, after someone she loved dearly. That's all I know." I thanked her for taking the time to tell me what happened. She asked me if I knew Carolyn's friend Linda. I said I had met her once over a year ago. The neighbor looked at me and asked my name. I told her it was Babe. "No, not your nickname, your real name." I told her my real name was Jerome.

"Jerome," she said. "Jerome sounds like . . . ." Just then she raised her voice and said, "Then you must be the one." I turned and walked off the porch in complete shock. I could hear her piecing my name together with Linda's baby's name, I could still hear her call out to me, "You must be Jerry, the one Carolyn was talking about." Why didn't Carolyn tell me any of this? It's obvious to me now that Carolyn was only spoon feeding me information about Linda. Why? I could hardly function. I couldn't stop thinking about Carolyn and Linda, and Linda having a baby, not married. Why wasn't I told anything?

I don't remember my journey home, I just remember going up the stairs to bed. It was only 5:00, but I was too sick to work. Menny woke me and said it was my turn to work, but I told him he was going to have to take my place, I was too sick to get out of bed. He took one look at me and could see that. Little did he know I was really in shock and mourning, having lost two very close friends? I just couldn't believe I would never see them again.

I woke up around 9:00 in the morning. I could barely move and just lay there and cried a few minutes. It was very tough because I didn't have anyone to share this with. I finally got up, but my legs were very weak. I knew I had to get over this. I didn't feel like doing anything, not even caddying. I just sat around for a while and then went out back for a smoke. I saw Joan, who was lying out and asked me to join her. I told her I wasn't feeling that good and didn't want to make her sick. She said, "Babe, you can make me sick anytime, I don't mind." I told her, "Not like this; you don't need this sickness."

I had to be at the store by 6:00 p.m., so I had to start feeling better. I'd cried enough. If I cried any more it would show in my eyes. It was all I could do to get ready to work. My mother was very concerned because I was rarely sick. That whole night I kept looking to see who was coming in to the store. I was thinking it would be Carolyn or Linda. Mommy kept feeling my forehead, so I lied and told her I was starting to feel better. This was going to be the hardest night shift I would ever have to work. It was horrible.

I went right home to bed and when I woke up, I was a new man. The sadness was gone and I was going to be in good shape. I would get my strength back and caddy in a few days. Menny said he could use the money to spend on his beat-up Pontiac wagon. Every time he stopped the hood would slide off into the street.

We went up to the Rock and checked in with Grumpy. He told Menny and me to go down to ten and hawk balls. He said he wanted everyone else to leave or come up to see him. It was a first for us for Grumpy to assign us on ten. This meant that Menny and I had it all to ourselves. What a deal. Menny and I made dimes and quarters hand over fist. We got to see everyone, good or bad. We stayed there till 3:30 and made $4.50 each, which wasn't bad for six hours. We went back Sunday and found Kautz already down there, so we checked in with Grumpy to caddy. It was backing up already, and wasn't that long before we got a job.

A couple was standing by the rack. Menny took the man, and as usual I got stuck with the woman. Betty looked like a big mean woman who had some authority like working in a concentration camp. It would have to be an awfully dark room to climb on that thing, or even kiss her. I said hello and she just mumbled hello back. This was going to be bad. I looked at the husband and thought that he looked like she kicked the shit out of him just for something to do. Menny was making faces at me, as if to say, "Do we even want to take this job?" If we didn't we would definitely be kicked down the road. We accepted it just to see where it would take us. But Betty could really hit a ball. When she walked I could hardly keep up with her because she took big steps. Her husband stayed away, and I didn't blame him. It was bad enough he had to get in bed with her. On the long, par five first hole, she was on in three. So when I was holding the pin, I got a lecture on how to hold the pin and put it back in the hole. I only wished I had the nerve to kick her in the ass. She pared the first hole. Instead of handing me her club, she dropped it on the ground.

On the third hole, a short par three, she hit the ball into a trap. When she came out, she slipped on some mud, which forced her legs open, causing the seam in the back of her pants to come apart. I wouldn't say anything, nor would Menny or Bob, her husband. Betty was now walking around with her pants coming apart. Her ass was so big that a toilet would cringe to see it coming. It looked more like a crack in the earth.

Betty was really not a nice person and didn't try to be, but she could play golf. Bob was trying to avoid her every chance he could. She told me on the sixth hole that she wasn't going to call me Babe. She didn't think that a golfer should call her caddy Babe; it just didn't sound good. She said she would call me Caddy. I never said anything. She said, "You can call me Mrs. Hardmass." I just looked at her. She never asked me for anything, such as the distance to the green, nothing. but I had to wash her balls and give her a tee on every tee.

Menny came over and asked me how I was holding up. I said she was really a bitch and could use a good screwing. He said that the closest thing that could mount her would be a bull from behind. We were giggling. She spun around and told us to be quiet. As she turned back around to hit a tee shot, we could see that her pants were torn from her waist to her crotch. Her husband was staying as far away from her as he could.

We finished nine holes and there was a backup on ten again. Betty came out with a hot dog and a drink, never asking me if I wanted something. Bob got Menny something and Menny felt funny, but I told him to enjoy it. On the tenth hole her ball went out of bounds. Boy was she pissed. I told her it went into the thick bushes and it was impossible to get. This just made her worse, if that was possible. Then she hit a big drive on the thirteenth hole. The ball fell in the creek, which was full of boulders. If you stepped on one loose stone, it would tilt and you would lose your balance and fall in the water. She came down to the creek and asked me where her ball was and if I was going to get it. I said there were snakes in there. She pushed me aside and stepped onto the tilting rock, and suddenly she was on her big ass in 18 inches of water. She asked me to help her and I said I was afraid to. She was cursing me and trying to get out of the creek. She fell in two or three times more.

She finally came out of the creek, wet all over. The only place dry on her was the top of her head. Menny and I were standing on the green and could see her dripping wet. When she got to the green, Bob asked what happened, and she said she had fallen into the snake-infested creek and her caddy was too afraid of getting his hands wet for fear of being attacked by some snakes. I was laughing because she looked so terrible and had five holes to go.

Those wet pants were hard on her crotch. She was starting to walk like it was on fire. As we were walking up the eighteen hole, she had smoke going out of both ears. She walked up to mark her ball and bent over. The crack in her pants was now about three inches wide. I tried not to look. She finished putting and dropped her putter on the apron and walked off. I said, "I'll get your putter, Mrs. HardAss." She stopped in her tracks and I was rolling on the grass laughing, and Menny was laughing, too. She stormed back to me and asked me what I had said, and this time I said, "I'll get your putter, Mrs. Hardmass."

She looked like she wanted to fight, but she knew I would hit her back. Bob caught up to me and thanked me, saying he was going to catch hell all night because it didn't take much to set her off. He apologized for her not getting me a hot dog. He said, "Thank God she is not paying you. Here is two dollars, like what your brother is getting. Somehow I think you earned yours." I thanked him and walked away. She kept calling Caddy, Caddy, asking me to come over to her, but I wouldn't pay any attention. Bob was at his car in the parking lot before she took the hint and to go home.

At the time, I was also practicing my driving and getting ready for my driving test. On the big day, I parked easily with the test supervisor, so we rode all over Bancroft Parkway and Little Italy, where there were a lot of stop signs and red lights. All you had to do was to miss one and you would fail, but I was very cautious. We got back to the Division of Motor Vehicles. The instructor told me to come inside. He took me up to the window and turned and said, "You passed. Drive carefully." I could have screamed, but I had to hold back. I had my license and didn't have to ride my bike any more! Soon after that Mommy sold our bikes for $40 each. Raleigh bikes kept their value.

15

I was a little nervous about going to P.S. DuPont, even though I knew most of the kids, I was still scared. The teaching staff was first class. They took a big interest in the students, so I knew this was going to be a wonderful experience. One day Menny and George came looking for me after school. They both told me that the gym teacher I yelled at in his convertible got both of them. He had thrown George up against the wall and was choking him. George said he couldn't breathe. Menny said that the man had him pinned up against the wall of their home room. He wanted to know which one of them yelled out that insulting remark about being a Jewish rat and disrespected him in front of his wife, who was with him in the car. They had said they didn't have anything to do with it, that it wasn't them. I am sure they told him it was me. I think this guy scared them to death. A few months later, he came in the gym during lunch and asked me to come in the gym office. He told me to close the door. He said that he knew I was the one that called out to him that summer evening and for my punishment, I was not allowed in the gymnasium until after the Christmas holidays.

I asked him how he could punish me for something that happened before I was a student at P.S. DuPont High School. Then he asked me what I thought he should do. He said, "I can't hit you; I told him that this was personal." He was using the school to punish me. I told him that if he made an inquiry he would find out that I was right and he could lose his job and career over this punishment on public school property. I continued, "You want me to stay out of the gymnasium during lunch, if that's what you want, this would still be involving the school, this is personal and we can settle it personally." I opened the door and walked out.

A few days later I was handed a note to meet the gym teacher out back after school. I went out and found him standing against the wall. I walked up to him. He tried to scare me and came up in my face. I knew that if he touched me because of this incident he would lose his job. He said he had a lot of time to think about what I said to him in the gym office and that I was right. "It took a quick mind to think of that so fast. I was really hoping you would apologize to me and I wouldn't have to punish you through the school," he said. I told him that I knew as soon as I said it, I was wrong. "I couldn't retract it, but now that you are calmed down, I apologize." He said, "Your dislike of Jews probably can be traced right back to your religious teachings. They tell you that we killed Christ or are responsible for His death. That was 2000 years ago, so let it go. You'll be a better man for it." We shook hands and walked away. I rarely saw him for the next two years.

One weekend we had a family get-together, where I saw my cousin Joe Elwood. He told me that when Father Dougherty was calling the role at Sallies for the junior year, they had no way of knowing who was coming back and who wasn't. This great school just calls the roll and sees who shows up. When they got around to the Toners, some one called out that they weren't coming back this year. He looked over his glasses at the students and said, "Good riddance." At least three or four hundred students were sitting there to hear that. It would be fair to conclude that maybe we were bad people for a priest to say that. What this told me was that he never heard a single word of what Rev. Dunn said to him, and had no intention of doing the right thing. When they are calling the roll upstairs he will have to answer for this and other abuses that he did to some students at Salesianum.

He knew that I never did one thing at that school for two years to ever get in trouble, and he could have gone on to the next name on the list of names and that's all their would have been to that. That would have been the Christian thing to do. Someone told me that some years later Father Dougherty went on a self-imposed penance for his past sins; they say it was in Africa. What about the three to four hundred students to whom he gave the impression that Menny and I were undesirables and that he was happy to see us not return for our junior year. From what I remember of the church's teachings he would have had to tell all of the students present that day that he was wrong in saying Good Riddance and giving the impression that we were undesirable in order for him to be forgiven by God. It didn't do anything for my pain that he was responsible for. He was praying for forgiveness, but I wonder if he prayed for the forgiveness from the people that he hurt. Probably not. This was only one incident about Fr. Dougherty; there were hundreds more.

One evening we were all in the kitchen at home, laughing, when my father walked into the room. You could tell he had been drinking and was looking for a fight with someone, so I guess his wife and children would be a fair match. My mother was at the sink washing some potatoes. She had taken a break from the store and had come home to make dinner for us. I said to my father, "You're home early." Now that set him off. He grabbed me by the arm and started pounding his fingers into my chest. Mommy started screaming, "He's going to kill Babe!" Menny ran up the back steps and came down with his .22 bolt-action J.C. Higgins rifle. He walked over to my father and stuck the gun barrel under his jaw and pushed up hard. He asked him if he wanted to die. Then Mommy started screaming. "Maneen, don't, it's not worth it. Put the gun down!" My father was practically standing on his toes, with the gun still pushed under his jaw. Menny asked him again if he wanted to die. My father's face was chalky white with the fear that Menny was going to shoot him. Menny had pushed the rifle up so hard he knew Menny meant business. He gave a final gulp as Menny pulled the gun back. I was still lying on the floor where he dropped me.

Mommy was really upset over this. It had taken a gun to finally straighten him out once and for all. He had pushed his children to the point where they were defending themselves with guns. So after ten years of terrorism, the King Terrorist walked out of the kitchen a defeated man. The look on his face was pathetic. Never again would he lay a hand on any of us again. A few weeks later Mommy told me she was going to have him put out of our house by the Family Court. She said the Court was going to investigate her children to see how they were affected by all of this. She told me that my wood shop teacher told a Family Court investigator that I had snapped at him one day. She said it was starting to show that we were all affected by this treatment, and it was clear that something had to be done about this.

On the morning we went to Family Court, we arrived and were asked to sit on the bench. Guess what? That guy who gave me a hard time during the Sallies games, the guy at our luncheonette who I told that Sallies was the worst school I had ever heard of, was standing in the service area handing out the case papers and courtroom assignments. I knew he saw me, but he never gave me or any of us a second look or a sign of comfort. How could he when he didn't have it in him to give anyone comfort in their hour of need?

It wasn't long before Mommy was called into the courtroom before Judge Reardon. About forty minutes later Mommy came out and said we could leave; the judge didn't need to see any of us. She said that she was going to the store, where she had left Theresa. She said that Judge Reardon told our father to pack his bags and be out of that house by noon or he was going to hold him in contempt of court. We were so relieved to hear that. Menny told us to get in the car and he would drive us home in no time. Menny went back for Mommy, who waited on the courthouse steps for him.

When we got home, I sat in my favorite chair by the front door. The three girls were sitting on the sofa and no one was saying anything. We were just sitting there enjoying how peaceful it was and going to be. I could hear someone step onto the porch; it had to be him. He opened the door and walked in; the three girls immediately stood up and left the room, leaving me alone with him. He sat in the chair next to me on the other side of the door. If I wanted to, I would have to turn my head ninety degrees to the right to talk to him. So now it was me and him. He knew by the look on my face that he had a serious problem with me. He would have to have amnesia not to know how he failed as a father and a husband. He started crying to me and that he couldn't believe that my mother was having him kicked out of the house. He was actually trying to blame Mommy for everything that happened. Sniffling, he said again that he couldn't believe she had him kicked out, and he had to be out of the house by noon today. I turned to look at the old clock on the mantle and looked back at him and said, "You only have 15 minutes left; you better get a move on."

With that he stood up and went upstairs. He was gone about ten minutes and came down the stairs with the worst looking suitcase I had ever seen. It couldn't have held much. He walked out the door, never saying a word and never looking back at me. He didn't even say goodbye to his three girls; he had left a beaten man. He had no wife, no children, no house, no car, no more Toner's Luncheonette, no job, no money, and nowhere to go but out of our house and out of our lives, and he did all that on his own., with no one to blame. That was a lot to lose for a man who met a young woman from Ireland and wanted to marry her. I guess he needed someone to do his washing and ironing and someone to screw when ever he fancied it. Why were we so lucky to have him? That's a good question. What was he doing that he couldn't have done as a single person? He could have had anything he ever wanted with a woman like Mommy and children like us. He could have made money all the time with his painting and our store, and we could have lived anywhere we wanted, including stylish Westover Hills, but I guess he didn't want it. If you really study how this happened, you come up with the fact that he had no examples from his drunken father, but to me that's no excuse because everyone knows right from wrong and in their hearts, whether they are doing the right thing or not. I never had any examples given to me from my father and I know all the right things to do, because I want to do the right thing. It's hard to believe he wouldn't get off the merry-go-round. He acted like a man possessed by a devil.

We all slept well that first night. He was gone, and every night after that he was gone, too. We all pulled together to help my mother and we were going to have a good life thanks to Toner's Luncheonette. With the right help, Mommy could work two places; the store and the house. We were talking her into taking private driving lessons, and it wasn't long before she got her license. Look out, Bina is on the road! She bought a used Buick and never bought any other cars but Buicks.

One day my father contacted my mother about wanting to get the rest of his clothes. She put them in brown bags that we got from the grocer. She put them on the porch. We were not interested in talking to him, so he finally got the message and stopped making inquiries. Honey was the only one who wanted to see him. That was understandable, but that wore off also. He just didn't know how to be a father to his children until it was too late.

Menny and I continued to feel good about going to P.S. DuPont. I loved my gym class. We were always playing sports, whether inside or outside, such as baseball, softball, touch football or basketball. I couldn't wait for gym class, which was once a week. We had wood shop five days a week. We learned a lot from our shop teacher, who we called Pops. As usual as soon as I took a liking to someone they would pass away. He did. We kids were all in shock and missed him a lot. I knew the boys from Sallies didn't have wood shop or would miss their teacher like Pops was going to be missed. By the end of my first year at P.S. (junior year) I did really well. I had a C average, not too bad for a dummy. It was good to know with just a little more effort I could get all B's. I was so relaxed there; I was never late for school and I am sure you know why.

I had a 1939 Ford sedan, which I drove to school every day and parked in the same spot. I loved my car, even though it had no chrome and a high tank aerial. It was fast through the gears but not on the long run. It was black and everyone knew who owned it; my car was popular. I still had some money stashed away, so I could join Rock Manor as a junior member. It only cost s$17 a year for anyone under 20. When I joined I was going to be a big shot; I could just hear Luther: "Look out, Babe's a club member now." The first thing I did was to tell Grumpy that I was a junior member now, but when I told him he didn't appear to be too happy about it. Now he had to treat me a little better instead of showing his grumpiness. He was going to have to show me some respect. He did shake my hand, though, and said good luck.

I signed up for my second Delaware state junior golf championship tournament. I wish I had better clubs, but I didn't. I had to make the best of it. I couldn't wait to see how I would play. I hadn't done that well at my first junior tournament at the Newark Country Club because every one of my balls had a cut in them. It was a bad day but good experience.

My notice finally came in the mail about the Delaware Junior Tournament, which was going to be at Concord Country Club. That day, I drove up and went to the sign-in table. A nice guy from Rock Manor, Huck Donahue, was helping out. He told me I was paired with Mike Walsh and pointed to a fellow on the putting green. He said we were going to tee off in seven minutes. Mike walked over to me and asked me if I was Babe Toner. I said I was, we shook hands, and he said let's play some golf. I told him I was nervous and he said he was too.

I teed off first and hit the worst shot you could ever hit off the first tee in a tournament. It was to be a metal play round, which meant score every shot. About six of us were there from the Rock. I had to shoot the worst round, a 96. Can you believe it? The course was hard but not that hard. Mike and I talked a lot. It was surprising to find out how we knew the same people. I couldn't have been paired with a better person. I probably ruined his day, but he didn't play that well either. Mike would later be elected sheriff of New Castle County.

The next day I was paired with a boy named Ted whom I played with at the Rock. He beat me badly. I was five holes down with four holes to go. It was a good ass kicking, but I deserved it. I hadn't practiced enough and it showed. I was eliminated fast. I went back to the Rock to play some more.

I played golf every day rain or shine. I had my car and could get to the Rock with no problem. The guy from the pinball company who serviced our luncheonette knew I played golf. He must have told the owners. One day when he came in our store to check the juke box, he asked me if I wanted to play golf with the owners at Spring Haven Country Club in Pennsylvania. I said yes and what did I have to do? He said just show up at noon on Wednesday. He said to look good and play good because it was a private club. He gave me good directions and I drove right there.

I carried my bag to the drop-off rack, and someone ran out and took my bag. I was carrying my shoes. He lay my bag down over by the putting green. He told me to go in the locker room if I wanted to change my shoes. Just as I sat down, a man brought me a cold glass of milk. I put on my shoes. I walked toward the putting green where my bag was, and three guys walked up to me and asked me if I was Babe Toner. They were sweaty because they had been on the driving range hitting balls and they heard I was good, so they wanted to make sure they could stay up with me.

I told Vinney I hoped I could live up to the rumors. I felt I had really improved since my collapse at Concord in the Delaware State Junior. I felt a little pressure but not enough to bother me. I was confident I could play well, and I was hitting the five irons really well. Sy and Louie asked me if I wanted to hit some balls, I told them that all I needed was some warm-up swings and I would be ready to go.

My caddy carried my bag along with Sy's bag. Boy was I on. I was out-driving them on every hole. My chipping was good, getting me close enough to one-putt a lot. I ended up shooting an 83. Sy told me, "Babe, with a few small breaks you should have broken 80." He reached for my hand and put a $20 bill in it. He said, "This is what we won, Babe, thanks to you. We beat those guys and they were really trying to win." I told him if I knew I was playing for that kind of money I would have choked. He laughed and said he didn't want me to know. We sat around in the nineteenth hole. I drank a Coke and thanked them for this memorable day that I would never forget. They wanted to buy me dinner, but I told them I wasn't hungry.

Sy walked out with me and told me he appreciated our family's business and was looking forward to a long relationship with us. I drove home with $20 in my pocket. I stopped at the store and sat with Mommy, telling her about my win and how they picked up the whole tab. I told her they have big money and we should stay on the good side of them, and she agreed.

One day a bunch of older guys were playing basketball behind the #30 school at Baynard Blvd. and Van Buren St. Three of them, whom I knew because they went to school with Theresa, wanted to play us younger guys. We agreed to play three against three, but they didn't say they were going to play really dirty and try to hurt us. They stepped on our toes on purpose and elbowed us every chance they got. They constantly fouled us with their hips and asses to prevent us from rebounding. It was starting to get serious. I was really getting hurt under the boards and I had to do something about it, so I went for a ball that flew up in the air and was heading toward the outside line. I ran after it and was going to try to stop it from going out of bounds.

As I got close to the ball, this big fat-ass was bearing down on me. I could see he was going to try and hurt me. I timed the bouncing perfectly so when the ball was in mid-air, I grabbed it and threw it as hard as I could with my right hand as he was diving at me to do me no good. I threw that ball at least 50 miles an hour, and it hit him square in his face. He dropped down onto his knees. Blood was gushing all over his face and from between his fingers covering his face. I wasn't worried about him coming after me because he had a lot to take care of before he could see me. We younger guys left and walked over to our store and had a Coke. His friend came in and asked for a towel, and I offered him some napkins to clean up his hurt friend. Mommy wanted to know how he got hurt and I told her he got hit in the face during a basketball game. His buddy said that it looked like the guy's nose was broken. I told him that the way they were playing it was a wonder we didn't have something broken because they were definitely trying to hurt every one of us. I hoped these guys learn something.

The friend came up to me and said that what he learned today, that I was a wise ass. I told him not to pick on people who would fight back and that if the game had gone on any longer he might have been next. Oh boy, he didn't like that. He looked shocked, as if he were thinking, "Who is this little shit talking to?" Mommy told him to get out of her store and never come in again.

The next day at the Yard I saw the guy I hit in the face with the ball. He was standing on the sidelines watching the game. He had a big white bandage with gauze across his nose and two very black eyes. He never said anything to me. He wasn't in any shape to fight me even though he outweighed me, and he was taller and three years older. He couldn't take another hit to his face for a long time. I heard his friend call him Skip. I was hoping he wouldn't skip any doctor's visit

16

In September of 1954, I was looking forward to my senior year. Ralph Burnley said we could get jobs on Faulk Road at an apple orchard called Faulklands. So Ralph, Menny, and I went up and got the job, mostly grading and very little picking. The owner had pickers during the day, and we were part-time after school making 75 cents an hour. I thought that was a lot of money. Along the rows of apple trees I could see white bee boxes stacked about three feet high. I had a good arm and I could hit them with an apple from 50 feet away. I would let an apple go and when it hit it sounded like a gunshot. Then I would take off fast.

One day Mr. Faulkner asked me if I could get three or four guys together to help get some apples picked the next weekend, before the frost. I got four more, for a total of seven. It was hot and hard work picking apples, and some of the new guys wanted to quit, so I told Ralph I was going to take the pick-up down and talk to Mr. Faulkner about a pay raise. Ralph said, "Babe, why can't you be happy with the 75 cents?" I told him the work we were doing was worth a dollar an hour. Ralph was scared and didn't want any part of this. I told Ralph that the only reason he was against this raise was because he was probably already getting a dollar an hour. He turned blood red and said, "That's a lie!"

I said I was going anyway. I told Ralph that if he didn't want the extra 25 cents, he could give it to me. He didn't want me to see Mr. Faulkner, but the other five did. I took the pick-up down to the barn, where I found Mr. Faulkner by the freezer. He was very nice. I told him that the fellows asked me to talk to him about our pay, that we should be getting a dollar an hour and not 75 cents. He broke out in a big smile and then laughed and said "OK, Babe, a dollar it is." I drove the pick-up back and told the guys that we were now making a dollar an hour. We were all happy except Ralph. I could never find out why he was shook up.

The next Friday the wind started blowing hard. We were sent home from school around noon because Delaware was going to be hit by a hurricane called Hazel. We were supposed to go home before it got worse, around 7:00 p.m. I saw Ralph outside and he asked Menny and me if we wanted to go up to the orchard and put in around five hours before the storm hit. He would drive, so we agreed to go. He picked us up at our house and we got there by one o'clock. We started bringing bushels of apples in from the big truck outside the grading room. We graded apples most of the time and were in the process of unloading another truck. The wind was getting very loud. We worked up to 6:00, when Mr. Faulkner said we had better quit before the storm got any worse. Ralph was a nervous wreck; he was much more serious than we were. Being a nonsmoker, Ralph didn't want anyone smoking in his car, but I was nervous, never having been in a hurricane before, so I couldn't help but smoke and that was that. Ralph drove down the driveway and turned onto Faulk Road and the storm got really intense. Ralph could hardly keep his car in his lane. The cross winds made him have a death grip on the steering wheel, thank God there wasn't anyone on the road. The street lights were on, and the traffic lights were swinging back and forth.

Ralph kept saying he was going to stick to the main roads. By the time we got to Route 202, it was raining hard and blowing us almost off the road. In a way it really looked good with the street lights on all down Route 202. We could see big tree limbs breaking off and blowing across the road, and the rain swept the road way like never before. Ralph still had a death grip on the wheel as we started down the hill toward the city. The water was running down the hill faster than we were going. It couldn't go in the drain at the bottom of the hill because it was going too fast, so it was flooding badly at the bottom of Route 202 and Broom Street. We told Ralph not to stop or we would be walking home. He kept going and hit a wall of water, sending the water rolling down Concord Avenue.

Wilmington had a lot of trees along its streets before Hazel came along, but I saw a lot of them down. Ralph wasn't too happy about driving us home, and by the time we got to 29th Street it looked like a war zone. He let us out and we ran to our house. We only lived halfway down the street, but when we got to our porch we were totally drenched. My shoes were full of water.

I stood on the porch and told Menny I couldn't get any wetter, so I took off my shirt and said I was going to run around the block. I jumped down the steps onto the sidewalk and took off. Trees were falling down or being sucked out of the ground as I got to them. Debris was everywhere. I had to jump the limbs across the sidewalk. The water was warm and felt good on my bare chest. I was scared but not scared enough not to do it. I had to be able to say that I ran around the block in the middle of a hurricane. When I got back to the house my chest was red from the wind and the driving rain. I went up onto the porch and told Menny he had to do it. He pulled off his shirt and took off; when he got back he was red and happy, too. He did it. We were the only two people or dummies outside.

Big limbs fell on cars blocking the streets. Houses were damaged and some roofs were off, but we still had electricity. We couldn't believe it. It probably lasted till 11:00 p.m. I am glad I ran. What a rush, and no one would believe that we did it. I know you will, won't you?

When we went back to school our gym teacher, Mr. Jake Warner, wanted everyone to get up a team for full contact tackle football. He called it the intramural league. We would play six games on the high field in back of the scoreboard. I formed a team and I was quarterback, what else? We had some good players and some good plays, every one of our games were exciting. I was throwing the ball with hair-splitting accuracy. After one game, Mr. Warner asked if he could take me down to meet the varsity coach and play on the varsity team. He said, "Babe, you can play down there," meaning the lower field where the varsity team practiced and played. He said, "I have watched you and you can make that team with no problem. I haven't seen an arm like that in years." I told him I appreciated his kind words and they meant a lot to me but I couldn't. I had to help my mother in our store and I needed the money. I told him that with the part-time job at the apple orchard, I couldn't play varsity and do all I was doing. He said he respected my decision but would love to see me in action. He patted me on the shoulder and said good luck.

I played both offense and defense in those intramural games. I loved defense because I loved to hit hard. I would grit my teeth so hard it's a wonder I still have them. I wanted to win our last game badly and was doing everything I could. I pulled off a quarterback sneak. that had everyone faked out when my thigh hit the ball it was knocked out of my hand on to the ground, as I was looking behind me I saw it, I could have walked into the end zone. I had to be happy to recover my own fumble, but we failed to score and lost the game. I threw two touchdown passes, and it really hurt to lose.

As I was walking off the field at the end of the game, Mr. Warner ran over to me and said it was a shame I didn't have a team to back me up. He liked me a lot. He was one of the most respected teachers in P.S. DuPont. I had some other good teachers, Mrs. Casey, Mrs. Allison, and Mrs. Farron, who were molding us for the future. My art teacher, Mrs. Klund, was quite a flirt. She loved to see me blush, so every class she would come up to me and rub her boobs on my shoulder. I would light up like a Christmas tree. My friend Ann Walker laughed at me for blushing. She would see me after school and tell me that Mrs. Klund was really having a good time with me. She just wants to see you blush.

Menny and I worked at Faulkner's as much as we could. I was saving my money to rejoin the Rock as a junior member again for another year. I was doing well at school and wasn't going to have any trouble graduating. I was also on an intramural basketball team. We won the honor of playing in front of the junior and senior classes for the championship. What a thrill; at least 400 people would be watching. I played a lot, nervous as hell, and scored seven points. Everyone was cheering and making a lot of noise. It was fun and probably my last sporting event at P.S. DuPont.

Sometimes Menny and I would ride our motor scooters around North Wilmington. We would ride down Weldin Road and stop at the Weldin Farm and talk to the two Weldin brothers, who sat on the front porch almost every day. One day I asked Mr. Weldin if I could ride his horse, Maude. He told me if I could catch her, I could ride her. I couldn't catch her so I never rode her. Mr. Weldin took us through his stable where he had coaches and a car and hitches and things. The Weldin brothers were very nice to me.

That year we had a wonderful Christmas. After our early dinner, Mommy wanted to open up the store by 4:00. We weren't open ten minutes before all the regulars were coming in. I think they wanted to get out and do something different than to sit around the house all day. It broke the monotony of the day.

Mommy was spending some time with Theresa, who was getting married to Bob Jones, a Marine she had been dating. I am not saying that Theresa didn't love Bob, but she just wanted to do like a lot of girls wanted to do, get out of the house. He was a Korean veteran with a Purple Heart. I didn't know it but Bob grew up in a group home on Todd's Lane for children whose parents couldn't take care of them. I used to serve papers there. I sometimes wondered how close we children came to going to that home, but it would have never happened as long as my mother was alive.

Theresa had to decide who was going to give her away. It ended up being my father. I was very uneasy about it because he didn't deserve it. I can't imagine what Theresa was thinking of; in all honesty he should have never been invited. My bad memories were still real in my mind. They would have to shore up the church walls when he walked in because he just didn't belong there. He was no father to her or us children. On May 14, 1955, Theresa and Bob were married at Christ Our King Church. Menny and I were in the wedding, wearing white tuxedo jackets. When Theresa came out of our house to get into the car to go to the church, someone told her to hold her dress up so she wouldn't step on it. She had it so high in the air you could see her stomach. The women were screaming with laughter.

The reception was at a union hall on Fourth Street. Theresa and Bob had picked out a live rock and roll band. The instructions to the band leader were not to suggest that the parents of the bride and groom dance together. We didn't want my mother to be humiliated by dancing with my father and giving the wrong impression. That band was good; they played for almost five hours. Lots of people from the neighborhood were standing outside the hall and dancing on the sidewalk, that's how good the band was. Later Theresa and Bob snuck off; I don't know where they went but I did know what they were doing.

My father was completely ignored by most of his children that day. He had to have felt it. He was proud of us, but we weren't proud of him. Mommy, on the other hand, was very happy and laughed a lot. She also paid for just about everything, including Menny's and my tuxes. That was the only time our store was ever closed.

Menny's girlfriend, Anna Roberts, asked Menny to see if I would take her girlfriend, Mary Ann, to the prom. I had seen her couple of times up at the driving range. She was cute, but I was still my shy self and had never been on a date with her. I called her on the phone to try to get to know her. On the night of the prom in the Gold Ballroom at the Hotel DuPont, everyone that thought they were someone was there. You should have seen their faces when I walked down the steps with Mary Ann on my arm. All I heard that night was, "Where did you find that girl?" and "Hey, Babe she's a good looker." Franny Lewis was the most impressed. I guess he didn't think I could get a date. But Mary Ann held back with me and I held back with her, which made for a very bad evening. I didn't know how to dance and she never insisted on a slow dance. I really felt bad because I knew I wasn't a bore, and she had to take some blame for this evening. The chemistry was good; it just wasn't the right time or place to have a first date. We should have gone on a date together first.

My friend Ann Walker wanted to meet my date, so I introduced her to Mary Ann. She told me how beautiful Mary Ann was and how much she liked her just from her short meeting with her. She told her how much fun I was in her art class. She invited Menny and me and our dates to her house for an after-prom party. She lived in a big house in a nice neighborhood called Alapocas. We drove there after the prom and had some punch and snacks. There must have been twenty couples at the party. But Mary Ann and I were getting nowhere, so I asked Menny for the car keys. I wanted to park somewhere with Mary Ann and maybe make out. Menny said no, he didn't want me to use Mommy's car, so this evening was a big flop. I drove Mary Ann home, stopped in front of her house, and she ran to her front door like she was in a track meet. I never saw or heard from her again. It was obvious to me that we should have never dated; there weren't any electric sparks between us. Menny thought that his girlfriend wanted Mary Ann to keep her company at the prom.

It was getting close to graduation. I stopped everyone I could and got at least 85% of the kids to sign my yearbook. On Menny's and my graduation night none of my family showed up. Mommy was keeping the store open. I remember that the two-hour ceremony; was a long time to see so many people honored and I wasn't one of them. Was this how life was going to be for me, I knew I had to do something about it because I was going to get a kick out of life, and not let life kick me. As we turned in our caps and gowns after the ceremony, people were asking each other to come to their parties. Nobody asked me to go anywhere. I really felt bad. Maybe I wasn't good enough to be invited to anyone's party; I quickly put that thought out of my head because I knew that wasn't true.

Menny and I drove to the store. It looked like I wasn't the only one not invited anywhere; loads of people from my class were there. Mommy wanted to see our diplomas. She was very proud of us, but for her it ended up being just like any other day. Menny and I never sat around waiting for anything; we made it happen. A group was going down to Rehoboth for a cookout on the beach and a blanket party, which was going to give some of those guys a bad case of blue balls, for having a hard-on for eight hours and nowhere to stick it. Heaven forbid that it would be in their dates; the girls in those days wanted to wait for Mr. Right. Other guys sat around distraught because they weren't invited. Hey, you want to have fun, make your own fun.

There was a lot of talk going around that if you didn't go to college, you would probably get drafted into the army. That didn't sound good to me. Joe Dawson told me he was going into the Air Force and that they treated you better than the army or marines. The Air Force sounded good to me, so I was going to look into it.

Meanwhile there were so many things to do. I wanted to do them all. Golf was my first love, so I played as much as I could. I also signed up for the Delaware State Junior Golf tournament. This time it was being hosted by Rock Manor, my home course. I had no excuse now; I knew every blade of grass, but I still needed to shoot a good round on opening day. I couldn't wait.

I played golf every day. We would gamble all the time, and a black guy named Willie would join us. We had some good matches, and I won more than I lost. I hadn't caddied in over a year, but I didn't miss it. I had a lot of memories. One beautiful day there wasn't anyone to play golf with. I decided to go out by myself, around 2:00 in the afternoon. I bent over to tee off on the first tee. I heard someone say, "Excuse me, do you mind if we join you?" I turned around and saw six guys. I told them the course only allowed foursomes. One guy spoke up and said only three of them were playing golf; the rest were going along to watch. I said sure, come on. The golfers introduced themselves as Dave Mahoney, Lou Silvesti and Joe Vaccaro.

We were walking down the first hole when one of the caddies, who looked more like a bodyguard, said to me, "Do you have any idea who you're playing with?" When I said no, he said they were three of the Four Aces, a popular '50s singing group. The only one missing was Al Albert. I changed my attitude after I heard that. The Four Aces playing with me! Wait till I tell everybody about this! When they walked together down the fairway, they sang, just having a good time.

Then I hit a ball out of bounds right where some bums were standing. In fact, we saw one of them pick it up and put it in his pocket. When we got to him he denied it. One of the bodyguards, I mean caddies, dropped the bag and walked up to the bum and asked him if he wanted him to put him to sleep because if we don't get the ball, that's what was going to happen to him. The bum reached into his pocket and gave it back to him. The bodyguard said something in Italian to him, which I didn't understand.

I thanked the bodyguard for helping me out and asked how he was going to put the bum to sleep. He said I can assure you I wasn't going to sing to him. I played well and we had a good time. The Aces said they were out for some exercise and a walk in the sun. We took the usual four hours, and as we shook hands and said good bye, I wondered how this guy could put someone to sleep without a gun.

On the day of the Delaware State Junior Golf Tournament, I checked in early. That guy Huck Donahue was working the table and handing out the official score cards again. It was eighteen holes of metal play, just like before, every shot counts. I shot an 83 and finished 13ᵗʰ. Wow, only 12 guys were better than me. I had come a long way. I got beat in my first match by the kid who came in second or third with a 74. I wished I could have won a match, but I didn't. I had an opportunity to compete and that was priceless. The top four golfers went to the junior nationals, with all expenses paid. I think Jack Nicklaus was playing in that national tournament that year.

One day no one was at the Rock; everyone must have been at the beach. Grumpy asked me to play with a couple from out of state. He introduced them as Hans and Gisela Lueb. They said they had a pharmacy in West Chester. Hans was really friendly and laughed a lot; Gisela was a little more serious. They were originally from a small town in Germany named Leudinshied and spoke English very well. When I told Gisela to watch out for the puddle of water by the trap, she didn't know what a puddle was. We laughed a lot that day. Hans liked my jokes.

He did something and I said "bullshit" and he said back to me in German accent "bullshit" if I told him it was his shot or anything. It was "bullshit" all day. We were standing outside the pro shop when Grumpy came up to him and asked Hans how it went. He said "bullshit" and Grumpy's teeth almost fell out. I assured him that Hans didn't know what he was saying. He learned a new word today. Hans said he would like to play with me again. He said that it wasn't easy to get away from a business and two small children. As he was leaving, I could hear him in the parking lot, still saying "bullshit."

I saw Stanley Bodan the next day. He asked if I wanted to join the Air Force with him. We would go through boot camp together, He said we would have to talk to a recruiter and find out more. I knew that Menny was talking to a Marine Corps recruiter also. The Air Force recruiter was a nice guy. He was fair and frank on what to expect from boot camp and life in general in the Air Force. Stan and I agreed to sign up and report in

30 days, on October 11, 1955. When I saw Menny, he said he was going in on October 4th.

Now we had to tell Mommy. We went up to the store and sat with Mommy and told her we had signed up for the Marines and the Air Force because if we didn't join we would be drafted into the army, and we didn't want that. We wanted to choose, not be chosen. We weren't going to college, so eventually we would have been drafted. We told Mommy that Menny had to report on October 4th and I had to report on October 11th. She started crying and saying how she couldn't get along without her two boys. I told her that it would work out fine and we had to get this service out of the way when we were young, before it got in the way. I told her Menny had three years and I had four years.

Menny left without any fanfare, and that was the last time we had much contact with each other, like we did when we were growing up together, sleeping in the same bed and all. We would see each other at weddings and funerals. We were never close again. He would never come to our family get-togethers and has stayed away for 40-some years now.

I was leaving seven days later and was to report to the Schuylkill Arsenal. I put my golf clubs away. My mother wasn't the type of woman to make a fuss, but you could feel the love anyway. I can never forget how she took the punches from my father just so we wouldn't get hit. The morning I left no one was around to say goodbye. Stan knocked on the door and we caught the bus to the train station. We had the train tickets given to us by the recruiter and waited on the platform for our train to come. I looked down the track and could see what I thought was our train coming. It rolled up slowly; Stan and I stepped on too the train and sat down.

I sat there looking out the train window. I don't know how, but the train window turned into a giant picture screen. All of a sudden I could hear voices and see the faces of all the people that were close to me. There was Mommy sitting at the end of the counter in the store with her usual cup of tea, she said, "Goodbye, Babe, I'll miss you." Mommy never said to me, "Babe, I love you," but that's all right. I knew she did. She knew that I loved her also, even though I never told her. I would miss her a lot. I could see all the people in my life starting to appear on the screen, as if they were in the train with me; it was like a live slide show. Old Grumpy appeared and was calling out my name for a caddy job, and all the neighborhood kids were sitting on our front steps calling me Jew Bab (their nickname for me). Donald's mother was saying, "What can I get for you today, Lucifer?" Donald told me she thought I was a little devil. Oh my God, there's my first girlfriend Maria. She had a beautiful smile on her face that changed to a plea asking me to please come find her. There was Joan, waving to me. As pretty as she was, Joan looked sad to me and threw me a kiss. Then Carolyn appeared smiling, saying she missed me a lot. She was waving to me and asking Linda to join her in saying goodbye to Babe. Linda looked like her old self; now that I could see her again I realized how lucky I was to know her and Carolyn, and Carolyn was right, she did lose that weight. Linda was holding her beautiful little girl up to wave to me; she looked just like Linda. The pain that I felt from the loss of those two was a lot for a young man to suffer on his own. Even Sister Francis Letitia appeared to me saying, "You can do it, Babe. I want you to come see me when you come home."

This was a highly emotional experience for me. The whole time this was going on I could hear Perry Como singing Ave Maria. My eyes were full of tears and I started to cry. I felt the train jerk to a start. Some teardrops fell from my eyes onto the back of my hand. Suddenly the picture screen went blank as the train started to move slowly out of the station, heading for a life I freely volunteered for, to serve my country in the United States Air Force for four years. Although it would be the unknown, somehow I knew life was going to get better for me. I could make it. I was strong.